In the early eighteenth century the increasing dependence of society on financial credit provoked widespread anxiety. The texts of credit – stock certificates, IOUs, bills of exchange – were denominated as potential "fictions," while the potential fictionality of other texts was measured in terms of the "credit" they deserved. Sandra Sherman argues that in this environment finance is *like* fiction, employing the same tropes. She goes on to show how the work of Daniel Defoe epitomized the market's capacity to unsettle discourse, demanding and evading "honesty" at the same time. Defoe's oeuvre, straddling both finance and literature, theorizes the disturbance of market discourse, elaborating strategies by which an author can remain in the market, perpetrating fiction while avoiding responsibility for doing so.

FINANCE AND FICTIONALITY IN THE EARLY EIGHTEENTH CENTURY

FINANCE AND FICTIONALITY IN THE EARLY EIGHTEENTH CENTURY

Accounting for Defoe

SANDRA SHERMAN

Georgia State University

CAMBRIDGE
UNIVERSITY PRESS

CAMBRIDGE UNIVERSITY PRESS
Cambridge, New York, Melbourne, Madrid, Cape Town, Singapore, São Paulo

Cambridge University Press
The Edinburgh Building, Cambridge CB2 2RU, UK

Published in the United States of America by Cambridge University Press, New York

www.cambridge.org
Information on this title: www.cambridge.org/9780521481540

First published 1996
This digitally printed first paperback version 2005

A catalogue record for this publication is available from the British Library

Library of Congress Cataloguing in Publication data

Sherman, Sandra.
Finance and fictionality in the early eighteenth century:
accounting for Defoe/Sandra Sherman.
p. cm.
Includes index.
ISBN 0 521 48154 6 (hardback)
1. Defoe, Daniel, 1661?–1731 – Knowledge – Economics.   2. Economics –
England – History – 18th century.   3. Finance – England – History – 18th
century.   4. Economics in literature.   5. Finance in literature.
6. Fiction – Technique.   I. Title.
PR3408.E25S54   1996
832′.5 – dc20   95–9217 CIP

ISBN-13 978-0-521-48154-0 hardback
ISBN-10 0-521-48154-6 hardback

ISBN-13 978-0-521-02142-5 paperback
ISBN-10 0-521-02142-1 paperback

for Steven
You Never Know

[T]hese People can ruin Men silently, undermine and impoverish by a sort of impenetrable Artifice, like Poison that works at a distance . . . and the poor Passive Trades men, like the Peasant in Flanders, are Plundered by both sides, and hardly knows who hurts them.

Defoe, *The Villainy of Stock-Jobbers Detected* (1721)

Contents

Acknowledgments

Finance and Fictionality argues that during the early eighteenth century a credit-based market dissipated the author. "Nobody" could be identified with discursive production. It further suggests that authors were complicit in de-authorization, foregoing identity to stay in the market, producing fiction for which they could not be held to account. I therefore posit an irony: if the market made authorship possible by circulating texts, the texts produced could not lay claim to authorship.

This argument is speculative, and may be a fiction. I am tempted to retreat behind tropes that (so I claim) the market furnished to stockjobbers, MPs, and Robinson Crusoe. However, academic protocol requires an acknowledged provenance. Thus my first "acknowledgment" is that if *Finance and Fictionality* is fiction, I am the author and must be held to account.

But *pace*. Since I trained as a lawyer, and appreciate that Cambridge did not contract for fiction, I preemptively invoke *Crusoe* itself: is there such a thing as "fiction?" My text, like the market it describes, assumes epistemological uncertainty as its justification. It enacts the argument I describe below, that an infinite regress of fictionality is the sum total of the real. All fictions, including *Finance and Fictionality* (if it is fiction), are on a continuum towards truth.

I should like to deepen the potential irony of this text by suggesting that if the credit-based market dissolved authorship, then in my case only because people *gave* me credit did I become an author at all. I owe the most to David Norbrook, without whom I would not have fancied leaving the Law. David rescued me from positivism before I heard of New Historicism. He accommodated me to the uncertainties of imaginative projection. He is the subtext of this text. *Finance and Fictionality* reflects on the uncertainties we inhabited. If it is a novel, it is a roman à clef.

It seems gratuitous to say that my next debt is to John Richetti, since virtually every study of eighteenth-century literature acknowledges him in some fashion. But John helped me from the start. He directed my thesis and saw it through as this book. When I had no sense that credit was a credible pursuit, I called Santa Fe in panic from Oxford. John's encouragement was crucial: this might have been a book on Margaret Cavendish. Indeed, John's moral, intellectual, and strategic support has been over the top: this was almost no book at all.

I also want to thank Margreta DeGrazia, who knows the subtext of this text. When my ideas were implicit, she articulated them. Her readings were incarnating. Peter Stallybrass read my thesis with his wonted brilliance, and confronted me with a basic crux: is this homological or causal historiography? He provoked many sleepless nights, and made this a more complicated text.

My colleagues – Murray Brown, Peter Herman, Bart Palmer – were generous with encouragement and advice, and my friend Randa Graves assured me I was making sense. Her frankness, rigor and excitement inspired me.

Of course, since I argue that fiction in the market projects prior fiction, I should credit the source of that assertion – the site where I realized that fiction proliferates fiction to hide fictionality. I refer to the Washington bureaucracy. Before I ever knew I would write *Finance and Fictionality*, I engaged the phenomena it concerns. In the world's greatest fiction factory, nobody signs his name. It was thinking about that trope that finally led me here.

Since I always hoped to thank Daniel Defoe, I shall take this opportunity. When I started thinking about credit, I joked about going to bed each night with The Compleat English Tradesman. But Defoe turned out to be compelling, our engagement a love affair. I had never met an author whose audacity so amazed me. This book reflects that amazement. It is less about Defoe than the experience of reading him.

Portions of this text appeared in *ELH*, *Criticism*, *Texas Studies in Language and Literature*, *Eighteenth-century Life*, *Mediations* and *Prose Studies*, and I thank the editors for granting me permission to reprint. Material from *Texas Studies* appeared in "Lady Credit No Lady," 37:2 (1995), published by University of Texas Press.

Finally, if this text pursues the irony of the textual condition, the fiction that we ever escape fictionality, then as a text myself I am bound to its purport. For a while I seemed clear of *Finance and Fictionality*, but David Meyer proved it is the story of my life. Because I really have no choice, this book acknowledges him.

Introduction

This is not a study of The Rise of the Novel, although Defoe's fiction plays a crucial part in my analysis.[1] During the early part of the century, "fiction" was not a formalistic concept, but a broad epistemological crux fusing all sorts of writing – "literary" and nonliterary – into a forbidding phenomenon that disabled apprehension of the real. In recent years, critics have assimilated into the novel's "rise" texts with little or no literary pretension, whose relation to "truth" was unstable.[2] I am concerned with conditions affecting the culture's acceptance of fiction in *any* genre, "news," "novel," "romance," financial credit. Indeed, *Finance and Fictionality* is about a retrograde resistance to fiction even less accommodating than the grudging acceptance of "moral fables" by Protestant critics.[3] In this sense, my study finally connects with Rise of the Novel criticism in that it adds a substrate of irony: just when *Robinson Crusoe* arguably leaves the first footprint in the sands of an emergent genre, the culture – even Defoe – is withdrawing from an overdose of fiction.[4] My thesis explains why therefore, apart from moralistic strictures, a literary fiction (such as *Crusoe*) does not acknowledge its fictionality.

The central feature of my argument, which accounts for its title, is that the marked instability of Defoe's truth claims did not result from a dogged attempt to reconcile fictive intent with "naive empiricism"[5] (an ur-novelist's incapacity to sever cosmos and heterocosm[6]); it recapitulated the logic of market-generated texts whose unstable truth claims baffled resistance to their own potential fictionality. The market, a congeries of bills, notes, stocks, annuities, reports on the National Debt, accommodated readers to an equivocal, impenetrable textuality – to Air-Money, Defoe's term for financial instruments floating beyond apprehension. I suggest in this study that Defoe's texts (intensely conscious of their commodification) instantiate the condition of the market, deferring representational integrity as much as any text whose payoff was speculative. Defoe's articulation of tropes affecting apprehension in the market, casts "literary" and "financial" texts as undifferentiated tokens of epistemological opacity. Insofar as they were all potential, elusive fictions such categories were moot.[7]

If a text could not be denominated a cheat, its author – a stockjobber, tradesman, MP, Defoe – could not be called a liar; he could remain in the market, generating more (potential, elusive) cheats. Moreover, if texts are perceived as nodes of discourse, outworkings of a depersonalized market, then the "author" of potential fiction cannot be identified, interrogated, held to account.[8] I shall argue that the market disperses authorship as it does genre: fiction proliferates fiction to hide fictionality, palimpsest promises pile up against no visible, originary Fund. This deracinating expansion and diffusion of textuality within an early capitalist market configures Defoe's defense; it is deployed in *Crusoe*, pondered in *Roxana*, recuperated in *The Compleat English Tradesman*.

I argue that the public sphere – the market in ideas, in literature – and the market constituted by commercial paper (both developing during this period) generate a mutually inflecting discursive field around the notion of "fiction." Within it, a self-reflexive discourse elaborates a shared concern: texts whose provenance is remote, whose authors are unaccountable, are potential fictions that escape accountability. As credit instruments become complex embodiments of financial relations, issues of credibility arise homologous with the "credit" owed to literary texts. Texts floating in the market detached from apparent authority, estrange readers irrespective of purport ("literary" or "financial"). A common provenance in the market avows a potential to disorder apprehension.

As this market develops, credit creates a vast, reticulating network of players, indeterminate in time and space; it imposes a disorienting distance between authors and readers of financial texts.[9] Likewise, in a market exploding with commercial publishers and writer/entrepreneurs, most authors become distant figures without a local context, lacking the traditional responsibility to a patron.[10] Readers of such "edited" texts as *Crusoe* are in no better position – epistemologically – than frequenters of Exchange Alley. In the same entropic motion, literary and nonliterary texts evince the uncertainties of the market, its inherent potential to generate fiction.

In light of recent junk bond and Savings and Loan scandals, the

MMM fiasco in Russia, and the perpetually receding paydown of third world debt, it should be no surprise that in the eighteenth century "literary" and "financial" texts configured a single problematic: "fiction."[11] There was shock at the time, however. As E.P. Thompson has observed, traditional face-to-face markets were still common.[12] Literature surrounding the South Sea Bubble evinces this older "moral economy." Purchasers felt tricked, incredulous that government-sanctioned obligations could dissipate in graft. The liminality of this new credit-based market provided Defoe with endless didactic opportunities in *The Review*, *An Essay Upon Publick Credit*, *The Chimera*, and *The Compleat English Tradesman*. That the tropes of this market jibe with his strategies of literary evasion is a stunning irony, situating Defoe at the center of an elaborating notion of fiction valenced to both literature and finance. At both valences, potentially lurking "fiction" was said to breach the contract between author and reader guaranteeing textual transparency.

In my account of epistemological disorder, the market is a secular, coterminous economy to that constituted by Puritan doctrine, suspicious of "anything fictional – a suspicion deriving from the Puritan conception of the world and events as emblematic. For the Puritanism of the late seventeenth century, fiction simply falsified the detailed world of fact and event – and thereby obscured the clear message that God wrote for all men in 'real' happenings."[13] When I argue for a fear of fiction, therefore, I do not minimize the impact of Puritanism, but I do suggest that the vast number of accounts that depict Defoe struggling with his own morality – or against that of his readers – must acknowledge another dimension.[14] It may be that what has always been assumed to have been a late religious troping in the publication of fiction, was engaged with secular phenomena to a greater degree than previously thought.

Since my argument derives from the materiality of texts rather than from moral or formal concerns, it suggests that resistance to fiction (against which Defoe's texts react, but to which they also contribute) was materially based. It was a phenomenon of experience: resistance to fiction was a response to resistant texts. In this sense my thesis extends the work of J.G.A. Pocock, who has identified financial credit as a source of epistemological malaise, but has sited its impact within a landed class that saw "new men," made rich by trade, speculation – "imaginary wealth" – as a threat to traditional establishments.[15] I demonstrate that irrespective of class, readers were disoriented by texts whose veracity could not be computed based on "face value." Pocock, in other words, must be read against the discourse surrounding credit, in which "imaginary" value attributed to *texts* goads consumers to ignore "intrinsick," true value. The strategies of credit cited by this discourse, whereby credit texts elude proper valuation and maintain a market for themselves, are deployed by Defoe, whose fictions conspicuously signal their own provenance in the market.

In applying and extending Pocock's work on the relation between "imagination" and credit, I take a crucial turn. In my analysis credit is not a "context," a background for literary "texts." I give equal weight to both as epistemological vectors, mutually informing the resistance of "credibility" to accountability. To *impose* such a distinction would artificially isolate discourses of "fictionality," distorting a discursive formation constituted transgenerically.[16] Instead, I "read" culture as an integrated text, grounding the relationship between "literature" and "finance" in concrete, market-based phenomena that propelled textuality towards a generalized crux. By elaborating this discursive continuum, I affiliate with New Historicism, which challenges the autonomy of the aesthetic.[17] However, while I obviously concur in that view, I do not propose that different discourses "can" (at the critic's option) be read together towards some new, speculative cultural synthesis – a charge often levelled against New Historicism.[18] I argue that such synthesis existed historically.[19]

Since I invoke a synthetic, homologic approach to "literary" and "financial" discourse, my method arguably excludes economic determinism, i.e. the priority of financial tropes relative to their literary equivalents. However, the mere contemporaneity of financial and literary sites resistant to self-disclosure, does not preclude evasive "financial" texts from some degree of influence on "literary" texts constituting the same market. Indeed, New Historicist work acknowledges causal modes, even where "causality" is unquantifiable.[20]

Nevertheless, merely "coincidental" homologies strike me as improbable: discourses configure an episteme, and at some level they inflect each other. Indeed, one might argue that the non-(dis)closure of romance influenced credit's proclivity towards concatenating fictions. Indeed, Defoe seems to make that case in Lady Credit's narrative. Thus while I think that "homology" more nearly describes the relations between "financial" and "literary" texts in the market, I still acknowledge the potential for causality. Unlike conventional Marxism, my work suggests that if the market was in some sense anterior to literature, then the reverse may also have been true. In the end, the issue of sequentiality is secondary, since I want to explore the *phenomenon* of a shared financial/literary discursive.

How was this phenomenon experienced? I argue that long-term credit implicated the culture in a new kind of narrativity, since promises in stocks, annuities, and negotiable instruments were verifiable only with time. Until the moment of payoff, narrative verged on potential fiction. The homology between a bill endorsed by a dozen signers, drawn against a remote promissor, and a narrative like *Crusoe*, was grounded in the experience that both made representations that were unverifiable; both continually recontextualized themselves in serial iterations (*Crusoe* in three volumes); both receded further and further from an originary authenticator, who might demonstrate the "truth" of the text by paying up or turning up (in the flesh). The coyness of a text like *Crusoe* was reciprocated by Defoe's "Coy Mistress," Lady Credit, herself a text (as I shall show) weaving in and out of avowing her "honesty." The crucial object for all such texts, literary and financial, was to remain in suspension, never disclosing their value or their provenance, forcing the reader to suspend his disbelief . . . and wait. Textuality aspired to the condition of epistemological opacity, which readers could not negotiate without extratextual aid. The market became a site in which readers and authors pursued mutual adverse projects of detecting (with no great conviction) and evading (without being convicted for) fictionality.[21] The perpetual contingency of texts produced demands for transparency. Voidable contracts became the ideal text, cited in pamphlets and treatises as the proper paradigm for author/reader relations: full disclosure at the time of signing was required, both parties could assume positions of equality, and failure of such conditions restored the parties to *status quo ante*.

Defoe was quick to argue that the primary factor shifting power between creditor/readers and debtor/authors was that since promises were by nature uncertain, the author of an unpaid bill could not (definitively) be said to lie. Time mediated the intent behind any promise, transferring agency from the individual to an unpredictable market. Elevating the modalities of the market into a prescriptive, Defoe argued that "intent" was contingent; an imputed "lie" was a category mistake. Readers learned (and should learn) that it was impossible to decipher – to isolate – intent. It was obscured – attenuated – in the intertext of credit relations. No one was responsible if those responsible to him failed of their own promises. In *The Compleat English Tradesman,* Defoe wrote:

> To break a solemn promise is a kind of prevarication, that is certain . . . But the Tradesman's answer is this; all those promises ought to be taken as they are made, namely, with a contingent dependence upon the circumstances of trade, such as promises made by others who owe them money, or the supposition of a week's trade bringing in money by retail, as usual, both of which are liable to fail, or at least fall short. . .
>
> I am under affliction enough on that account, and I suffer in my reputation for it also; but I cannot be said to be a liar, an immoral man, a man that has no regard to my promise, and the like. . .
>
> It is objected to this, that then I should not make my promises absolute, but conditional: To this I say, that the promises, as is above observ'd, are really not absolute, but conditional in the very nature of them, and are understood so when they are made, or else they that hear them do not understand them as all human appointments ought to be understood.[22]

Citing credit's destabilizing tendencies, such logic attenuates the moral implications of causing epistemological confusion. It asserts that promises *are* conditional, like the human condition itself. The ideal transparent contract is subject to certain implied terms, exculpating commercial actors from moral (perhaps legal) consequences. The passage argues that uncertainty in credit relations instantiates the inescapable randomness of things, that in the market (as in every setting) conditionality is normative. Defoe does not misdescribe the uncertainty of commercial promises, nor their embeddedness in networked commitments that frequently obscure the cause of default. He provides a gloss, invoking a structural basis for diminished moral culpability when commitments are not fulfilled. It is a crucial move. Even though *Crusoe* promises authenticity, its prominent, proliferating references to the personae of commercial publishing suggest a network of blue pencils inscribing an intertext. *Crusoe* is an artifact of the market. Everyone and no one (not Crusoe, not Defoe) is responsible if the text is a fiction.[23]

Recent scholarship recognizes that narrative fiction was implicated in debates over how much "credit" should be accorded texts of indeterminate veracity.[24] It does not notice, however, that the potential fictionality of credit provides a logic to engage with the moral/epistemological credibility of texts. In *The Origins of the English*

Novel, Michael McKeon comes near this approach, but his suggestive analysis is contained in only two sentences, involved with a separate argument concerning the morality of fiction:

> Our difficulty in deciding Defoe's stance concerning the relation between capitalist credit and aristocratic honor reflects a real uncertainty on his part about some of the more disquieting features of the world of exchange value of which he was, in general, an enthusiastic supporter. The analogy with his posture on questions of truth is worth noting, for there, too, the basic solidity of Defoe's naive empiricism becomes vulnerable to doubts about the false claim to historicity, in which the stability of moral ends is undermined by the "imaginary" status of pedagogic means. (206)

McKeon argues that the Novel was developed to negotiate epistemological uncertainty, that it epitomizes *generic* uncertainty and can therefore accommodate unstable perceptual paradigms. My study takes a ninety-degree turn, suggesting that Defoe's "fiction" (which includes more than his "novels") was self-reflexively exploiting epistemological uncertainty, negotiating it for the text's own advantage. McKeon's "noting" an "analogy" between Defoe's stance on credit and his attitude towards truth, could have been extended into the epistemology of credit itself (rather than its bearing on "aristocratic honor"). In such a case he might have found that credit and literary fiction maintained a market by deploying the "disquieting features of the world of exchange." The "blind spot" in McKeon's analysis suggests that just as historians have considered credit as a financial, political phenomenon unrelated to the processes of reading, so critics concerned with truth claims in literature have not considered the involvement of such claims with financial discourse. I propose to tie these two skeins of scholarship together, deriving a new approach to the economy of reading in the eighteenth century.[25]

The "financial" texts that I consider engage with the potential fictionality of credit at a quotidian, rather than a partisan level. They are generated by Parliament, anxious investors, an anonymous public concerned with the mounting Debt and the Bubble that burst as a deluge. In language reinforcing the same terms over and over, these pamphlets, treatises and reports define a discourse in which long-term credit is described as "fiction," a phenomenon appealing to "imagination." Its victims emerge as disappointed readers. As I encountered these texts on endless reels of microfilm, it seemed as if I were watching unfold the unmediated anxieties of a culture afraid of texts. The authors betray an emerging, chilling self-awareness. They accept credit as inescapable, but articulate the crux at the heart of emergent capitalism: credit necessary to sustain trade exacts the price of diminished apprehension. To engage in the market (and how could one not?) was to accept a phenomenon implicating reading in uncertainty. The concern addressed in these texts is epistemological. They are not baldly "financial," even, if as seems clear, the authors had no "literary" intent.

The "literary" texts that I consider are primarily Defoe's. More than any oeuvre of the period, Defoe's texts instantiate the homology between financial credit and literary credibility, and engage both the discourse of emerging capitalism and the theory and practice of fiction. While Defoe is famous for *Crusoe*, *Moll*, and *Roxana*, he produced hundreds of texts addressing contemporary financial issues. These texts engage questions of credibility; they are not narrowly "financial." However, the epistemological purport of Defoe's topical tracts has never been addressed. To do so radically alters how Defoe is read, moving to the center of his canon works regarded as peripheral and specialized.

Undeniably, Defoe supports credit, arguing against resistance and apathy that it is crucial in public and private affairs. Nevertheless, following through Defoe's explication of financial instruments (for example) complicates conventional views of Defoe as the champion of bourgeois culture.[26] He emerges as sensitive to the market's capacity to disorganize the self by thrusting it into other people's narratives.[27] At the same time his texts deploy the uncertainties of the market so as to remain in the market unidentified as fiction. Defoe's ability to instantiate cultural anxiety; to contribute to epistemological uncertainty which is its cause; and to use such uncertainty to evade interrogation, creates a complex persona "trapped" in culture but exploiting the trap. Defoe's persona – addressing public concerns but deflecting direct address – challenges rational debate in the public sphere. I shall take issue with Habermas' paradigm of the public sphere as the site of "rational" discourse, arguing that it does not fully account for assaults on rationality such as Defoe's.[28]

In his radical ambivalence, Defoe epitomizes the cultural problematic of a positive engagement with credit that is matched by the disengagement of resistance. While Defoe's serious concern for public credit is straightforward, it takes a turn. At a different angle, Defoe is the stockjobber's counterpart, disseminating potential fictions while employing strategies to resist accountability. Yet even as he supports imagination so that credit (honorable or not) will continue, he opposes imagination, to which the fictions of credit appeal. Thus unlike Swift, who resists the "imaginary" element of credit from outside the practical discourse of credit, Defoe resists from within: he explicates its motions, even supports its operations, in works like the *Review* and *The Compleat English Tradesman*. Defoe represents the complexity of the period's epistemological dilemma with regard to market-generated texts. He instantiates discursive limitations – and strategic possibilities – in a market where unstable representation militates against fiction but insures that it remain unaccountable. In this sense Defoe is a phenomenon of discourse, not an authorizing will located outside and prior to language.

Yet I do not argue that Defoe is without intent. The discourse that constructs "Defoe" requires that Defoe deconstruct himself, embracing congruity with discourse. I treat Defoe as a "trope of selfhood," if not precisely an "author," since (in his fiction) Defoe actively resists being known as an author.[29] He cannot seek credit for fiction, since fiction would discredit him. If his object is to remain in the market, he must seem not to be there. Thus while Defoe is theoretically available to instantiate an author function, he does not (in his fiction) acknowledge such function and the culture cannot easily find him. He disappears as an author before he is reified as one.[30] This disappearing act interests me: it enacts the concatenation in Defoe's oeuvre between credit and fiction.

However, I shall argue that Defoe's de-instantiation as an author is itself unstable, and that his texts betray this. The paradox of marketplace epistemology is that fiction's claims to truth respond to demands for certainty, while the market disables perceptual assurance. If the reader attempts to isolate truth with intratextual cues, he remains stymied. While Defoe's fictions avail themselves of this impasse, they finally evince a sense that the impasse is potentially passable, vulnerable to a reader who breaks through bafflement by importing extratextual data. The famous ending of *Roxana* is a terrified acknowledgment of the persistent reader, unrestrained by disappointment with marketplace texts. Defoe's nightmare reader is Susan, threatening to expose Roxana, and so evict fiction from the market.

I am concerned with the epistemology of Defoean texts, both the problem of reading them and the problem of "reading" as they self-reflexively address it. Thus I consider the prefaces to Defoe's novels, where truth claims are radically uncertain; various impersonating memoirs, which infiltrate the public sphere as "true"; and *The Compleat English Tradesman*, brilliantly theorizing evasive fiction as a commercial program. Instead of tracing development in Defoe's oeuvre towards narrative fiction, or even development from *Crusoe* to *Roxana* – strategies typical of formalism, which reify Defoe as an author – I proceed analytically, positing fiction as a constant problematic. I therefore discuss Defoe's theory of fiction most extensively in relation to an ostensibly economic text, *The Compleat English Tradesman*, and discuss *A Journal of the Plague Year* as it relates to the discourse of accounting, which reacted against the non-(dis)closure of credit.

The problem of reading bears on the formation of the autonomous bourgeois subject. In my analysis, the "economic man" evoked by Defoe – dependent on his "credit," his reputation – is subject to fictions constructed by others. Their perceptions supersede his ability to maintain an integrated, nondependent self. In *An Appeal to Honour and Justice* (1715) Defoe links the market, the public sphere, and processes of fiction into a single dynamic. In a complex conceit, he claims that his real intent has been dispersed in Opinion, his name commodified, "hackney'd about the Street by the Hawkers, and about the Coffee-Houses by Politicians, at such a rate, as not Patience could bear" (46). In Defoe's texts, conflation of the market with a distorted public sphere configures the market's corrosive effect on reputation, and indeed on one's sense of agency. Defoe presents an ironic riposte to Habermas' view that by the eighteenth century, the market conferred an experience of independence:

In a certain fashion commodity owners could view themselves as autonomous. To the degree that they were emancipated from governmental directives and controls, they made decisions freely in accord with standards of profitability. In this regard they owed obedience to no one and were subject only to the anonymous laws functioning in accord with an economic rationality immanent, so it appeared, in the market. These laws were backed up by the ideological guarantees of a notion that market exchange was just, and they were altogether supposed to enable justice to triumph over force. Such an autonomy of private people, founded on the right to property and in a sense also realized in the participation in a market economy, had to be capable of being portrayed as such.[31]

For Defoe, the *irrationality* of the market, infiltrated into discourse, subjects the self to chronic contingency. "The right to property" does not equate with "autonomy," since credit – antecedent to property –

binds the self into discursive matrices that invite caprice and preempt self-assertion. Property in one's own name is contingent, since reputation can be alienated involuntarily. This perception becomes prevalent after the South Sea Bubble, as the market's disorganization "sinks" credit irrespective of an individual's worth.

Yet as I have suggested, by assimilating credit tropes, Defoe's texts take an ironic, opportunistic turn on the self's contingency in the market. If credit dis-integrates "economic man," if he cannot author himself, so authorship as an economic category is destabilized. The market's co-optation of intention becomes the ultimate rationale (for the Compleat English Tradesman, for Defoe) by which to elude accountability as an author. The text in the market constitutes authorial absence, testifying to the dispersal of intent in a ramifying intertext. As a consequence, *The Compleat English Tradesman* is my central exhibit: it theorizes the absence of agency in the market, and hence the inaccessibility of an author's intent.

My approach, informed by the irony of Defoe's approach to texts, is necessarily ironic. By concentrating on Defoe, I deconcentrate him, dispersing his persona in discourse (a project that finds him a willing accomplice). In chapter 1, I elaborate the discourse of public credit, its connection to private credit, and Defoe's personal identification with the regime of credit through the narrative of Lady Credit.

Chapter 2 discusses Defoe's political fictions and the prefaces to his novels, examining how these texts incorporate strategies deployed by credit. I argue that Habermas' definition of the public sphere is too linear, too dependent on "reason" to accommodate texts that do not disclose their intent.

Chapter 3 concerns *The Compleat English Trasdesman*. The text is highly self-reflexive, recapitulating tensions that permeate Defoe's texts: if Defoe is constantly claiming to be credible, yet constantly throwing up barriers to rational inquiry, the *The Compleat English Tradesman* projects this trope into a comprehensive market rationale. On the one hand, the text presents itself as forthrightly providing a version of credit that is stable and transparent. On the other, Truth and Lies collapse as independent categories, engulfed by a notion of "intent" that recedes into impenetrable subjectivity. The "intent" of the text – to define credit so that it can be measured objectively – is obscured, drawn into the exculpatory logic of credit where intent is unhinged from performance. The text pivots around the nexus of credit/credibility/fiction, insulating the author from definitive determinations that his intent is to *produce* fiction.

In chapter 4, I argue that if credit destabilizes epistemological categories, the culture offers a competing (if artificial) regime, a Fiction of Stability in which truth is always fixed, stable, accessible. This is the artifice of double-entry bookkeeping – "accounting" – by which the trading classes calculate daily financial standing. In the ideology of accounting, there is almost no such thing as misrepresentation. The system detects and expels "Error," militates against "After-cheats," producing texts that are absolute "Truth." Reading such texts (in the context of their ideology) is the mirror image of experiencing credit texts; it weakens the market's discipline against expecting transparency.

As a consequence, accounting threatens a market-based textuality that depends upon uncertainty to obscure "fiction." In *The Compleat English Tradesman*, Defoe offers a version of accounting that departs from convention. His own accounting texts are not self-adjusting; they assimilate with the very texts they would regulate – negotiable instruments – and so undermine the possibility that any text is invulnerable to credit's mystifications. The turn is brilliant, absolutely necessary, consistent with Defoe's disarticulation of Truth. As a means of dismantling barriers to the unfettered production of Defoean fiction, *The Compleat English Tradesman* challenges bourgeois culture in its most basic instrumentalities.

In chapter 5, I discuss *Roxana*, arguing that it tests the durability of fictive personae. I shall argue that *Roxana* explodes the credit/fiction homology, opening up the possibility that readers, unpoliced by a daunting market, can expose the author of fiction. In his meanest, but most authentic fantasy, Defoe has Susan killed (or apparently killed, in a final wink at the infinitely regressing obscurities of market-generated texts). Susan's crime is that of threatening the (anti)-interpretive community of the market, even after she is warned. Her relentless pursuit of Roxana, and her apparent murder, reveal that the (anti)-hermeneutic of the market is vulnerable – if not to accounting, then to rogue readers. But Defoe cannot kill all the readers.

In the end, *Finance and Fictionality* concerns a cultural moment suspended in paradox: it would hold market-generated fiction to account, while maintaining a system of credit that prevents its being found. The only way around this paradox is by violent transgression, Susan's and hence Defoe's. In *The Compleat English Tradesman*, Defoe opts to remain in paradox: one cannot kill all the characters.

Moreover, it becomes apparent that even as he dismantles the absolute integrity of accounting, its pretensions remain attractive, a barrier to the uncertainties of credit. Defoe's ambivalence regarding accounting configures his address to credit, and indeed to the market: while he resists their inclination towards fiction, their tropes merge with his own fictions as he flees accountability for fiction. For Defoe, as for the culture, credit becomes a site for enacting the limits of discursive integrity.

In suggesting an homology between credit and narrative fiction, I am not proposing a paradigm applicable to novels that begin emerging towards mid-century. Once novels openly avow their fictionality (even while claiming faintly to have been "found" or "edited"), the homology breaks down. Richardson and Fielding, for example, no longer eschew accountability for fiction by confusing (and so discouraging) efforts to identify it.[32] The homology also breaks down at the financial end: while public finance is still characterized in terms resonating with fiction, there is an ebb in the acute sense of textual crisis that pervaded the early part of the century. In this sense, the "market" contracts, assuming the generic isolation with which discourse now credits it. My discussion is therefore time-bound. It concerns the experience of reading just before "literary" "fiction" becomes the novel, the final anxious moment when fiction is uncontained.

CHAPTER I

Credit and its discontents: the credit/fiction homology

PUBLIC CREDIT

A brief history

For twenty-four years beginning in 1689, England was almost continually at war with the Continent, radically increasing the National Debt.[1] The unlikeliness of a prompt discharge was implicit in the proposed "Fund of perpetual Interest" to carry the Debt.[2] Long-term annuities for periods as long as ninety-nine years, with interest as high as 14 percent, proliferated. Lottery pay-outs extended to sixteen years. "The Government appear'd like a distress'd Debtor, who was every Day squeez'd to Death by the exorbitant greediness of the Lender."[3] By all accounts public credit was "sunk." Long-term debt in 1708 exceeded £8 million. Another £2.5 million were added by 1710, supplementing short-dated bills exceeding £9 million for naval supplies, general war necessities, and miscellaneous expenses.

Defoe reflected the growing anxiety during a series on credit that appeared in the *Review* between 1710 and 1711. His main argument, a theme that was to dominate discourse during the coming decade, was that financial "securities" were valenced with insecurity, binding the nation to an endless entail of crushing obligation:

It is very evident, that in the present Circumstances of Britain, fifty Years Peace gives us no Breath, nor are we one jot the more able to begin a War again, after 50 years rest, than we are now to carry it on; all our Capital Branches of Income, are actually mortgag'd for an Hundred Years, that is, in one Sense, for ever; the Customs, the Excise, the Salt, the Stamp Paper, they are all Anticipated, all Engag'd . . .

[H]amper'd with Chains of an Entail'd Debt, [we] must feel that Wound to Ages to come, and have no Relief by the Length of Time; this would be worth considering, at least in our Future Taxes . . . [I]f all our Securities are actually Sold and Convey'd, and the Time absolute, if they are determin'd

for Ninety nine Years ... they cannot be Redeem'd, and by Consequence the
Nation cannot wear off the heavy Burthen, till such a length of Years as is so
Limited.[4]

The prospect of being bound to generations of unseen, demanding
others, condemns the Nation to debtor's prison, where it is stifled
("fifty Years Peace gives us no Breath"), "hamper'd with Chains,"
unable to pay its way out ("our Capital Branches of Income ... are all
Anticipated").[5] Defoe's conceit conveys credit's defining crux. One is
enmeshed, inscribed into narrative ("Ages to come," "such a length
of Years") written on others' behalf; one's volition is (con)scripted by
the market. The metaphor of being bound, abdicating liberty to an
enchaining institution, conflates the creditor/jailor with potential
enemies to whom the Nation concedes sovereignty ("nor are we one
jot the more able to begin a War again").

Indeed, in *Fair Payment No Spunge*, Defoe argues that a swollen
National Debt is incompatible with freedom:

It is in vain to talk of the Liberties and Privileges of a Nation that is in Slavery
to Creditors, and chain'd down to the miserable Consequences of an
insupportable Debt: No Liberties can be long supported, when the Means of
resisting the Power of Enemies is out of our Hands; For while the Nation is
overwhelm'd in Debt, she lies bound Hand and Foot, a Prey to every
beggarly desperate Invader.[6]

As credit compounds, so does the debtor's servitude. "Liberties and
Privileges" abdicated "in Slavery to Creditors," entail lost civil
liberties, abdicated to a "desperate Invader." As the debtor remains
"bound," one loss yields another in a course of decreasing agency.
Defoe's rhetoric, valencing financial and civil liberty, suggests that
credit ramifies and complicates loss – the "chain'd down" debtor is
"invaded" (ironically by beggars). Britons urged to free "themselves
and their Posterity from a Burthen which they are not able to bear"
(introduction), are weakened further by worry: "Our Debts are the
main Article that darken our Circumstances, and makes every
Rumour alarm us; every Conspiracy, tho' supported by Beggars and
Mad Men, seem formidable to us" (17). Debtors "credit" erroneous
discourse ("every Rumour"); they are cowed by baseless imposition
("every Conspiracy"); hysteria co-opts judgment. Yet in theorizing
credit within a scene of lapsed rationality (and base opportunism),
neither Defoe nor his readers envisioned the fiasco to ensue when
long-term debt was "retired."

In 1711 Parliament sought to manage the short-term debt. It chartered the South Sea Company. With the momentous consequences of this decision still a decade away, the government's short-term creditors were incorporated in the Company, their claims cancelled in return for the equivalent in stock. By authorizing the Company to trade with South America, creditors were bought off with the lure of high profits. The accessibility of these profits was uncertain, however, given Spain's exclusion of foreigners. Moreover, though the Company was to receive over half a million pounds a year in government annuities, the government fell behind. For two years, its stock traded at around 70, reaching par only in 1716.[7]

This fanciful expedient had no impact on the government's long-term debt, which by 1714 had mounted to over £14 million. Outstanding lottery obligations would clearly never be paid from dedicated funds, and to a degree it was still government practice to charge debts against funds already subscribed. In 1718, Archibald Hutcheson, MP, complained to Parliament that:

Debts contracted since [1714] have been all charged on the old Funds, which had before been appropriated to other Purposes. I have ever thought, that the raising the current Supplies of the Year, by imposing new Duties, and mortgaging the same for long Terms of Years, to be a practice very ruinous to the Publick; but to create any new Debts, without new Funds, and to charge the same on those which were appropriated to the Payment of other Debts, is certainly much worse; for this seems to bear hard on the Publick Faith, and evidently tends to make the discharge of the Publick Debts altogether impractical.[8]

"Bear[ing] hard on the Publick Faith" by adopting financial schemes that are "incredible" (but assert their regularity), that are fictions (but audaciously claim what they cannot deliver), was a normative complaint in discussions of public credit. In Hutcheson's account, "old Funds" are sites impacted with fictions, which make claims discounting prior, competing claims, so that each is supported by a willed (and shaky) credulity. His argument, citing lack of originary, authenticating support for Parliament's representations ("new Debts, without new Funds"), implicates credit in the logic of fiction: both produce signs without referents, ciphers with no payoff in the world of phenomena. Hutchesonian fictions of credit inhabit a discursive space ("old Funds"), a few lines in an Exchequer ledger. But as they accrue they crowd the text with mutually discrediting promises to pay: claims pile up *seriatim*, straining funds and credulity in an intensive, opaque, palimpsestual discourse that renders textuality increasingly remote from rational efforts to read Parliament's intent.

In Hutchesons's view, the Funds' lapsed transparency exposed the ironic relationship between expanding credit and shrinking credibility, which intensified even as Parliament attempted to breach the gap. Could methods purporting to clear the National Debt be *given* credit? Were they real; likely to work? Hutcheson's rhetoric anticipates the charge of "blue smoke and mirrors" by which Reaganomic tax cuts would raise revenues. His analysis recognizes credit's epistemological dimension – the "real" and the "imaginary" – arguing that schemes to retire new debt could not sustain Publick Faith because (like the Funds themselves) they could not sustain inquiry into their own reality. He asserts that credit produces a kind of dissipative narrative, a discourse in which the originary *situs* of debt retirement ultimately evaporates:

[I]t now appears . . . that the great sinking Fund, with which we were so charm'd for a while, is vanished into Smoak, and that we run some Risque of a great Deficiency even in Annual Payments. And at best, that there will be no sinking Fund. . .

To get rid of some present Pressures, and to dispose the Parliament to the granting of such great Taxes as were thought necessary for the Support of the Government, was a present and great Conveniency: But surely this might have been obtained without the Amusement of a pleasing Dream, and which, in a short time, must appear to have been entirely vain. The Nation, indeed, should have been plainly inform'd (and so they must at last) that they must groan for ever under the present heavy Load of Debt . . . By [making the Funds equal to the annual charge against them], and the Reducement of Interest, instead of an Imaginary, there might have been a Real and Substantial Sinking Fund towards the Payment of the National Debt.[9]

Hutechson suggests that the Fund, the authenticating ground of credit, seemed real (for a while) because Parliament was "charm'd" by "the Amusement of a pleasing Dream." Credit-as-fiction, like the literary genre, misrepresents: the passage resonates with Puritan distaste for fiction. Both amuse, distracting the senses from the real. Thus the "Reducement of Interest" was an "Imaginary" measure, seeming "Real and Substantial" only until the Fund blew away as Smoak.

While Hutcheson pictured the vanity of public finance, both trading and landed interests complained that debt and high interest

diverted capital from circulation, depressing land prices, choking off
trade, enriching foreign investors. While the gentry claimed that it
bore the burden of the Debt, in *Fair Payment No Spunge* Defoe argued
that the poor and middle classes suffered most from high taxes. Duties
on imports were also high, forcing traders out of business.[10] Several
pamphlets asserted that moneyed interests would oppose efforts to
help the burdened, since that would make interest rates fall.[11]

Indeed, speculators were prospering. Between 1717 and 1720
investment in joint-stock companies climbed from £20 million to £50
million. Stockjobbers, as well as the Bank of England and other
holders of government debt, were accused of profiteering. The Whigs
favored credit and the emergent "paper'" economy, and Walpole
pushed through a series of measures that untangled government
obligations, lowered annual charges, established the Sinking Fund,
and cleared certain old encumbrances.[12] The relative reprieve set the
stage for tackling the intractable problem of high, virtually perpetual
interest owed to annuitants.

In 1719 annuities accounted for about three-fifths of long-term
debt, which had by then risen to almost £50 million. The annuities
were of two kinds, those redeemable at the government's option, and
the "irredeemables," which could not be terminated or reduced
except with the annuitant's consent. No annuitant would agree to
redemption, however, unless offered terms at least equal to retention
and hence of no value to the government. Nevertheless, since
irredeemables had yielded such exceptional profits, Walpole and
Hutcheson, among others, argued that it would not be unjust if these
securities *were* redeemed on terms less favorable than retention. Defoe
agreed, arguing in *Fair Payment No Spunge* that with a reduction in
interest rates, the debt could ultimately be retired. Parliament
responded to the challenge as politicians do, finding a solution that
seemed painless.

Rather than lowering interest rates, another way round the
impasse was one that appeared to have worked when incorporating
the South Sea Company: exchanging debt for stock on the prospect of
capital appreciation. In 1720 the government tried it again.
Parliament proposed an act to empower the Company to offer
holders of redeemables and irredeemables new South Sea stock in
exchange for their annuities.[13] The proposal was not regarded as
painless by everyone. Sir Richard Steele, MP, argued that the
annuities were contracts, an absolute promise by the government to

perform, and that any potential reduction in annuitants' rights would be confiscatory. He discounted claims that the exchange would be voluntary, and argued that it imposed a condition on rights that ha⸀ been purchased unconditionally:

[T]wo Contractors always understood each other to be, and covenant to be, Equals, and never to use any Advantages for Evasion; and I appeal to all the World, whether they think these Annuitants would have purchas'd under a Reservation, that forty Years after, the Publick should have an Equity of Redemption . . . The mention of this at the time of making this Sale would have broke the Bargain, and therefore it is not supportable by the Rules of Honesty to mention it now, and to subject their Fortunes to the same imaginary and changeable Condition, which Moneyers put upon the intrinsick Value of the Money lent on the rest of publick Securities.[14]

Steele asserts that credit must repel the impulse to render promises fictive, malleable, subject to subsequent desire. The credibility of credit rests on credible texts – contracts inscribing debtor and creditor into a mutually intelligible, binding commitment. His concern, central to the deepening crisis in credit, is epistemological as much as moral: contracts must be transparent, disclosing all terms and conditions at the time of execution.[15] If the government were to meddle with its contracts, demonstrating that an ostensibly stable intent were fragile as paper itself, then credit would founder: "according to my notion of Credit, whatever Power gives occasion of Distrust of Safety to the Creditor, must of Necessity become Bankrupt, and who can raise a greater Suspicion, than they who assert, that the Right and Disposal of any part of what they have borrowed, is yet in themselves?" (20–21). Steele's premises for consenting to be bound, that both sides "never . . . use any Advantage for Evasion," link credit to a theory of scriptive integrity based on scriptive stability. The annuities must not be mere puffs of Smoak. They must not be turned into fiction *après la lettre*.

Yet despite such opposition, the act passed, in part because of well-placed bribes. The price of the exchange-for-stock was specifically omitted from the legislation, to be agreed upon later by the parties. This became the basis of a stunning irony (discussed below) when annuitants, confident they would be able to negotiate an exchange, failed to read subscriptions that transferred this right to Company functionaries. The Company was ambitious for the act, and for the various loopholes, since it saw the chance to make the fortune that had not materialized in South America. The higher it could push the value of its stock, the less on a proportional basis it would pay the government creditors. Thus if the whole £31 million of subscribable debts were exchanged for £15.5 million in new South Sea stock valued at 200, the Company's capital would increase by £31 million, and it could sell the other £15.5 million of stock at whatever the market would bear. If the stock were valued at 400, the Company's profits doubled again. From the annuitants' point of view, a rising market in Company stock meant higher profits when they unloaded their shares.

Though there were warnings, purchasers were not deterred by thoughts of a market slide.[16] As it happened, the Company began inflating shares even before annuitants' subscriptions took place; exchanges occurred on three dates in 1720, when the stock rose as high as 1,050. The frenzy in South Sea stock fuelled speculation in all sorts of "mushroom" projects. Angry at the competition, the Company loaned huge sums so that buyers could buy on margin. It suffered a liquidity crunch when required to pay dividends on earlier subscriptions. Then it sued an important company, the Sword Blade, that was lending *it* money, claiming that the firm engaged in businesses not authorized by its charter (which, incidentally, had attracted speculators away from South Sea shares). The suit succeeded all too well. By late 1720 the South Sea was out of cash and overcommitted. There was a run on its stock when people sold off to cover other obligations (undertaken, ironically, in the general frenzy inspired by South Sea's advance). Company shares plunged to 155. Thousands of annuitants were devastated. Exchange Alley collapsed. Then came the threat of bubonic plague, raging in Marseilles.

The South Sea Bubble, as it has become known to posterity, seared into the English imagination.[17] It exceeded the US's Savings and Loan scandal in terms of the proportion of people affected and ruined. But like that scandal, it exposed brilliant and ruthless financial manipulation, unbelievable incompetence, and a relationship between government and business that depended on bribes and insider trading. Parliament set up a Committee of Secrecy, which quickly discovered that Company directors had sold "fictitious stock" – stock which had not yet been issued – to influential persons, so as to insure passage of legislation authorizing the scheme. If the stock went up, these individuals would profit; if it went down, the sale would be void. The names of such purchasers were deleted from Company records; when the sale was discovered, the Company cashier fled to the Austrian Netherlands, safe from extradition by dint of a £50,000 bribe to the Netherlands' governor.

In the real world the Bubble struck at every quarter of society, wiping out marriage portions, impoverishing orphans. Sir Isaac Newton lost £20,000. It bankrupted investors and those to whom they owed money. Rich men were suddenly penniless, their fine horses sold for drays. Two famous newspaper accounts tell the story:

You may see second-hand coaches; second-hand gold watches, cast-off diamond watches, earrings to be sold; servants already want places who were, but a little while ago, so saucy and so insolent, no wages and no kind of usage could oblige them. The streets are full of rich liveries to be sold, nay, and full of rich embroidered petticoats, rich, embroidered coats and waistcoats; in a word every place is full of the ruin of Exchange Alley.

The far greater number who are involved in this public calamity appear with such dejected looks, that a man of little skill in the art of physiognamy may easily distinguish them. Exchange Alley sounds no longer of thousands got in an instant, but on the contrary all corners of the town are filled with the groans of the afflicted, and they who lately rode in great state to that famous mart of money, now humbly condescend to walk on foot, and instead of adding to their equipages, have at once lost their estates.[18]

William Chetwood's comedy, *The Stock-jobbers: or the Humours of Exchange Alley* (1720), was too close for comfort. At best, the following may have provoked a nervous twitter:

MONEYWISE: . . . We are all ruin'd, all undone.
WEALTHY: Why, what's the Matter? What's the Matter? No harm in the South-Sea, I hope.
MONEYWISE: No, but there's a damnable Calm; it has ebb'd no less than a hundred and fifty per Cent. since Morning.
WEALTHY: I had rather you had told me of a Civil War, Earthquake, Inundation, or a general Massacre – The Devil has long ow'd me a Grudge, and now he has paid me Home, Sue.
SUKEY: Sir.
WEALTHY: Here's the Key of my Study. On the Shelf behind the Door, lies a Blunderbuss ready charg'd, prithee fetch it. I'll shoot myself instantly. (33)

Even if one heeded calls for restraint, one succumbed with the unrestrained. Tradesmen failed when their debtors collapsed, inscribing the credit/domino effect of conscription into other people's narratives. Worse still, even rational behavior, the attempt to cut losses by unloading falling stock, proved disastrous to the market as a whole. It accelerated the sell-off, depressed prices further, and exacerbated everyone's losses. It precipitated what is known as the Fallacy of Composition, in which the impact of a phenomenon as a whole differs from what should be the combined effect of its parts: "the action of each individual is rational – or would be, were it not for the fact that others are behaving the same way."[19]

A pamphlet published as the Bubble exploded, anatomized the mutual entanglement of individuals characteristic of a credit-crazed environment. The author renders a sense of chafing, as people caught in each other's narratives construct – and deconstruct – each other:

Every body began to fear that Paper would not prove real Money, when they wanted it: seeing those who had the best Reputation failed, they run on the Bankers, many of whom were immediately blown up, and those some of them thought past all possibility of Danger . . . Our Merchants, whose Cash chiefly lay in the Bankers Hands, was there lost, could not pay the foreign Bills drawn on them, which thereupon went back protested. The Foreigners finding their Bills not paid here, refused to pay those drawn from England on them; and so it has gone round, till an universal Stop is put to that Credit which circulated our Commerce; and every Note and Bill . . . is now become a mere piece of waste Paper, as if a Prayer or a Creed was writ on it instead of Money . . . Every considerable Man that stops Payment, draws a multitude after him.[20]

Helplessness before this ripple effect caused numerous comparisons with the plague: the pamphlet suggests that "the Infection spread like the Pestilence" (16). Such comparisons (which I discuss in chapter 4) premise a new kind of community in which the ills of credit are contagious, inescapable except by leaving the community of trade altogether. For merchants, this was impossible. They were tied to their financial neighbors as much as the poor had been yoked together in cramped cities, unable to escape the plague as it raged from house to house. In this regard, the trading community became an abstraction, located nowhere and everywhere, a "market" defined only by the extent of reticulating mutual promises. *The Compleat English Tradesman* dramatizes relations within this new community, where no one necessarily knows anyone, but where everyone has literal life-and-death effect on everyone else. Bankruptcy is equated with death in the text, as tradesmen go bankrupt through no fault of their own.[21]

The contingency of a world configured by credit inspired plays, poetry, and cautionary tracts (of which *The Compleat English Tradesman* is the consummate example). The Bubble became a metonym of greed and corruption, played out against a speculative frenzy in which hundreds of lesser bubbles competed for capital and gulled the unwary. Some of these were incredibly absurd, and Anthony Hammond remarked that "it's more fashionable to own one is ruin'd by the South-Sea, than by a Bubble; as if there was something more brave in being wounded, or almost kill'd by a great Bear, than by a ridiculous Mouse."[22] A contemporary pamphlet portrayed a mood of soured bemusement:

It is but a few Weeks past that whoever had taken the liberty to talk rationally of the State of the Nation, to warn his Countrymen of the sudden Destruction that was coming upon them, would have been laughed at as a whimsical odd Fellow, or contemned as a poor Wretch, who having nothing to hazard in the Lottery, envied the prosperity of the Lucky Adventurers. The greatest Patriots, Men whose Honour and Wisdom had entitled them to the highest Regard, who with the strongest Reason and most lively Eloquence endeavored to save their Country from Ruin, might as well have made Speeches to Sticks and Stones as to those that heard them. The Frenzy rose so high, that even Mathematical Demonstrations (of which this subject was always capable) were slighted, and the Authors of them treated as if they had been Quacks or Ballad-Singers.[23]

Credit "Frenzy" is portrayed as preying on credulity – on wishful thinking – so that Reason seems "whimsical." The passage suggests perceptual distortion: Patriots trying to "save their Country" are seen as Quacks, phony doctors railing at nonexistent Plague. Mathematics looks like romance, a mere ballad. Such carnival inversion suggests that credit induces a hermeneutic at variance with material phenomena, dislocating responsibility for aberrant interpretation from inditer, to reader, to a market configured by aberrant readings. This shift in the situs of authority, indeed of meaning, attended by the subversion of rational discourse, turns reading into a Lottery for Lucky Adventurers. The average reader, swayed by market discourse, might blame himself; will probably blame the market; and laughs at warnings to resist the market. The passage is a classic iteration of how credit's web-like relations were seen as disempowering, shifting agency among numerous actors so that no one and everyone is responsible for a discourse that defies accurate reading.

In France, Scottish expatriate John Law was orchestrating a

scheme to exploit the Mississippi while alleviating government debt.[24] It was a model for the South Sea scheme, even as the English ridiculed it.[25] Defoe wrote a brilliant, ironic pamphlet about French finances, *The Chimera: or, the French Way of Paying National Debts, Laid Open* (1720), drawing specific parallels between Law's errors and South Sea Company conduct. Yet there was a mentality in England whereby chauvinism, greed, and a certain innocence created a split consciousness. It prevented the English from connecting French flamboyance to their own potential improvidence. Indeed, shortly after *The Chimera*, Defoe issued a pamphlet, extraordinary for its timing, which supported the South Sea scheme, *The South-Sea Scheme Examin'd: and the Reasonableness Thereof Demonstrated* (1720). It appeared when the stock was already depressed. Defoe inverted common claims that "madness" had driven the stock *up*, claiming that "an universal Infatuation, has so far seized on Mankind, as to run down the Stock much below its Value" (8). When the Bubble burst he was unabashed, complaining in *The Case of Mr. Law, Truly Stated* (1721) that no one had issued a warning. Law's scheme blew up slightly earlier than did the Bubble, and in England, Parliament was left with the sticky business of investigating its own.[26]

In 1722, Defoe wrote a scathing, ironic denunciation of Parliament for its role in the affair, *A Brief Debate Upon the Dissolving the Late Parliament, and Whether We Ought Not to Chuse the Same Gentlemen Again*. He suggested that MPs had been bought, and hence had truncated the investigation that followed the Bubble. More grandiosely, critics suggested that the Glorious Revolution had liberated Britain from the irresponsible, unresponsive financial management associated with absolutism, and that the Bubble had decimated this progress:

Credit has been working up ever since the Revolution, and was this Year got to a vast height. It is now fallen on a sudden, and we are at present much where we were a hundred years ago. It must require a great length of Time to restore it again, and some part of it I think can never be restored to any great degree, especially that of the Bankers, which made a large article.[27]

The restoration of credit was an effort to restore credibility: the public saw misrepresentation by South Sea principals as "fatal . . . to the Credit of our Legislators."[28] Hutcheson hinted at venality.[29] Pamphleteers demanded that Company contracts be declared void, claiming that Necessity was a higher "law." The reaction called into question the transparency of the legislative process, and of the law itself. For the first time, government seemed to have authorized a company to betray "Justice and the Publick Faith." As the polity sought to inspect the parlous relationship between credit and credibility, it confronted an even more basic relationship between epistemological and psychological stability:

> Credit is nothing more than that mutual Confidence, which one Man reposes in another, and till that Confidence be restored, Credit can never be; nor will that Confidence ever be restored, till each Man's Property is settled and ascertained. While Property is (as now it is) unsettled and uncertain; while no Man knows, what to call his own; while no Man can even trust himself, but lies under constant Agonies of Mind and Fears to morrow may bring his Ruin; who will trust him? . . . Something must be therefore done to settle and ascertain Property, and to compose the Minds of the Unfortunate.[30]

The passage was nostalgic. The discourse of credit in the early eighteenth century acknowledged that efforts to "settle and ascertain Property" *within* a credit-based regime would stumble over the fact that credit, resting on promises, was shifting and contingent. Property constituted in more credits than debits could evaporate overnight. Defoe called such property Air-Money. The "constant Agonies of Mind and Fears [that] to morrow may bring . . . Ruin" were not local phenomena (a sort of post-Bubble jitters); they were intrinsic to economic life defined by credit, which the Bubble clarified for some people and exacerbated for many others.

When the Bubble broke, the perception that property was unstable brought extraordinary proposals, such as passage of an act "as a formal Guarantie and Security for quieting the Minds of the People." The proposal contained an elaborate new design for "Parliament Money," including size, inscriptions, and how the King's face and Sign Manual should be engraved.[31] "Security," it would appear, was to be constituted by piling up concrete details, a tangible materiality equal and opposite in logic to piling up debts against "old Funds." The pamphlet's concern is with representation (phenomenalogical and political), the assurance that a text *represented* an unassailable reality, i.e. a fund of money guaranteed by Parliament. Ironically, it sought to enlist Parliament in precisely the same enterprise at which Parliament had just failed: acting as origin for textual promises, the ultimate point of reference that validated their veracity.

It is apparant that Steele's fear for the viability of contracts; the complaint that "Every body began to fear that paper would not prove real Money"; the "constant Agonies of Mind and Fears" over unsettled property; the proposal for "quieting the Minds of the People" with elaborate bills, concatenate to link epistemological uncertainty with the instability of texts. The annuities exchanged for South Sea stock that collapsed were emblematic of an endemic problem, a credit/credibility crunch in which finance, mediated through texts, made texts the object of mistrust.

The discourse of public credit

J. G. A. Pocock and the credit/fiction paradigm

J. G. A. Pocock, who first defined credit as a discourse, suggests that "credit" was absorbed into debates over political theory conducted by professional writers, partisans, and genteel authority.[32] I have already shown that the discourse was broader. The ensuing discussion considers the relationship of Pocock to this more inclusive discourse.

While Pocock recognizes the epistemological crisis at the heart of Britain's encounter with credit, his insights register the high political implications of this crisis. However, hundreds of texts suggest that credit disorients the mundane affairs of individual lives. While such texts ultimately broach the integrity of government, they are not (as are many read by Pocock) ideologically self-conscious; in the first instance, they issue from actual, practical engagement with credit. They formulate epistemological crisis in terms of a person's encounter with potential fiction in actual credit *texts*. Indeed, credit-based misrepresentations in *texts* were denominated "fictions," reified when contracts, certificates, books of account were seen to be less than reliable disclosures of their authors' intent. Beyond its political ramifications, this (broadly conceived) discourse, concerned with specific issues such as how annuitants should be compensated, influenced proposals for textual construction, and the notion of how "fiction" should be understood.

In *The Machiavellian Moment*, Pocock argues that writers such as Charles Davenant viewed credit as dislocating the counters of value: land gave place to movable, abstract forms of property which depended for their worth on the opinions of others. Objects of knowledge literally decomposed, and were recomposed from others' perceptions. They become less than real, a projection of the shifting, uncertain views of strangers. Pocock's central, crucial insight is that

Davenant proposed an "epistemology of the investing society" (440), wherein

> the language in which we communicate has itself been reified and has become an object of desire, so that the knowledge and messages it conveys have been perverted and rendered less rational. And the institution of funded debt and public stocks has turned the counters of language into marketable commodities, so that the manipulators of their value [political agents, stockjobbers] are in a position to control and falsify "the intercourse of speech." (441)[33]

Language becomes an autonomous reality, discontinuous with the Reality it once represented. It is reified in manipulable tokens that are themselves sites of value, desired, bought and sold. Their value, however, no longer reflects the intrinsic value of real, solid things, but only abstract "values" contingent on the whims of others. The attack on credit is an attack on its capacity to dislocate and disorganize the real, to destabilize knowledge and the means to knowledge.

Pocock argues that Davenant's was a rearguard political reaction to the rise of a "monied interest . . . constantly striving to promote, through war, the extent of the public debt and its value to them" (448). Credit became a symbol of revised power relations in emergent capitalist society, where opinion, passion, fantasy – embodied in the market for stocks – eroded traditional, stable values embodied in land. Men who owned land were displaced by men who owned paper. The potential for corruption amongst such "new men," who manipulated imagination to get money and whose money influenced the government, became an obsession of the rearguard.

Pocock's analysis engages the political implications of credit from the point of view of a class whose values and hegemony were threatened by it. However, the perception of epistemological decay was not restricted to a landed elite; it was, so to speak, common property. Such decay, when transposed from the sphere of high politics to the scene of everyday reading, was expressed as a concern for the relationship between truth and fiction in the texts of long-term credit. In this regard, credit affected the individual qua individual, rather than as an actor competing for status. The epistemological uncertainty attributed by Pocock to a political nation consciously resisting credit was recapitulated at every wrung of society, as bewildered readers of financial texts despaired over tarnished transparency. The leap from Pocock to this more encompassing theory derives from the fact that credit discourse was not confined to the political nation, but extended to all of it, to readers of stock certificates, annuities, even the law underlying them. Because credit was involved with texts accused of being "fictions," and literary "fictions" represented themselves as potentially true, the textual formations of early capitalism constituted an homologous market with emergent literary forms.

In *Virtue, Commerce, and History*, Pocock examines the politics of credit by elaborating its implication in the elapse of time:

The National Debt was a device permitting English society to maintain and expand its government, army and trade by mortgaging its revenue in the future. This was sufficient to make it the paradigm of a society now living to an increasing degree by speculation and by credit: that is to say, by men's expectations of one another's capacity for future action and performance. (98)

Pocock argues that belief in such a future was grounded in imagination; one imagined the desirable future. When the sequential component of credit is acknowledged – as it must be, since only cash and barter subsist in the present instant – credit entails narrative. Within a regime of credit, where reality-in-time is configured by imagination, reality is recessive, a speculation on what might be. It "exists" as a representation. There is no way to measure whether it will be instantiated in actuality, since revelation is postponed to an indefinite, perhaps perpetually receding futurity. Like an "old Fund," credit is always a potential cipher, a fiction with nothing behind it. Credit narratives, homologous with literary counterparts, appeal to imagination for consent to their truth claims.

Pocock's argument is suggestive:

[F]rom the inception and development of the National Debt, it is known that this date in reality will never be reached, but the tokens of repayment are exchangeable at a market price in the present. The price they command is determined by the present state of public confidence in the stability of the government, and in its capacity to make repayment in the theoretical future. Government is therefore maintained by the investor's imagination concerning a moment which will never exist in reality. (112)

Pocock's analysis of investor psychology develops a theory of narrative where the investor – the creditor/reader of financial texts – invests in promises that may or may not pay off, but that appeal to imagination. The reader makes a long-term commitment, as he would to narrative in a literary text that he has given "credit." In both cases, he buys the text (creating a market); initially persuaded, he hopes to sustain belief. The crucial point is that under Pocock's logic, the market in potential narrative "fiction" cannot be restricted to literary fiction.

Credit texts precipitated narrative as their real value emerged relative to a purported but actually imagined value projected by the reader. The discovery that credit texts were potential "fictions," that apparent value was time-sensitive and might be an illusion (or at least perpetually elusive), surfaced in discourse as the Debt mounted and the Bubble blew up. In the run-up to 1720, encounters with suspected literary fictions raised questions of credibility; so did encounters with credit.

Credit/fiction/texts

The author of *Considerations Upon the Present State of the Nation* argues that under a regime of credit, a man's worth is (de)constructed in others' imaginations:

[N]o one at this time knows whom to trust for a Remittance of Money, or Goods. It's impossible to remedy this Evil, while one merchant goes off after another. Traders are so linked with one another, that unless a man knew his Correspondent's Affairs better than perhaps he does his own, he could not know how to venture upon dealing with him . . . [W]hen the bankrupcys [sic] are over, and the several Accounts made up, I dare say it will appear that many of those who have stopt Payment, are not insolvent, but able to pay even double what they owe. What shall we then think of Schemes and Projects, that by their Mischievous Consequences, are able to break the best of our Merchants, at a time when they are worth a great deal more than they owe? (18–19)

Inability to know a person's capacity forces people with whom he deals to imagine that capacity (probably for the worse). The pamphlet's author resents fictive discourse, consequent upon Schemes and Projects, by which individuals are constructed. A person's individuality, his ability to project an intrinsic worth, is dispersed in others' assessments. These assessments, or rather imaginings, cohere into an impersonal Opinion having no identifiable source; it cannot be stopped or even addressed. In this passage, the resentment of Opinion that Pocock attributes to an ideologically self-conscious reaction – concerned that credit destabilizes worth and disorders perception – is grounded in quotidian experience. People are victimized by fictional representations of themselves, compounded by a radical uncertainty that elides the fact they could "pay even double" what they owe. The victim, an extension of others' perceptions, is bound into others' narratives as they too experience a credit/credibility crunch. At this level, the discourse of credit is mundane, but it evinces a discursive formation in which debits and credits are unreadable. Accounts are *assumed* to be in flux since perception is devalued.

The notion of a value apart from that constructed by Opinion – the "intrinsick" value – was a staple of mundane credit discourse. Individuals in their reputation, and financial tokens in their market price, were affected (one might say "effected") in the same practices of valuation: "imagined" value was opposite "intrinsick," and overtook it. Hutcheson observed of the run-up to South Sea stock:

It is certain, That nothing so extraordinary has ever appeared in this Nation, as the Madness by which the imaginary Value of South-Sea Stock has been raised to the present Heighth: But, that the Frenzy will pass all Bounds, is not conceivable and, in Honour to the good Sense of Englishmen, cannot be supposed. We may put what Value we please upon our Paper, and raise it . . . but we cannot hope always to make it pass with the Nations with whom we have trade and Commerce, for more than its intrinsick worth.[34]

Hutcheson ridiculed the scheme whereby "the South Sea Capital may be raised to a greater Value than the Wealth of the whole World." He called it a "Philosopher's Stone" (63). Through elaborate calculations, he demonstrated how the stock's value had been manipulated, how "by Art-Magick" the Company's advocates had "compute[d] other people out of their Senses" (31). Crucially, the Company prepared its texts (its "Books") so as to hide the stock's "intrinsick Value," raising suspicions about value but leaving no textual (as opposed to extratextual) means to ascertain it:

But is this an Account fit to be given of the Value of this Stock, by the Directors of so great a Society? Surely, they ought to have set forth, The money due to them from the Publick; The Money gained at those respective Times by Subscriptions; and the Profits made by their Home and Foreign Commerce; and to have likewise set forth, The Debts due from them; and, That on the Ballance of their Books, their Stock was then worth such a certain Sum. By this they would have dealt candidly and uprightly with all Mankind, and the intrinsick Value of their Stock, as was only fit for them to give: And their omitting to do this, must necessarily give the strongest Suspicions, that the Value of their Stock is not able to bear such a Light. (86)

The passage raises a complex of considerations: the Company's efforts to confuse apprehension of its Books by manipulating and withholding data; a strategy of deflecting apprehension from the real towards a false, imagined value; the reader's Suspicions of an opaque text. Within the discourse of credit, Hutcheson describes textual posturings and evasions, and delivers reader responses that, I will show, inflect the dynamic between Defoe/Crusoe/Roxana and their readers. The credit text, *potentially* fictive, elicits epistemological confusion at the level of pragmatic, quotidian concern for representational truth.

In *A Modest Apology, Occasioned by the late Unhappy Turn of Affairs, With Relations to Publick Credit* (1720), Hammond describes the slow emergence from the "Infatuation, Lunacy, Or Phrenzy" (4) surrounding the run-up of South Sea stock:

> Then they began to wake out of an Eight Months Dream; and finding the Stocks tumbling down, such of them as were by Authority, and had some Foundation, drawing near to their intrinsick Worth and Value, and others dissolving and sinking into their Original Nothing; the scene is soon chang'd from Joy in the greatest Affluence of Imaginary Wealth, into Complaints of, Want of Species, Decay of trade, and universal Poverty. (5)

A Modest Apology recounts emerging from a Dream into materiality that is dematerializing, seemingly solid stocks "dissolving and sinking into their Original Nothing."[35] In the dream-state induced by credit, the process is reversed: "Imaginary Wealth" seems to materialize into substantial "intrinsick Worth." States of consciousness pivot on a stock certificate, whose purport defers discrimination between "Imaginary" and "intrinsick" until an extratextual phenomenon (the falling market!) triggers a reality check.

But how can an Original be a Nothing? This is the essential paradox of credit, the notion that at the center of discourse there is a blank, a blank that can mesmerize, supporting unsound obligations. Hammond notes that "fictitious Losses" emerged over time from Value that never was, as the narrative precipitated by credit demonstrates that "Wealth" was only "fancy'd":

> In this great Distress among the several Traders in South Sea Stock and Bubbles, some complaining of their fictitious Losses, because they had not sold out in Time, and realiz'd their fancy'd Wealth . . . many indeed sinking under the Weight of Real Contracts and various Engagements. (6)

Fancy is an operative principle, imparting false solidity to the value of credit texts; their evanescence contrasts with "the Weight of Real Contracts." The pamphlet identifies the reader as proximate cause of his own misconstructions, and suggests that "universal" folly and greed – the market's madness – engross the reader:

> [T]he complainants, who are those Numbers trading in stocks and Bubbles, are in some measure Delinquents in universally contributing to raise them to the imaginary Values by their Folly and Avarice, which, in the Consequence, have been so fatal to themselves and others. (6)

Epistemological disorder emerges from a willing suspension of disbelief; prompted by texts that appeal to imagination; in a market where readers' vices mutually reinforce their delinquency. Hammond's text demonstrates that credit engages the imagination beyond ideological concerns of class realignment, addressing itself to the scene of reading.[36] The market, where reading occurs, constructs individual response, inflecting motivation with the impulses of others.

The idea that we read something into Nothing, prompted by other readers inclined to do likewise, is the talisman of credit discourse. We follow desire, willing to impart Value to texts that are not "Real Contracts." Credit is thus the agent of reader bemusement, inducing a collective readership to impart "credit." Hammond's pamphlet is significant in that within a discourse of finance, it articulates a theory of reader response suggesting that a text is just a starting point. However, the text does not contain cues signalling its own right construction. Rather, it seduces the reader, provoking his desire to "imagine" a false purport seemingly validated by other readers' motions. The credit text constitutes around it an interpretive community that is against interpretation, at least insofar as that requires dispassionate assessment of discourse, subordination of the self to a linguistic artifact. By projecting the self into a text, the reader becomes complicit with the text's intent to hide its nonrepresentational status.

The equation of credit schemes with fictive discourse is formulated legalistically in *The Pangs of Credit: or, An Argument to Shew Where it is most reasonable to bestow the Two Millions . . . By An Orphan Annuitant* (1722). This "Orphan," familiar with Latin, the civil law, and Locke, claims to be among those having signed dissimulating subscriptions transferring to Company clerks annuitants' authority to negotiate an exchange. He argues:

> So that if the Directors and we, in our own Persons, had agreed for Stock at a Rate which they knew to be above the real Intrinsick Value of it, we should not, according to Grotius, be obliged to stand to such Contract, but should,

in the Nature and reason of the thing, be released from it, and have had a good Action in Equity against them for cheating us. This casuist makes it the first necessary Preliminary to a Fair, just and binding Contract, That either Party concerned must discover to the other the Faults and Imperfections of the thing contracted for, so as that the other may have such sufficient Knowledge of its Worth, as to treat for it RATIONALLY AND INTELLIGENTLY ACCORDING TO ITS INTRINSICK VALUE.

But now whether the Directors took a Method to inform Men of the intrinsick Value of Stocks; nay, whether they used not many Artifices to raise false and fictitious Notions of its Value, is too well known and felt to need any Remark. (42-43)

Consistent with Steele's logic, the "Orphan" argues that the contract which set the value of annuitants' stock should not be enforced (i.e. the parties should be returned to *status quo ante*) since it cannot be construed "rationally and intelligently." The contract, a fiction that hides its fictionality, should be subject to a protocol by which credibility in credit texts might be assured: "intrinsick Value" would not be effaced by "Artifices [that] raise false and fictitious Notions" of value. Like its predecessors, the pamphlet situates the discourse of credit within the scene of reading, and argues that readers cannot be presumed to consent to a nontransparent text. Power is an issue, not in a Pocockian, sociopolitical sense, but with regard to the parties' equality in making contracts.

Issues affecting contract penetrate the discourse of credit. In *Time Bargains Tryed by the Rules of Equity and Principles of Civil Law* (London, 1720), Sir D. Dalrymple examines the legal principles of consent applicable to the purchase of South Sea stock. He argues that "The Buyer, by the Law of Nature, which requires an exact Equality in all Contracts, is free from his Bargain in as far as the Price exceeds the real Value of the Thing bought" (12). Like the "Orphan" and Richard Steele, he looks to a recoverable time when mutuality of intent can be determined. Moreover, he refutes the idea that mutuality is implied in the phenomenon of marketplace noise, in the general reinforcement of mistake constituted by external manipulators. In this connection, he treats Opinion not just as a modulator of social relations, but as a force to be denied in the construction of texts: "Opinion of the World regulates it self, when it is not led into Error by the Artifice of Cunning and designing Men: The Rule is, to Fix the Value according of the thing sold" (19). The distance between Opinion as it constructs "new men" and new texts, marks the valences of the discourse surrounding credit. At the level of Sir D. Dalrymple, the credibility of "Time Bargains" – texts that develop a narrative – is at issue; texts that deceive out of "Artifice" should not be enforced.

To redress their damages, the annuitants presented to Parliament *A State of the Case Between The South Sea Company, and the Proprietors of the Redeemable Debts* (1721), in which circumstances leading to execution of the false power of attorney, transferring bargaining rights to Company clerks, were outlined for purposes of legal disposition. There were

certain loose Sheets of Paper, lying at the South-Sea House, on some of which appeared something printed; but what it was, or whether it was designed for a Preface, or Preamble, could not be read, both by reason of the Croud, and because the Sheets were doubled in such Manner, that but one half of it appeared either written or printed. (3)

The "sheets" deliberately conceal the authors' intent with "little mean Arts of Tricking and Shuffling" (4). The annuitants state that they had no reason to expect fraud or concealment, since the Company had previously seemed to act honorably, and was invested with a parliamentary trust. The disjunction between what the law seemed to promise, and what the annuitants derive from "certain loose Sheets of Paper . . . [that] could not be read," foments their indignation. The *State* suggests that the materiality of textuality, its capacity to be rumpled, folded, printed on and written over, is the crux of a credit discourse where "intrinsick" and "imaginary" values radically elude apprehension.

The likelihood that authors of credit texts will exploit this materiality comes to a head in the episode of the "fictitious stock," sold to potential supporters of the South Sea Bill to gain its passage. *The Several Reports of the Committee of Secrecy To the Honourable House of Commons, Relating to the South-Sea Directors, &c.* (London, 1721), is an extraordinary account of physically corrupted texts. It concerns "the Disposal of the fictitious South-Sea Stock" (4) that had not been issued, but which appeared in the Company's books as subscribed.

The *Reports* notes that in order to obscure the fraud, "in some of the books produced before [the Committee], false and fictitious Entries were made; in others, Entries with Blanks; in others, Entries with Razures and Alterations; and in others, Leaves were torn out" (1). Examining the cash book, the Committee notes efforts to distract from the lying entries through an appearance of regularity: "The whole Accompts comprehended in these two Pages of the Cash Book, and enter'd in this concealed Manner, appear, nevertheless, to have been stated and ballanced by the Company's Committee of Treasury, without expressing the Day when such Accompts were stated" (2). The Company kept two sets of books: "the said Accompt laid before this House, is not a true Account . . . there are many fictitious Names therein, as the Names of several Brokers and others, which are made Use of to cover the Names of other Persons, who had the real Benefit of such stock, and who nevertheless are not mentioned in that Accompt" (3). The very existence of dual ledgers, kept to preserve "original" intent as purely contingent, functions as a signifier in itself, signifying that real, concrete signifieds do not characterize credit discourse.

The *Reports* state that:

[S]ince the beginning of this Session of Parliament, the examinant and Mr. Knight [the company cashier] discoursing about the Company's fictitious Stock . . . the Examinant asked how he would conceal that? Mr. Knight replied, He would go through thick and thin, rather than discover it. (4)

Reflecting on such textual corruption, the Committee concludes that the directors "had chiefly in View the raising and supporting the imaginary Value of the Stock, at an extravagant and high Price, for the benefit of themselves, and those who were in the secret with them" (16). The *Supplement to the Reports of the Committee of Secrecy* (1721) denounced these practices as "corrupt, infamous and dangerous" (6); profits from the purported sale were ordered disgorged; an MP was committed to the Tower. The reaction against submerged "fiction" – literally so called – evinces extreme repugnance. The *Supplement* recites from a petition that attributes to the Company's action "a great Damp" on Public Credit, which it hopes may be "restor'd" (9).

The Company's books were rogue texts, which unlike the contracts for exchange of *issued* stock, lacked even the color of law as justification. The books were pure, unmediated fiction, drawn up to *produce* a law favorable to their authors. The "fictitious stock," constituted in texts that did not exist, reported in "Accompts" intended to be misread, was a double-sided fiction, a type of Möbius strip where one misreading entails another. Fiction upon fiction becomes a credit-based trope, a strategy of texts to elude interrogation.

At the end of the affair, Defoe wrote a brilliant pamphlet, *A Brief Debate Upon the Dissolving the Late Parliament*, which turned the committee reports on their head, alleging they were themselves fiction, a cover-up of Parliament's laxity in pursuing Company directors. Defoe suggests that the *Reports* – texts begotten by the body that initiated the South Sea scheme – evinced the same evasiveness as the account books they castigated. With biting irony, he asks:

How can we look .upon the several Elaborate Works of that August Assembly, and how vigorously they attack'd that Monstrous Hydra, or many headed Beasts, call'd South Sea Men. How they trac'd the fatal Conspiracy, even to the very Confines of the Court; nay, we may say almost into it, and how they laid open so much of it as served to let us see that it was too deep for our Search, and out of our Depth. (15)

Defoe's intervention, read together with Parliament's own texts, configures a highly public discourse suggesting that an evasive law (not specifying the terms of the exchange), adopted in response to bribes, produced evasive "Accompts"; that evasive accounts of the affair disabled a penetrating Search back towards the source of the cheat. In the deep structure of credit, a capacity to proliferate discourse stymies identification and interrogation of those who authored a cheat. Only the authors can unwind such discourse so that its mystifications are "laid open." The reader can make gross assumptions; he can throw out the suspects *en masse* when the narrative, played out, has (d)eluded everyone:

If they [the MPs] form'd the happy South-Sea Scheme, and brought it to bear in the Shape of an Act of Parliament, opening a Door for the Company to pay all the Publick Debts; what though the South-Sea Directors (deficient in the Execution) drew the whole Kingdom into it as a Bubble, yet the first Scheme certainly draws your favour, and the making a Law of such a Capacity, to make us all Rich calls loudly upon us to show our Gratitude to the Old Members when ever we shall be happy as to come to a new Election. (8)

A Brief Debate is Defoe's "theorization" of the South Sea debacle. It argues that once a text – even a Law – engages the processes of credit, it precipitates textual outworkings that disorganize a linear, fully-informed inquest into original intent, even as they purport to promote it. The South Sea Law, elaborated in discourse, becomes the phenomenological equivalent of the Company's dual books. In each case, representation is short-circuited. When some sort of disclosure is forced, it becomes apparent that the will or the capacity to deliver on a representation has been absent. The "fictitious stock" is cognate to a Dream in that it could just disappear, leaving a vacuum. The legislation seemed backed by the credibility of Parliament, but that disappeared with the slump in public credit.

In subsequent chapters, I argue that the tropes of credit diagnosed by Defoe are homologous with literary tropes deployed by Defoe himself. Defoe's strategy is possible because credit functions as ideology: "it imposes (without appearing to do so, since these are 'obviousnesses') obviousnesses as obviousnesses, which we cannot *fail to recognize* and before which we have the inevitable and natural reaction of crying out . . . 'That's obvious! That's right! That's true!'"[37] Faced with the tropes of credit in *any* marketplace text, even one apparently "literary," the reader assumed an inherent generic uncertainty, and an author who could not be found or interrogated.

Defoean complications

Though Defoe participated in discourse that denounced the fictive potential of public credit, there was a tension in his attitude. He believed in the *utility* of credit's appeal to imagination, its resistance to empirical address. Credit forced the mind into a *creative* mode: imagining the future. In a credit economy, imagination supports the suspension of disbelief underlying investment. It initiates economic narrative. For Defoe, the impulse to invest was involved with a base of imagined data by which to formulate possible, successful narratives. If imagination could conjure the unreal and unverifiable, which could corrupt rational exchange, it could also facilitate exchange that was rational but (because its payoff was deferred) not verifiably rational. Defoe's engagement with the discourse surrounding credit, which rejected imagination, was therefore complex. He impugned imagination because it disordered apprehension of the real, but justified imagination because it provoked apprehension into economically predictive/productive modes. In other words, Defoe recurs to the logic of credit, an either/or proposition that might be a swindle or a windfall (if we could only tell!), and recognizes both possibilities equally. The popular discourse downgraded (to "the Prosperity of Lucky Adventurers") what was necessarily implied in the logic of credit, that *half* the time, *at least in theory*, an imagined payoff paid off. While Defoe does not change the logic of credit, he situates it within a discursive formation that preserves the positive potentialities of imagination. Thus while everyone wanted to restore public credit, and recognized its impact on the private sector, Defoe was singular in promoting the imaginative substrate of credit as the foundation of sucessful credit-based finance. For Defoe, credit transformed economic enterprise into an hypothesis answerable in imagined/unrealized realities – projections of the mind.[38]

In his *Essay Upon the South Sea Trade* (1712), Defoe imagines the creation of American colonies and projects great profits for the South Sea Company. Imagination breaches time, accommodates the future to the present. I take issue, therefore, with Pocock's suggestion that Defoe "busied himself, especially when challenged by Swift, to show how opinion and passion might be grounded upon experience rather than imagination."[39] Defoe never wholly accommodated imagination to the empirical – it remained a functional, useful category. Defoe's valenced logic, defining the imaginative component of credit as pointing towards fiction *and* truth, is homologous with inscribing literary fictions that *conflate* fiction and truth. Defoean credit posits a narrative theory premised on the fluidity of fiction and truth, an enterprise that defers to the reader's imagination while it claims to invoke history. In fact, credit always defers to the reader, and such deference is the quintessential credit trope deployed by Defoean fiction (even as it instructs the reader how to read). The desired result is that if the reader can imagine narrative that is as likely to be "true" as not; if he remains suspended in an Air-Money regime of equally possible outcomes; then the text of a fiction never emerges as a detectable fiction. The author can never be held to account.

Defoe's resistance to credit's potential fictionality was apparent early in his career. Typically, he privileges "intrinsick" over "imaginary" value:

Credit is the certain Knowledge of an Established Fund, on which the assurance of punctual Payment, either of Interest or Principal, or both, in any Loan is Founded ... It is true, Opinion is the Rate of Things, but this is a *deceptio visus* upon Reason; as Fancy is the Judge of Ornament so then Fear is the Guide of Credit; but all this is setting the World with the bottom upward, for all Things have some Intrinsick Value, for which they really ought to be Valuable ... This is real – all the rest is Whymsie, Apprehension, and meer Imagination.[40]

The bivalence of credit, its seeming ability to precipitate alternate potential outcomes, is a *trompe l'œil*. Speaking of stockjobbers, Defoe suggests:

[T]hese Gentlemen added 625,000 l. of Air-Money to the Bank, they give a new Imaginary Value to the Stock – And what is the Consequence, but whenever they please, they can with the same Breath of their destructive Mouths blow away this, and carry away 625,000 l. more of real Value along with It? Thus like true Chymists, they can condense and rarifie at Pleasure; in short, they can condense their own Vapour, and make you take it for Money; then they can rarifie your Money, and make it evaporate into their Pockets.[41]

If credit is narrative in suspension, it is only because the cheat is not yet apparent. The Chymists decide when it will be; they eventually take one's money, extruding narrative while they mock one's senses. In *The Anatomy of Exchange Alley* (1719), Defoe accuses stockjobbers of gothic mayhem to the senses by "Trick, Cheat, Wheedle, Forgeries, Falsehoods, and all sorts of delusions; Coining false News, this way good, that way bad; whispering imaginary Terrors, Frights, Hopes, Expectations, and then preying upon the Weakness of those, whose Imaginations they have wrought upon" (3–4).[42] He raises the spectre of the Bubble *avant la lettre*: "when Statemen turn Jobbers, the State may be jobb'd" (42).

Yet in *An Essay Upon Publick Credit* (1710), Defoe argues that while credit is inaccessible to empirical methods of inquiry –

[it] gives Motion, yet it self cannot be said to Exist; it creates Forms, yet has it self no Form: it is neither Quantity or Quality; it has no Whereness, or Whenness, Scite, or Habit . . .

CREDIT is a Consequence, not a Cause; the Effect of a Substance, not a Substance, it is the Sun-shine, not the Sun[43] –

this opens it up to imagination, which is *useful* to motivation. He compares credit to the hands of a clock, which are evidence of an honest, efficient mechanism; we do not see the mechanism, and while the hands "tell us that the Wheels are good, perfectly made, exactly plac'd, and move to a Truth" (16), it is imagination that facilitates belief in the mechanism. In this extended conceit, knowledge is circumstantial; it cannot be verified and its utility is in projecting the future. The clock is a narrator, and if it is accurate its "honesty" may continue, but we imagine – we project – this continuity. Imagination, the progenitor of fictive narratives, permits us to believe in an extended "Truth" that would otherwise not be apparent.

Ironically, if credit is manipulated by alchemists to whom we surrender rationality, it is also subject to praise for the same reason: "It is the best Philosopher's Stone in the World, and has the best

Method for Multiplication of Metals; it has the effectual Power of Transmutation – for it can turn Paper into Money."[44] This "power of transmutation" infiltrates Defoe's configuration of credit, in which credit's appeal to imagination transits between gothic horror and mercantile soundness. The fluid mutability of credit under Defoe's pen, homologous with a Defoean textuality that resists generic fixity, is reified in Lady Credit, the female incarnation of credit on whom Defoe projects his textual style. She is both impenetrable – a literal virgin – and provocative, giving the impetus to enterprise. Lady Credit, the most underrated narrative subject in Defoe's canon, gripped his imagination.

Lady Credit
A decade before the Bubble, opposition to credit was already nostalgic: the National Debt was rising, and credit had become the basis of late mercantilism. The dressing table of Pope's Belinda registered the compass of English trade, which her body reformulated aesthetically.[45] Defoe observed that "almost every Man we Converse with now Talks of, *The Balance of Trade*,"[46] and he recognized that the emergent system of finance, dependent on the "credit" of public and private negotiants, needed popular (if partisan) explication. In order to address himself to credit from the standpoint of winning the war and maintaining trade, Defoe launched his *Review* into a phenomenology of credit. For reasons that would not have been lost on Belinda's creator, who also wrote

> Ladies like variegated Tulips show
> 'Tis to their Changes half their Charmes we owe[47]

Defoe embodied in a "Lady" the indispensable but mercurial phenomena of financial credit. Lady Credit, variegated as any tulip of the Dutch tulip craze (and as prone to wreak as much havoc on her fanciers' finances),[48] was the first female narrative subject that Defoe created, the one which (in her various "Changes") obsessed him the longest.

Yet "Lady Credit" is an oxymoron: a female narrative subject who embodies Credit cannot sustain ladylikeness. Lady Credit can be no (consistent) lady because, embodying the whimsicality of the market, her female "honesty" is a punning, metaphorical register of the mercurial honesty of marketplace representations – i.e. texts in the market, paper promises written on stock certificates, annuities, the myriad instruments of financial credit. Her personal narrative rings all the changes in marketplace honesty through her sexual deportment.[49] It depicts an abused woman with a regenerative hymen, whose ostensible sex life of blandishment and repression is punctuated by a politic whoredom.

This reading of Lady Credit, focusing on her sexual conduct, is a revisionist approach to the "Coy Mistress" employed in Defoe's *Review* as a "meer Allegory of CREDIT," a woman not ostensibly conceived as a red-blooded Moll or Roxana, but as a device, the emblem of an impersonal market.[50] Of course, one cannot regard Lady Credit – still little more than a cartoon – as comparable to the heroine of a novel. Nevertheless, the generic boundaries of "allegory" accommodate a gendered characterization more ample, more resonant than any heretofore proposed.[51] It is these confining approaches that I want to escape, and by so doing apply a notion of Lady Credit's sexuality to Defoe's perception that "credit," reified in marketplace texts, shares a logic with the "credit" owed to any text in the public sphere.

Studies of Lady Credit elide her perverse sexuality by focusing on her gender, her very femaleness. Such "womanhood" invokes stereotypes that jibe with a credit-based market which in variant versions is mystifying and irrational; vulnerable but useful; the model of stout British virtue.[52] However, Defoe's "meer Allegory" oversteps the stereotypical tropes of emblem-book womanhood, attaining a narrativity (however one-dimensional) anchored in a personal, idiosyncratic life of the body. Indeed, Lady Credit's sexuality entices Defoe: even as he continues to invoke her as Allegory, he elaborates his own involvement in her story, conflating allegory and history.[53] Lady Credit becomes a discursive site on which Defoe imprints his relation to the market – a market where Defoean texts make unstable truth claims.[54] Defoe's displacement onto a "Lady"/"mistress" of his own problematic discursive persona, initiates a trope wherein the parlous "honesty" of a female subject provides narrative material, operant as metaphor, that concatenates with Defoe's discursive honesty.

When Defoe introduces Lady Credit, he observes that:

This is a coy Lass, and wonderful chary of her self; yet a most necessary, useful, industrious Creature: she has some Qualification so peculiar, and is so very nice in her Conduct, that a World of good People lose her Favour, before they well know her Name; others are courting her all their days to no purpose, and can never come into her Books.

If once she be disoblig'd, she's the most difficult to be Friends again with us, of anything in the World, and yet she will court those most, that have no occasion for her; and will stand at their Doors neglected and ill-us'd, scorn'd, and rejected, like a Beggar, and never leave them: But let such have a Care of themselves, and be sure they never come to want her; for, if they do, they may depend upon it, she will pay them home, and never be reconcil'd to them, but upon a World of Entreaties, and the severe Penance of some years Prosperity.

'Tis a strange thing to think, how absolute this Lady is; how despotickly she governs all herActions: If you court her, you lose her, or must buy her at unreasonable Rates; and if you do, she is always jealous of you, and Suspicious; and if you don't discharge her to a Tittle of your Agreement, she is gone, and perhaps may never come again as long as you live; and if she does, 'tis with long Entreaty and abundance of Difficulty.[55]

Reflecting on this passage, Pocock observes that Credit is described in rhetoric that evokes literary goddesses of the Renaissance – Fortuna, Occasione, Fantasia. "Like all these goddesses," he states, "Credit typifies the instability of secular things, brought about by the interactions of particular human wills, appetites and passions . . ."[56] Yet to assimilate Credit to ancestral deities without acknowledging her frantic sex life as a mortal woman, reinscribes her as an emblem, a static signifier with limited narrative potential. Moreover, not even goddesses survive rape as a virgin, or career through myth as chaste, whore, and chaste again. Yet Lady Credit does. Even in this introductory passage, she steps out to "court" those who "have no occasion for her," flouting conduct books that counsel modesty and circumspection, displaying her dejection openly (in doors "neglected and ill-us'd") and with intransigence.[57] If she is "chary," she also chases men. Her erratic sexual deportment – she observes and disrupts gender norms – enacts uncertainty, preempting gender itself as a signifier.

As Credit's narrative proceeds, claims made on behalf of her chariness are subverted by revelations of a "past," of her consorting with Europe's most notorious royal lecher, the lover of actresses Moll Davis and Nell Gwynn:

Nor is she to be won by the greatest Powers; Kings cannot bribe her; Parliaments cannot force her; as has been seen by manifold Experience, among a great Variety of Ladies. King Charles II, had got her once for his Mistress, and she was very kind to him a great while . . .[58]

If Credit is an Augustan Fortuna, she is also a courtesan.

Indeed, in the same paragraph Defoe argues that Charles, "meerly by this Jades Assistance," might have encompassed all the nation's funds if he had not shut up the Exchequer, forcing Credit to flee. A "jade" is not "chary" or "nice in her Conduct," and this slippage in Defoe's rhetoric further unsettles any univalent inscription of sexual demeanor.[59] Defoe's rhetoric develops a double entendre, equating financial and sexual phenomena, suggesting that Credit's chariness on the one hand produces license (perhaps licentiousness) on the other. In William's reign, "Deficiencies happening... and having no Satisfaction, she took it so ill, that she made a second Elopement, and away she run and left us."[60] Bringing her history into the present, Defoe remarks that Queen Anne has been the first monarch, through "Husbandry and Vigilance," to have "added tha: thing call'd CREDIT, to the Affairs of the Exchequer; a thing of that Immense Value and Infinite Consequence, that I dare not Write, what to me seems contain'd in the Teeming Womb, of this Mother of great Designs."[61] Credit is involved with men, breeding in her body the fruits of economic passion. The convoluted narrative of her relations with men – Defoe's near contemporaries – forms the basis of Credit's persona, not stereotypes from the Renaissance. Credit is frequently in danger of being raped; patriarchal language of "possession" and "conquest" is applied to her; and in King William's reign she *is* "raped."[62]

Yet after revealing the rape, the *Review* claims that in Anne's reign Credit is a virgin.[63] The revelation/revision follows a remark that restoring credit is "almost as Difficult" as restoring virginity. The remark is self-reflexive. Defoe invokes the impossibility of actually regenerating a hymen, yet reserves to Credit – to marketplace discourse – the option of flouting the logic of narrative progression. As one inscribing Credit-as-woman, he is licensed to reinscribe discursive virginity when it reflects marketplace revisions, thus implicating authorial latitude in the shiftiness of the market:

I cannot confess but acknowledge, that to recover Credit to any place, where she has been ill Treated, and perswade her to return, is almost as Difficult as to restore Virginity, or to make a W[ho]re an Honest Woman; and therefore, tho' I am but a very indifferent maker of Panegyricks, yet I think I say too little, if I say, 'tis Superiour to all our Conquests of *Hochstette*, and *Catalonia*; tho' those Articles are also prodigies in their kind too.[64]

By reemerging from her history as virginal, Lady Credit becomes a narrative *tour de force*, a "conquest" of narrative that disengages an explicit narrative past. Lady Credit, constructed within history, a product of discourse, develops an ahistoricism that suspends recourse to discourse: she clearly has lost her innocence, and she clearly has not.[65] By contriving such narrative deracination, Defoe casts himself as Lady Credit's ultimate disappointed suitor, courting but not "possessing," unable to contain this "Coy Mistress" within norms of narrative practice. He becomes a subject of the text as he produces Lady Credit; in control but not; a phenomenon of the market, *like* Lady Credit, in the uncertainty of his deportment.

As the narrative deracination intensifies, so does the perception that Defoe as narrator is suspended in contraries, at any point credible/noncredible. Under threat of a French landing, the directors of the Bank during Anne's reign do all they can "to preserve the Honour and Chastity of their new Guest," and succeed in retaining her.[66] Honour? Chastity? The *Review* had already revealed that Credit was long since a victim of rape, set upon by stockjobbers when King William grew lax:

These Creatures growing numerous, and assuming Human Shape, the first Violence they committed was a downright Rape – For hearing the Lady, I am treating of, was got into *Holland*, they wheedled her over hither by a new Sham, *I might call it a Cheat*, call'd, A Vote in Parliament for supplying Deficiencies – The poor deluded Lady, thinking she might depend upon any thing Parliamentary, came away very readily; she was no sooner come over, but these new-fashion'd Thieves seiz'd upon her, took her Prisoner, toss'd her in a Blanket, ravish'd her, and in short us'd her barbarously, and had almost murther'd her.[67]

It was generally understood (despite some Restoration comedy) that when a woman was dishonored, even through no fault of her own, the taint was permanent. She almost never reclaimed the prerogatives of an unsullied woman.[68] Yet Credit's history is elided in assertions of Chastity and Honour. She expects an honorable marriage, hoping to preserve her "chastity" with a man who sublimates his libido in his shop. That is, she will marry:

[i]f she lights of a Young Man full of Application, sober, sensible, and honest, that lays his Bones to his Work, and his Head to his Business; that doats upon his Shop, that has his Heart behind the Counter, whose Mistress is his Counting House, and his pleasure is in his Ledger.[69]

Despite consorting with Charles II, her rape, and her simpering displays at the doors of indifferent men, Credit shrinks from sexual contact when faced with an "honest" match. She transits a bivalent sexuality: "chary," remote from sex, even ostensibly a virgin, but also sexually active, a "mistress," a flirt and the object of assault.

The radical ambiguity of Credit's narrative, the two strains of her personal life as a woman, corresponds to Defoe's endorsement/rejection of its imaginative potential, i.e. to the bivalence of credit itself: "Credit in Trade, like a Surfeit of Bread, is a most dangerous Evil, where it proves a Distemper; as it is the life of Commerce in some Degree, where it is duly observed."[70] The epistemological uncertainty of a credit-based market is bodied forth, as it were, in Lady Credit's deportment.[71] No Fortuna, this woman (on the one hand) "will stand at [her husband's] Door to invite his Customers," using her body to appeal, exceeding even the progressive norms of female propriety that Defoe would propose.[72] At the same time, she withholds her body, withdrawing from lawful conjugal sex.

The narrative of Credit (configured as a woman) deconstructs itself as it proceeds, never allowing the reader – the consumer, the consumer of narrative – to maintain a purchase on the underlying value of Credit herself. The narrative of credit-as-a-woman literalizes the tendency of paper credit to elude stable valuation. Defoe's jibes at stockjobber/Chymists suggest that the value of a credit transaction is subject to the whims of its initiator, who implicates credit in a narrative fluctuating through time. Value remains suspended, its consumers remain in suspense, until the authors (should they choose) declare its value (if any, which can always be ascribed to chance). The irony of Defoe's rhetoric is that the destabilization induced by stockjobbers, sworn enemies of Lady Credit, is consistent with her own instability, both as to gender norms and in terms of physical virginity itself.

As Air-Money, Credit may (at least in theory) precipitate radically antithetical outcomes. In the person of a woman, Credit recapitulates this propensity, holding in suspension chariness and Jade, elaborating a narrative that at any point features one, the other, or some unresolved combination of both. Her narrative represents marketplace credit because, just like it, it defies rational construction, resists narrative closure.[73] Most particularly, the value of Credit-as-woman is subject to the valuation, the manipulation, of Chymist/Defoe (though just like her, he is volatile, a narrator on whom it is difficult to place any value, whose discourse inscribes market shiftiness).

In perhaps the quintessential expression of Lady Credit's affinity to a credit that rarifies and condenses, and eludes stable construction (as narrative proceeding rationally towards an implicit end), Credit that begins as shadowy, bodiless, volatile, condenses in the same long paragraph into female pronouns. The transformation is striking, as if the narrator of the *Review* must evince irresistible pressures toward instability from the narrative subject. Defoe begins by stating:

That substantial Non-Entity call'd CREDIT, seems to have a distinct Essence (*if nothing can be said to exist*) from all the Phaenomena in Nature; it is in it self the lightest and most volatile Body in the World, moveable beyond the Swiftness of Lightning; the greatest Alchymists could never fix its Mercury, or find out its Quality; it is neither a Soul or a Body; it is neither visible or invisible; it is all Consequence, and yet not the Effect of a Cause; it is a Being without Matter, a Substance without Form – A perfect free Agent acting by Wheels and Springs absolutely undiscover'd; it comes without Call, and goes away unsent; if it flies, the whole Nation cannot stay it; if it stays away, no Importunity can prevail for its Return.[74]

This rhetoric of insubstantiality becomes unstable, however, as (in the same long passage) Defoe introduces gendered terms:

What has this invisible Phantosm [sic] done for this Nation, and what miserable Doings were there here before without her? She cuts all the Notches in your Tallies, and the obedient Nation takes them for Money; your Exchequer Bills have her Seal to them, and my L[ord] H[alifa]x sets his Hand to them in Her Name; 'tis by Her you raise Armies . . . and in short by Her you found your grand Alliances have supported the War, and beat the *French*: By this Invisible, *Je ne seay Quoi*, this Non-natural, this Emblem of a something, tho' it self nothing, all our War and all our Trade is supported. . . . 'Tis all done by the Aid and Assistance of this Machine call'd *Credit* . . . Pay Homage to her Image.[75]

Credit is fluid, disincarnate as "Je ne seay Quoi," incarnate as female; it disappears into "nothing," reappears as a female idol. The process is that of Air-Money, with Defoe as Chymist once again. The body of Credit registers the market's mystifications, elaborating a narrative that splays into independent variables, resisting (dis)closure. Defoe's rhetoric absorbs this mystification, rarifying (arbitrarily) into credit's neuter valence, condensing (arbitrarily) into the female, ambiguating itself through rhetorical identification with its subject. As I have suggested, Defoe assimilates his own narrative mode to that of Lady Credit. Her narrative becomes an "allegory" of his own relationship to the market, i.e. of his production of narratives that do not contain in their ostensible purport the outcomes they could ultimately display.

Lady Credit allegorizes a narrative style that would remain as Air-Money, never realized in a payoff or blown up in a Bubble, but hovering in epistemological limbo, neither obvious Lie nor verified Truth. Such narratives belong to the political arena of coy dissimulation; to the literary arena of fiction that claims not to be; and to that in-between sphere in which narratives (*Memoirs of the Conduct of Her Late Majesty*) ostensibly by others ("The Right Honourable the Countess of —") disorient political debate. Defoe practiced all of these, and I suggest it was his purpose to continue, to elude readerly curiosity by remaining unfixed, an author who could not be pinned down when he signed his name nor identified when he did not. In the area of politics especially, the credit-based market provides a paradigm for Lady Credit, who as text provides a paradigm for Defoe, who writes Lady Credit as ur-text for political/textual strategy.

In Defoe's own "relationship" with Lady Credit, she (like credit) *is* narrative, and so she can serve as an allegory of Defoean narrative. If she is descended from Olympus, she is also refracted through the *Review* as a heuristic device, executing impossible turns as respects elusive narrative structures. As a practicing propagandist, Defoe could anticipate operating under numerous personae (indeed, he already did), writing for different parties (the *Review* itself swung between Tory and Whig), and espousing different sides in debate in the hope that his "past" would not discredit him (a practice for which he was repeatedly taunted by rival journalists). He displaces onto the body of a woman the same inclinations towards elusiveness, and through Credit's sexual metamorphoses (some "honest," some suspect) he literally tests his own ability to survive in – even control – the marketplace of ideas.[76] Like Credit, Defoe's narratives must remain suspended as Air-Money to remain in the market: should they explode into bubbles, he is himself "undone," exposed as a liar and a tool.[77] Stemming from an insight that issues in Defoe's earliest, least appreciated act of narrative transvestism, Credit as a woman becomes yet another Defoean persona, enacting through the unsettling turns of her sex life Defoe's own parlous connection to narrative honesty.[78]

Indeed, by the end of the *Review* essay in which credit Is/Is Not, it/she firmly *is* a woman: Credit is twice a "Coy Mistress," and on the following page her infamous rape occurs. In addition, Defoe's preoccupation with Credit's body as a register of the market becomes involved with her very metabolism – a very ungoddess-like feature. The next issue of the *Review* states:

Now, while she is in this prosperous State of Health, it is great Pity to let any Body have the Management of her, or designs to do her Mischief. The Stock-jobbers, like Quacks and Mountebanks, are every day tampering with her; they flatter her with fine Words, feed her with Sugar-Plumbs as they do Children: and gorge her with luscious Diet – But the Design is murtherous and villainous, for they only seek to kidnap her into their own Power again, that they may dishonour and debauch her – Thus they run her up at first, prompt her Vanity, and make her swell 25 *per Cent*, above her usual Pitch: But without being a Sorcerer, I can tell you, if ever she get into their Hands, she is undone.[79]

Once again Lady Credit is in danger of being raped, dishonored, "undone," only this time she violates the first rule of modest womanhood: one does not take candy from strangers. Lady Credit succumbs to a sugar craving. Instead of offering "a snare to the Unwary Person,"[80] she is herself ensnared, implicated by her own corporeality in morally reprobate, unhealthy indulgence.[81] As she gorges and becomes fat, sinking into decadent luxury, it is her body – pitched upon by stockjobber "Quacks and Mountebanks" – that suffers. Credit contributes to her sexual vulnerability through an ingenue's credulity, almost as if she might consume nostrums hawked in the *Review*. In this anecdote, her physicality is deepened, becoming specifically human: goddesses are raped and even sweet-talked, but they never stuff their faces.

Paula Backscheider has argued that from 1710 Lady Credit "became a permanent, universally recognized symbol uniting fixed virtues with English history." She locates Credit's precursors in "polemical tracts dating back to the Middle Ages," and suggests that "[s]he might be Virtue, Pallas Athene, or Brittania."[82] Lady Credit's resemblance to goddesses and emblemata cannot, as I have argued, be dissociated from a mediating narrative dissonance. What I want to examine here is the suggestion that this Lady becomes a "permanent . . . symbol" with "fixed virtues." Over the course of the following decade, Credit defies fixity and lacks virtue: she becomes a whore in several venues, including one of Defoe's. In 1710 Lady Credit is not only a woman with a past, but a woman whose reputation is on the way down.

In 1710 Lady Credit is reintroduced in the *Review* on a notably classier note, the daughter of Probity and Prudence. Her "walk was daily between the Bank and the Exchequer, and between the Exchange and the Treasury; she went always Unveil'd, dress'd like a Bride."[83] Lady Credit's elevated (and univalent) demeanor begins to crumble, however, as the nation's credit is endangered:

[B]eing Infirm, and Unsound, afflicted with a Terrifying and Fatal Distemper, the *Falling-sickness*; her Spirits sunk, and her Strength reduc'd; I must acknowledge, there seems a great deal of Danger in the Case – I have been about the City, to enquire among her Friends – and really they are all more Disponding about her *than I am* – I went to the Bank among her own Servants, and *they say*, she cannot live many Days . . .[84]

Falling sickness – the contemporary term for epilepsy – designates Lady Credit as congenitally liable to unpredictable, uncontrollable metamorphic fits. A person who suffered it was literally in flux, subject to the whims of the disease.[85] In her very physiology, therefore, as she moves towards apocalypse in 1711, Lady Credit exemplifies – embodies – uncertainty, and becomes a narrative of protean infirmities.

Lady Credit succumbs in reaction to the ugly, abusive national mood. In language reminiscent of *The Shortest Way With the Dissenters* (1702), Defoe rails that Credit "has been barbarously Treated on both Sides . . . But *You Tories* have assaulted this Beautiful Virgin Lady, with all the Violence of a *Ravisher*, like the Men of *Benjamin*, on the *Levites Concubine*; you have brought your whole Rabble upon her, and attack'd her Chastity."[86] As Credit sickens, assaulted all around, Defoe becomes proprietary, moves closer, refers to Credit as "my Favourite Mistress" and "my Charming Beautiful Mistress."[87]

Finally, in an epiphanic encounter broaching mutual desperation, Lady Credit materializes, speaking with Defoe. She steps out of allegory. This encounter with ailing, shape-changing Lady Credit merges "allegory" with Defoe's personal history, the logistical outcome of a logical momentum of five years. The moment prefigures crisis:

POOR CREDIT! sunk and dejected, sighing and walking alone; I met her t'other Day in the Fields, I hardly knew her, she was so lean, so pale; look'd so sickly, so faint, and was so meanly dres'd. . .

Lady Credit intimates that she is leaving England, and when Defoe is startled, she replies:

[W]hy, What should I do here? I have staid too long here already; you know how I have been us'd, how I have been Mob'd on one Side, and Mob'd on t'other Side; Bully'd and Insulted by Parties and Factions, and yet I have born it all with more Patience than I used to bear such Treatment with; I have, in short, stay'd till I am quite Ruin'd.[88]

Lady Credit pours out her heart, cataloguing the country's abuses; Defoe urges, pleads that she reconsider; they resume in the *Review*'s next issue, with an almost scholastic inquiry into the High-Flyers' threat. Lady Credit assumes the worst, yet Defoe manages a cliff-hanger:

Well, says she, then this is the Reason why I am going Abroad, therefore pray do not stay me – But hold, Madam, said I – the Parliament – And with that she stop'd again – And what farther passed, you shall hear hereafter.[89]

This inconclusive tussling with Credit incarnate – who bursts the constraints of textuality, and eschews Defoe's own directions – releases Lady Credit into hypertext; she transcends fixity as *mere* text ("meer Allegory," an extension of Defoe's mind), entering Defoe's history as a determinant of the text he inscribes. In altering radically moving from text to hypertext, Lady Credit evinces falling sickness at the level of literary metaphysics.[90] She displays in her incarnation an independence of Defoe that marks Defoe's text as contingent, bound to the uncertainties of a whimsical market (embodied by Credit).

In this scene, the realization of Lady Credit; her separation from the mind that created her, the text that contained her; and her ultimate entrance into history, reifies the self-reflexivity of the *Review*'s engagement with the market. The discursive exchange between Lady Credit and Defoe, in which he inscribed on her body his relation to truth in a market for political speech, is now shown in reverse. Lady Credit will prescribe Defoe's text, which is still in suspense ("what farther passed, you shall hear hereafter"). What had been a patriarchal relationship between the two becomes companionate, a dialectic fusing the two into discursive mutuality.[91] Defoe's texts, deeply affiliated (through this dialectic) with the movements of the market, *avow* themselves as a type of Air-Money, suspended like Credit between assertion and proof. The text remains open, a narrative that aspires neither to lie nor to tell the truth, so much as to survive in the market for political speech, a consumable.[92] The drama with Lady Credit enacts the scene of Defoe's inculpability, his ideal state of epistemological nonresolution. The *Review* does not reveal whether Lady Credit departs from England: as hypertext her influence is not definitive because *as narrative* she embodies unsettlement. She apparently stays, persisting in uncertain health.

The involvement of Lady Credit in Defoe's relationship to textuality, to the "honesty" of his own discourse, continues as the narrative of Lady Credit's body colonizes new texts. A few months after Lady Credit's incarnation, she meets apocalypse. In *Eleven Opinions of Mr. Harley*, Defoe ridicules the Whigs for thinking they can control Credit, whose infidelity is manifest in a sordid revelation:

That was their Opinion, I believe no Body will question, and this Opinion was founded purely upon the belief that this CREDIT was their Mistress, sure to them only, and that no Body could debauch her but the Bank, &c. little dreaming, that in spight of all Mr. Defoe's Allegories of a Beautiful Coy Virgin Lady, called CREDIT, his Virgin prov'd a Whore, a meer Common Strumpet, will lie with any Body that has but Money to supply her insatiable Cravings; Nay, the worst sort of Whores, a mercenary Whore, for she forsakes her best Friends that have spent all their Estates upon her, as soon as ever their Money fails them, and will run after, and prostitute her self to those that have no manner or Occasion for her, always fawning upon, and flattering and hanging about them that slight and scorn her, while she is inexorable to the Entreaties of a poor Man, or a poor Nation, though they may be in Danger of ruine for want of her.[93]

Had the Whigs read the *Review* carefully, they would have perceived that "all Mr. Defoe's Allegories of a beautiful Coy Virgin," chased but chaste, were valenced with those of a woman with a "past." From her inception, Lady Credit might disdain conduct-book norms; she suspended her coyness with King Charles (or so Defoe said, before he dissolved the assertions in uncertainty); and she was no virgin anyway, having been raped in the reign of King William. She is/was a virgin, but she isn't/wasn't. Defoe's *avowal* that Credit is – and has been – a whore, merely extends the narrative fluidity that always figured her persona.[94] To suggest that Credit ever was, *tout court*, "a beautiful Coy Virgin Lady," is itself an instance of that fluidity, employed here for strategic effect.

More particularly, Defoe's avowal of Lady Credit's multivalent inclinations implicates his own persona in the narrative of Lady Credit's body: what the Whigs conjectured based on that narrative (delivered and ambiguated by Defoe) is subverted by an amoral inclination (now acknowledged by Defoe). The revelation announces that Defoe has produced a narrative that was neither truth nor lie but a delicate, indeterminate balance, obscuring the bivalence of Credit without exposing Defoe to imputations of lying. Because Lady Credit occupied multiple subject positions, she, like her creator, deferred any definitive revelation. She remained in the market, disorienting it (n.b. the Whigs), *as did Defoe.*

It is fascinating to speculate on why Defoe now explicitly denominated Lady Credit a whore, when in the *Review* she had never been so thoroughly of the *demi-monde*. Clearly, Defoe could have written *Eleven Opinions* short of going to such extremes. The answer, perhaps, is that by late spring, 1711, Defoe's speculations on his ability to sustain Air-Money narratives had become totally sublimated in the narrative of Lady Credit's body, in her capacity (endowed by Defoe!) to *em*body narrative without resolution. The dialectic between Lady Credit and Defoe, reified in his epiphany earlier that year, becomes institutionalized, configuring his other texts, taking them to new extremes that explore (extend) the incalculability of narrative modes derived from credit's gyrations. The ultimate turn in this heuristic exercise is that just as it seems to resolve itself, bodying forth an irreversible extreme statement, it seems not to: Lady Credit's apocalypse dissolves. In a *Review* that appears shortly after *Eleven Opinions*, Defoe opines that "To call these Things Credit [namely stockjobbing and cheating at lottery] is abusing Credit and our selves too: it is only calling a Whore by an Honest Woman's Name."[95]

The unfolding and refolding of Lady Credit's narrative, recapitulating the flux of a market driven by credit, constitutes a brilliantly elusive performance that self-reflexively assimilates Defoe to Lady Credit's coy lack of commitment, her epistemological opacity. Defoe becomes discourse, an extension of the unstable sign – Lady Credit – that represents the unstable signs – credit instruments – that constitute the market. In claiming to represent that market by inventing the elusive Lady Credit, Defoe acknowledges that the market produces his own elusiveness (insofar as he produces her unresolved narrative). Indeed, Defoe constructs a proto-Derridean regime in which Lady Credit becomes an uncertain sign deranged by interpretations (successive *Reviews*, *Eleven Opinions*) that are themselves uncertain signs, perpetually reconfigured by an interpreter reconfigured by the same marketplace discourse that he purports to interpret. Defoe deconstitutes the author function as it applies to him; he reconfigures it without responsibility.

In the next decade the bivalent Lady Credit persona that Defoe so delicately balanced falls precipitately. A female figure, embodying credit as instantiated in the notorious South Sea Company, is savaged in drama, poetry, and tracts which insist that this apparent "fine lady" was a whore in masquerade. The "fall" of Lady Credit parallels the fall in public confidence that in 1720 resulted from the run-up of South Sea Company stock and the collapse of the market with the South Sea Bubble.

In *The Battle of the Bubbles. Shewing Their several Constitutions, Alliances, Policies, and Wars; From their first suddain Rise, to their late Speedy Decay. By a Stander-by* (1720), Avaritia and Trickster spawn a litter of Brutes, the eldest of which is Oceana: "She bewitch'd Thousands to fall in Love with her, and to spend their whole Fortunes upon her: And what is monstrous in her, is, that tho' she has reduc'd 'em to Skin and Bone, yet her Lust is not one Bit abated; and she runs after new Lovers every Day" (10). A narrative ensues in which she is excommunicated by the Dutch, French, Swiss, and Irish. We are told that while she reigned, however, the rivals at Garraway's bid for her, and "the sawcy Slut step'd out a Dutchess" (13). She falls when "discover'd to be false at Heart, and unsound at Bottom" (14), even though "a Figure call'd Perjury, swore off all to his Face . . . if . . . Oceana was not one of the Honestest and most Vertuous of Women in the World" (15).

In *The South-Sea Scheme Detected; and the Mangement thereof Enquired Into* (1720), a serious examination of the financial crisis, the author still cannot resist a gendered slur:

The Chief Managers of a certain Stock, may dress up their Darling Mistress once more, and send her into the World not without a tempting Aspect; but People who have already been Sufferers by their Schemes, will look upon her with a cautious Eye. A fine Lady, who had deceiv'd a Man once, will for the Future be treated as a common Prostitute. As a very great Statesman, some time since, has observ'd, they may usher her in, as the Trojans did their Horse, with much Pomp and Applause; and the end prove like that, Treachery and Destruction. (19)

The equation of "a fine Lady" literally dressed to kill, with a Trojan horse bringing "treachery and destruction," makes the point.

In *An Epistle to His Royal Highness* (1720), the South Sea Company, embodying credit as a female, is figured as a whore whom other women could not decipher:

> See here Two ruin'd Countesses in Tears
> While there a *South-Sea* Upstart's Strumpet wears
> Two *Pendants*, worth two *Mannors*, in her Ears. (6)

During this period, the attack on credit figured as a whore is an attack on the credibility of credit-related representation. The textuality of representation – promises to pay inscribed on certificates of stock, ostensibly executed through powers of attorney – becomes the object of contempt: textuality is revealed as variable and uncertain notwithstanding its apparent fixity. In the form of a female degraded to the level of a whore, Credit becomes a version of these rogue inscriptions, as writers of the day write on Credit's body the record of their having been gulled. Defoe did not issue any major Bubble-related texts that join in vilifying credit as a female. However, as I show in the chapter on *Roxana*, Lady Credit did not retire in disgrace from his oeuvre after the South Sea Bubble. She was redeployed as the whore she had become, used once again to register Defoe's relationship to textuality, to fictions that inhabit the market without *declaring* their fictionality.

For the period of her existence, however, Lady Credit is a brilliant foray into Defoe's sense of the possibilities of narrative that aspires towards nonresolution, towards the suspension of contraries. As I shall show, Defoe's possibilities as a writer were enmeshed in the politics of fiction. They were dependent upon the limitations of interpretation, the capacity of texts to sustain nonresolution, and the capacity of readers to tolerate such a state without seeking outside the text to force (dis)closure. This is Defoe's real subject in the narrative of Lady Credit, and (as I show in chapter 5) it remains so in its modulation, *Roxana*.

CHAPTER 2

Defoe and fictionality

TELLING IT LIKE IT ISN'T: DEFOE'S IDEOLOGICAL FICTIONS AND THE SUBVERSION OF THE PUBLIC SPHERE

The preceding chapter argued that credit-based texts were untraceable to a provenance. Obligations charged to a particular Fund did not necessarily represent dedicated capital, but might float on ledgers like afterimages. An impersonal market allocated "credit" to a stock, its holder, or issuer. Discredit at one site redounded to another. The credit-based market was a web of obligations, and no indicia isolated nodes in the web. No agent dissolved the palimpsest of text and opinion that obscured originary, "intrinsick" value. Responsibility for texts in the market was perpetually deferred.

This chapter argues in its first section that strategies deployed by Defoe's political fictions are homologous with credit-based tropes. By "political fictions" I mean fictional narratives that are ideologically freighted and intended to persuade.[1] The distinguishing quality of Defoe's political fictions is that as with stocks, Funds, and credit instruments, they elicit epistemological confusion by disrupting attempts to determine their veracity. The author can neither be found nor held to account (without extratextual data), since the text is occupied by an ostensible "author." While the reader may have a different perspective from such an "author," and may doubt his reliability, no *hors-texte* suggests an hermeneutic that might indicate the text's provenance. The reader, limited by the text, interprets it as if the "author" wrote it.

Defoe produced dozens of such texts. Among them, *The Secret History of the October Club* (1711), "By a Member." *A Letter from A Member of the House of Commons* (1713). *An Apology for the Army* (1715), "Written by an Officer." *A Letter from General Foster to the Earl of Mar* (1715). *A True Account of the Proceedings at Perth*, "By A Rebel." *Minutes of the Negotiations of Monsr. Mesnager* (1717), "Written by Himself. Done out of French."[2] Collectively, they advance an epistemology that mocks the barrier between fictive and nonfictive, between rhetoric and phenomena, leaving only rhetoric. By disinscribing himself in rhetoric, i.e. in the text, "Defoe" is disinscribed in the world. In Defoe's political fictions there is only text: like the texts of credit, they make no reference to an origin, an author, a source of value or meaning accountable *for* the text. These fictions aspire to airtight textuality. In plain English, they aspire to the perfect hoax.

Swift's evasive fictions are a pointed contrast. Readers assume that *behind* the authorial persona is a "real" author, using the persona as a shield while asserting himself as untouchable. One attempts to locate this author, to interpret *his* views based on brittle textual cues. In *The Converting Imagination*, Marilyn Francus observes that in order to protect himself from public exposure, Swift deployed a characteristic satiric device:

[I]nstead of presenting himself and his opinions directly in his writings, he presents a series of outrageous personae to the public, personae who usually function as his immediate (though not final) targets – and by deftly exposing them, Swift could make his opinions known implicitly, without the potential backlash to which explicit argumentation would leave him open. In the presence of the uncontrollable, often morally suspect narrators [e.g. The Hack, Gulliver], the reader seeks a reassuring authorial temperament to stabilize the meaning of the text. Swift's absence from the printed page only reinforces the need for evidence of his existence, and by forcing the reader to locate him behind the written word, Swift paradoxically draws attention to himself. Perversely then, the schizophrenic use of speakers serves as a medium for Swiftian self-assertion.[3]

While Swift toys with the reader, directing him outside the text (possibly though not inevitably towards Swift), Defoe draws the reader into the text, deflecting him from an "author" other than the narrator.[4] The tactic has its risks: if the reader suspects the persona is a ruse, the whole text becomes a potential fiction, seeking to impose upon the reader while hiding its imposition. To continue the ruse, Defoe must proliferate more fiction, exculpating himself. The text assimilates the *modus operandi* of the market, in which recursivity is a condition of fiction reluctant to avow itself.

If the fiction is unsuspected, however, the text occupies the public sphere as an object of false cognition: debate centers on the views of a cipher. Defoe's authority to represent history expands to include every participant in history. Whatever he wishes to say is "authorized," even as he evades accountability for its purport.[5] "Defoe's" impressions of the Battle of Perth, especially from a Jacobin perspective, would be secondhand and unreliable – impressions "By A Rebel," however, are on-the-scene, their wrong-headedness imparting a perverse credibility. Defoe's evasions are therefore more evasive than Swift's. Swift's satire acknowledges that the "author" is the butt of an intelligence outside the text, that the text itself is fictive. Even if his tracts are coy as to provenance, and "destabiliz[e] intellectual notions and linguistic meaning,"[6] they do not silently co-opt discourse by miming transparency.[7] If Swift is elusive at the level of language, entrapping the reader into states where meaning is chronically imprecise, at the political level he is less epistemologically menacing than Defoe, who assaults discourse by seeming not to.[8]

As a "stealth" operation, Defoe's strategy calls into question theorization of the public sphere. In *The Structual Transformation of the Public Sphere*, Jürgen Habermas argued that during the early eighteenth century a bourgeois public sphere was constituted through rational discourse embodied in books, newspapers, pamphlets – print media circulating in the streets, by subscription, available in coffeehouses. The medium of political confrontation "was peculiar and without historical precedent: people's public use of their reason" (27). "Reason" is central to Habermas' conceptualization.[9] Terry Eagleton argues that in the public sphere, "[w]hat is said derives its legitimacy neither from itself as message nor from the social title of the utterer, but from its conformity as a statement with a certain paradigm of reason inscribed in the very event of saying."[10] Likewise, Craig Calhoun observes that "the idea that the best rational argument and not the identity of the speaker was supposed to carry the day was institutionalized as a valuable claim."[11] But what happens to "rational argument" if debate is drawn towards imagined phenomena made falsely credible by imagined authorities? What happens, moreover, when market-generated tropes of authorial elusiveness penetrate the public sphere? I suggest that in order to escape self-avowal, Defoe's political fictions challenge rationality, using conventions of marketplace discourse.

In 1714–15, Defoe wrote *The Secret History of the White Staff*, parts 1, 2, and 3, an anonymous account of events surrounding the Queen, Robert Harley, and the end of the Tory ministry that Defoe could not possibly have observed. An unsuspicious reader would attribute the text to a person with inside information. In the style of "secret histories," *The Secret History* has an intense, byzantine atmosphere, with many of the names symbolic – "Purse," "Mitre," "White Staff" – probably to avoid libel. Harley (the "Staff") is the protagonist of a tragedy, threatened by absolutist conspirators who favor the Pretender and seek to influence Anne against the Hanoverian succession. Harley stands for a politics of moderation; when he will not be co-opted, the conspirators instigate his removal by weak-minded Anne. Harley responds with grace, and Anne resolves to reinstall him, but dies before she can. At the last moment, however, she hands the staff of Treasurer's office to Shrewsbury, frustrating the plotters who reveal their nature in curses and blasphemy.

Geoffrey Sill notes that by historiographical standards, the text is a fabrication.[12] But if read ideologically, as the vehicle for a kind of transcendent truth, it becomes "an interpretation of faithful service and the tragedy of good designs thwarted by fate and bad men . . . Defoe's first major – and still probably one of his most important – works of fiction" (88). Sill correctly observes that the text is an integrated work of art, a "fiction'" rather than bald propaganda. But it is crucial that *The Secret History* is not intended to be *read* as fiction. It is realpolitick pretending to be political reality, without any of the devices that lend ambiguity to the *chronique scandaleuse*.[13] Unlike such fictions of court intrigue, obvious allegories frequently distanced by elaborate (even whimsical) frames, *The Secret History* invokes only the most superficial features of its nominal generic relative.[14] It purports to be History, and resists self-disclosure.

The text was quickly attacked as a lie, and Whig partisans suspected that Defoe wrote it. In response, Defoe invoked a logic for the literary/political homologous with that of financial markets. His defense, anticipating his exculpation of errant debtors, suggests that no "Defoe" could have written *The Secret History* since texts in the market of ideas are produced by means that suppress discursive agents. There could be no "Defoe" because there is only discourse. In Defoe's logic, the public sphere, like the financial market, is produced by individuals who are extensions of the market. Political texts do not represent authors, let alone authorial intent; they "represent" the market, more particularly the market's noise. Defoe's argument collapses the public sphere into Exchange Alley, where texts have no "intrinsick" value, except what is read into them.

Defoe's application to the public sphere of the ideology of credit challenges the public sphere in its basic assumption – that political texts, whether true or false, are reflections of a rational author. By arguing against rationality, situating truth *or* lies beyond rational contemplation, Defoe reduces the public sphere to a site of epistemological futility where the attempt to discriminate fact from fiction (and so to denounce the author of fiction) assumes an intentionality that does not exist. "Intent" is subsumed in market-driven protocols, which become their own "intent" and render texts mere ciphers. As an extension of the market's logic, the public sphere becomes paradoxical. Print texts that facilitate rational discourse and are spread by a capitalist market, also subvert discourse because the market cancels the individual, accountable voice. Thus, if credit's *modus operandi* dissipates originary discourse and dissolves authorial responsibility, then Defoe's defense of *The Secret History* recapitulates credit's operations, discrediting the public sphere as a site of intentional speech.

In view of *The Secret History*'s elaborate effort to shore up Harley's reputation in the face of detractors, Defoe's response to the firestorm that broke around the text may seem incredible. Yet it demonstrates the homologous logic of financial and literary/political texts where an underlying, market-based objective is to avoid avowing fictionality. Indeed, the Whig opposition to *The Secret History* seemed to acknowledge the homology, reinscribed it in their attacks, and attenuated their own arguments.

When part 1 appeared, the Whigs assailed it as outrageous, and while speculation was rife as to the author, John Oldmixon cited Defoe: "five or six days ago out comes *The Secret History of the White Staff*, written by Defoe, as is to be seen by his abundance of words, his false Thoughts, and false English."[15] Oldmixon justified his attribution on the basis of extratextual data, citing Defoe's "abundance of words" and "false English." He also offered a detailed refutation of its "false Thoughts," which was joined in by numerous others.[16] Defoe was undeterred, however, and in part 2 he refused to join issue, denying (still anonymously) that anything substantive had been asserted against the text:

Nothing has been offered to refute this Secret History, or to oppose the Matters of Fact related; as to the Gloss put upon them by Party-Men, it is nothing to the History; my Business is to relate, not to dispute; if what is contain'd in this Secret History is not True, no doubt we shall hear of it in Publick . . . (II, 70–71)

The statement that "Nothing has been offered" in refutation is already a fiction intended to deflect detection of a fiction; Oldmixon's reply is weighty and specific. More particularly, Defoe dismisses responses to the text as mere "gloss[es]," the private feuding of "Party-Men" that the "Publick," should it materialize, will weigh with candor. Existing discourse is discounted, the "publick" sphere cast as inchoate, a site of legitimate debate and potential resolution deferred by the public itself. The response invokes a credit-based logic where outcome is chronically deferred, and a text neither true nor false but a suspension, which if proven false is untraceable to an author. Yet while Defoe's response implicates the public sphere in the logic of credit, the full implications of that strategy remained to be articulated.

Reaction against part 2 was even more intense. Oldmixon issued a second part of his tract, again attacking Defoe. Francis Atterbury, alluding to the text's intent to disorder perception, vituperated against "the Mercenary that has been hired to raise a Dust in order to blind People's Eyes for seeing cleerly into the White Staffs true character," who "having acquitted himself of that Filthy Work, by a second endeavor," had perpetrated "Defamation and Falsehood."[17] Journalists such as Abel Boyer also weighed in.[18] *The Secret History* ran through several editions, and speculation continued as to its authorship and veracity.[19] Defoe's next response was astonishing.

The Secret History of the Secret History, purporting to be by a "Person of Honour," disabuses a populace taken in by ridiculous pamphlets produced by multiple Grub Street hacks:

[I]t is provoking to the last Degree, to see what Success these Men have had in the Trick they have put upon the Town, and how universally all sorts of Men have run into the Cheat, and been bubbled to accept these Romances for a true Narration, and have taken the Fable for History, without enquiring into the Things.[20]

The Secret History is a ruse. The position does not deny authorship, or even claim that the text is ironic. It attempts to deconstruct a politically powerful text that supported the interest of Defoe's former patron, claimed to be true, and disclaimed the need to refute charges against it. It is an assertion that romance and truth, Fable and History can be made to seem like each other, that the public sphere equals Grub Street equals Exchange Alley (where everyone is "bubbled"). "Bubbled" reifies the logic of credit as the controlling logic of ostensibly rational discourse. The public sphere is cast as a site where hack writer/Chymists delude readers into mistaking the phony for the real.

The Person of Honour suggests that while friends of the Staff were happy, and "Enemies of the Staff . . . could not avoid the Snare of taking the Books for Genuine, and for a Design of the Staff to start something into the World in his own Vindication" (7-8), everyone on Grub Street was hilarious:

> The Writers of Books sitting still all this while, had their Leisure to laugh at Mankind, and to please themselves with thinking how either Side fell into their Snare, and bought up many Thousands of the Books, which as shall presently be shewn, was the Summa Totalis of the Design, and to see with what eagerness the Party Writers on every Side carried on the Paper War which they had rais'd; and which confirms the Truth of what is here asserted beyond all Contradiction. It shall appear that the same People employing other Hands, have been the editors not only of the Books themselves, but also of several of the Answers to these Books, causing the deceiv'd People to Dance in the Circles of their drawing, while these have enjoy'd the Sport of their own Witchcraft; and like the Hangers-on of the Camp, have taken the Spoil of the Field of Battle, as well of the Victors of the Vanquish'd. (8)

In other words, *The Secret History* is not traceable to an author, but to a discourse factory.[21] It is fiction but without the animus of a lie, since it has no purpose but to sell more fiction. While it appears to be rationally constructed, its rationale is that of the market, which by means of appearance induces people to buy more fictions of no "intrinsick" worth.

The Secret History of the Secret History, itself a worthless successor text, "rationalizes" *The Secret History* as neither purposive lie nor Defoean lie by obfuscating its context, suggesting it has no political provenance. *The Secret History of the Secret History* – its very name an explosion of fiction upon fiction – replicates credit's trope of proliferating fictions to hide fictionality. Its strategy is one of deferral, imputing to the public sphere the galloping, strategic fictionality that the text itself deploys. Consistent with its logic, it suggests that even opposition texts – Oldmixon's, Atterbury's, Boyer's – are chimeras, generated in the same process of incremental fictionality. The text induces a type of discursive vertigo; the reader is left tumbling through a hall of mirrors. The final turn in its wild self-reflexiveness is the suggestion that even if the reader suspected fiction, he was wrong, since the text is *even more fictional* than anyone knew.

The argument is thus a radical variation on Defoe's defense of *The Shortest Way With the Dissenters* (1702). When Defoe was accused of having fabricated a High-flying diatribe, he advised the reader to decodify the text so that when literal was read as ironic, fiction would become truth. The text, admitted to be a hoax, was still said to retain a certain veracity, albeit oblique.[22] In the case of *The Secret History*, decoding is not just transposition to a mode where transparency is possible. The reader is advised that apprehension is not possible, that deconstruction – not decoding – propels the text past any possibility of intentionality, truthful or lying. The Sidneian premise, that in order to lie fiction must be rationally based, underlies the assertion that *The Secret History* is not rational: it is discourse distilled of meaning. Of course, *The Secret History* aspired to be taken for truth, but Defoe is retrenching. The author of *The Secret History* is erased as a subject, demoted to a nonvolitional nonentity abiding among "other Hands" in a market where "authors" are only Hands. The logical purport is that a text with no rational, moral content has no rational, moral mode of inscription – no author.

As the mere product of a profit-driven market, *The Secret History* (it is alleged) is scripted within an intertext of cipher-texts promoting each other with reciprocal fictions. In the market configured by this intertext, "authors" are nodes where demand and supply are generated and met. Since authors are extensions of the market rather than agents, no one is responsible for *The Secret History* because "nobody" wrote it.[23] The dismissal of authority, relocating the provenance of *The Secret History* from History to the market, not only deconstructs the text, but ventures a theory of political/literary production in which *The Secret History* becomes an exhibit, an artifact with *no* provenance (except discourse itself) rather than just an anonymous one.

In Defoe's analysis, politics is consumerism, political literature a commodity, instigating open-ended hermeneutic desire. The discourse among Defoe, his critics, and the Person of Honour supports this assessment, demonstrating that desire, perpetual in textuality, perpetuated *by* textuality, is reified (in texts) and sold in the market like any artifact. A reader following the controversy, buying text-and-response as each quickly appeared, would assimilate the argument through evidence of his own desire. Desire in this case is gendered. Just beneath the surface of Defoe's rationale, Grub Street's gender – its "Witchcraft" – implies an affinity with Lady Credit. She fascinates Defoe in the *Review*, where her narrative is protracted, perpetually unresolved within the categories of virgin, mistress, the subject of rape. She is the object of perpetual desire. In the market, Air-Money credit texts are similarly unresolved and make the same appeal. Thus I would argue that Defoe's gambit in *The Secret History of the Secret History* absorbs credit's *modus operandi*. It suggests that political literature is produced within a regime of commodification, provoking a desire homologous with that for financial texts. Both define a market of texts that elicit desire and defer payoff. They are cipher texts, remote from originary discourse and hence from authorial responsibility – but we buy them because we defer their fictive potential.

In the narrative of *The Secret History of the Secret History*, the Person of Honour meets a Quaker who assures him that *The Secret History* is a fabrication, that neither Defoe nor Harley "had any concern in Writing, or Composing those Books" (10). The Quaker reports that Harley told a friend of the Quaker that "many, if not most of the Facts in these Books were False" (15).[24] Thus Harley moves between *The Secret History* and *The Secret History of the Secret History* as a fiction of himself, a fiction claiming that he was a fiction in the prior text. Likewise, Defoe begins to disappear into his own texts, creating a persona that resurfaces two months later: the Quaker reports that Defoe was found in "a Fit of Apoplexy" (16), the same (highly incredible) observation attributed to the Publisher at the end of *An Appeal to Honour and Justice*. In these fictionalizations of historical persons, discourse withdraws from History into an encompassing textuality intent on severing the connection with history. The text aspires to block access to persons behind the text – most notably, Defoe.

The Person of Honour observes that critics, who presume a relationship between Text and History, are unwitting accomplices in fostering illusion, instruments of hack writers "likewise abusing very notoriously the Readers, by making them believe that these things are of Moment, which are the Conceptions of silly Mercenaries . . . to deceive the credulous Heads and inquisitive Tempers of the People, and pick their Purses of a little Money" (22). Public discourse is a tilting at windmills, giving "Conceptions of silly Mercenaries" substantiality they would otherwise lack. Texts in the public sphere are disjunct from reality; charge and countercharge have no purpose except to sell texts. The rationale suggests that such texts, like credit texts, are simulacra – lacking a provenance, representing only their own processes of obfuscation.[25] It suggests that in the market, the value imputed to texts hides "their Original Nothing" measured by financial or conventionally discursive standards.

As the narrative of *The Secret History of the Secret History* continues, its self-reflexivity becomes explicit. The Person of Honour claims that he is not interested in defending the persons slandered in *The Secret History*, but rather "howbeit, for the innocent common People, who are made to believe a Lie by those Men, for their sakes, I say, it is but just that such practices as these should be expos'd, as they deserve; that they may be better inform'd, and may be made to see who they are, that delude and deceive them" (38–39). Excoriating writers who "will defend one false Thing with another . . . covering a Fraud with a greater Fraud" (39), the text parodies itself, "deluding" as it claims to "expose," covering Fraud with a greater one.

In the world of credit, self-reflexivity is quintessential: obligations may pile up against a Fund, asserting a presence that is an absence. Self-reflexivity is paradoxical as much as parodic, since how can one recur to an absence, to an Original Nothing? Yet just such a motion makes the Fund a type of Air-Money, suspended in a disavowal that obscures the fictiveness of its impacted promises. In *The Secret History of the Secret History*, self-reflexivity functions in the same way, piling fiction upon fiction to hide an originary fiction. In the hall of mirrors that develops, the face of the author perpetually recedes.

Yet if *The Secret History of the Secret History* implodes into itself, sending *The Secret History* into a *mise-en-abyme* of texts, then *The Secret History* reinscribes the bivalence of marketplace texts by disinscribing *The Secret History of the Secret History*. Like bivalent Lady Credit, really "honest" and really not, part 3 of *The Secret History* emerges as if the market had never been "expos'd" as a Fraud. It silently conflates *The Secret History of the Secret History* with all the texts that *that* text dispatched, erasing it as substantive. The radical uncertainty that followed part 2 is compounded, turned back upon itself, so that fiction claiming to be true, "expos'd" as fiction, now reasserts its truth. Part 3 blandly asserts that "What has been said in the two previous parts of this *Secret History*, having therefore been so useful to the Illumination of Mankind, this Part, without retrospect to any thing mentioned before, proceeds to what is yet behind, of Moment equal" (4). Such claims to illumination impact the text into its own fictions, abstracted from the swirling controversy that accuses it of "blinding People's Eyes." Yet when read as part of the discursive continuum, part 3 is not so much a local fiction as a deliberate effort to derange perception of itself and the preceding texts. One might ask why part 3 was written, since *The Secret History of the Secret History* already threw the previous texts into doubt. Yet if proliferation of conflicting texts is itself a purpose, imputing to textuality an impenetrable ambivalence, then part 3, throwing doubt even upon doubt, makes sense. The technique of credit and Lady Credit, flummoxing the reader who attempts to assess veracity, arises from the same trough of mutually exclusive dodges.

The maneuvers prevail against the most hostile reader, Oldmixon. Launching against part 3 with wonted doggedness, he still cannot disentangle his substantive attack from the logic of *The Secret History of the Secret History*, which makes substantive attacks meaningless. He suspects that part 2 is mercenary. Part 3 is "so empty, so trivial, that one may plainly see the Writer had no meaning at all in writing it, but for the Bookseller's pay, and he lets us know at the end of it, that while the Commodity is in demand, he will take care to furnish us with it."[26] Oldmixon cites the commercialized teaser at the end of part 3: "There are yet several large Fields that are not mentioned, or entered into, and which have some Arcana of publick Matters to bring to light, before the History of the White-Staff can be said to be compleat" (80). He cannot imagine that the texts' flaunting their commerciality is a strategy, an antihermeneutical dodge that ultimately erases authority. He therefore does not connect *The Secret History of the Secret History* with the author of parts 1, 2, and 3 of *The Secret History*. Indeed, the invisibility of Defoe's ruse depends in part on the illogicality of the same author's inscribing all the texts, even though *The Secret History* (warning against its own practices) asserts that just such illogic is at work.

Oldmixon is too linear to imagine such dissonance in one provenance:

I do verily believe that Staff did encourage, if not emply him ["the Staff's Historian"] in the first Part of his Work, though there's plainly to be seen his own dirty Finger in every Page of it . . . I cannot agree with a viler Wretch than even the Staff's Historian, that the first History was written only for the Gain of Bookseller, what follow'd was probably produc'd with that generous View, but the design was form'd at first to engage the Whigs to think a little more kindly of the White Staff, and, if possible, to persuade them to take him when he was abandon'd by the Tories. (1–2)

Unwilling to concede that "the first History was written only for the Gain of the Bookseller" (if it were, Oldmixon joins critics "very notoriously abusing the Readers"), he acknowledges that the rest of *The Secret History* was spontaneously generated (like a grub) from Grub Street. Most of the blame for part 1 is cast upon Harley; the author is demoted to some vile Wretch. Defoe remains undetected behind "a viler Wretch than even the Staff's Historian," though at the same time Oldmixon credits the Wretch (who exculpates Defoe), reinscribing his views. The discourse among Defoe's texts, and between his texts and others in the market (those of his critics), confuses perception of provenance. Defoe's responsibility is displaced onto the market, which assumes authorial agency: it multiplies insinuation, operates as fiction's proximate source, and makes one's dupes dupe others. The strategy succeeds by maintaining the market in a constant state of irony: the Person of Honour's demand for transparent texts ("it is but just that such practices as these be expos'd"), proliferates fiction by claiming to resist it.

The same year that Defoe wrote *The Secret History of the Secret History*, 1715, he issued one of his most cunning "political fictions," *Memoirs of the Conduct of Her Late Majesty And Her Last Ministry, Relating to the Separate Peace with France*, "By the Right Honourable the Countess of —." These texts are aligned in logic, if not in subject, in that both warn against the practices they deploy, developing a self-reflexivity that implies candor even as it tries to exclude extratextual interrogation. The Countess' avowed purpose is to deter prosecution of Anne's last Ministry for advising and concluding a peace with France disadvantageous to Britain. She argues that far from receiving advice from her Ministers to intiate the treaty, the peace was Anne's idea and her Ministers followed suit. She suggests that they had reservations, persuading Anne to involve Parliament as negotiations proceeded. The Countess' unintended revelation, however, is that in abandoning their role as advisors, the Ministers capitulated to a weak sovereign. Moreover, in allowing themselves to be co-opted they covered their flank, since by obtaining parliamentary sanction they evaded legal, justiciable guilt for a treaty they would *not* have advised.

The Countess' argument, demonstrating that the Queen and not her Ministers advanced the treaty, absolves the Ministers of legal guilt only because it convicts them of moral laxity. Her logic is inherently ironic. Yet because the Countess so earnestly pursues it, barely stopping to qualify or to consider its obvious, disturbing implications, we accept her evidence as true, an admission against interest. That is, we understand that the Ministers were not in favor of the Peace, and we acknowledge that for that very reason they took steps putting themselves beyond guilt for concluding it. The Countess is "right," legally considered. But because we feel that our conclusion is more refined, imputing a measure of guilt that the Countess does not notice, we are induced to finesse the question of whether amorality is all the guilt there is – whether the Countess' story is true insofar as it dismisses an active (hence justiciable) role for the Ministers. I suggest that this dancing about the issue's penumbra is what Defoe intends, engaging readers in the qualification of data that they must therefore concede in essentials. The Countess' object, to convince us that Parliament buffered negotiations for a treaty the Ministers had not promoted, succeeds because she makes a botch, exculpating the Ministers by inculpating them in amoral conduct. The gambit wins because it is unaware of itself. The Countess, like the Queen, is not a great tactician, and so she gets her way.

The issue broached by the text – in its narrative and in its strategy – is deferred responsibility: the Ministers defer to Parliament (which succeeds in negating their potential authorship of the Peace), Defoe defers to the Countess (whom we are supposed to imagine as author). By calling attention to, indeed inducing us to condemn practices that the text would hide on its own behalf, the text preempts reader suspicion: in ferreting out the Ministers' protective cover, we dismiss any thought that the *Memoirs* would similarly be skulking past our scrutiny, hiding authorship behind a pseudonym. Had the text outright condemned amorality in the Ministers, we would not have felt so smart, so superior to the Countess as we do discovering it for ourselves. As a consequence, we do not consider that a mastermind is behind the text. Part of the Countess' credibility is that she *is* the Countess, the somewhat unsubtle author of the *Memoirs*, not merely a front for a calculating propagandist. It is essential that we do not suspect Defoe (or anyone), and since we do not anticipate the irony, the audacity of a secondhand text's pretending to be firsthand by eschewing a spokesman who would conscientiously make its case, we tend to accept the Countess. We do not assume that the text is *so* audacious as to bring us to a pitch where, having thought about a psedonymous author, we dismiss the possibility since the authorial persona succeeds so marginally. After all, a canny expositor would have dealt with the Ministers' amorality, explained, excused, or even just acknowledged it. Like Oldmixon, we do not imagine audacity sufficiently. We do not proceed nonlinearly. Defoe relies on this fact.

Nonlinearity is the *sine qua non* of credit, yet the reader reacts to its obliquity by attempting to enforce linearity, defying its bivalent/Air-Money operations, hoping that potentially "Real Contracts" will not sink "into their Original Nothing." The reader is conscripted by credit into complicity with it, in part because he will not, cannot imagine the audacity of an Air-Money text (be it stock, an annuity, a Fund with multiple self-cancelling obligations). Thus the Orphan is incredulous that government-sanctioned stock might flout Publick Faith; Steele insists that contracts be aloof from politics. Readers induced by the market to accept impenetrable texts come down on the side they want to, intuitively reimagining texts as less audacious than they really are. I would argue that audacity, pretending that each charge against a Fund is not just a fictive expedient, is the base line of credit texts and of Defoe's texts in the public sphere. In each case, the reader makes a judgment; he is the proximate cause of his own mistake, based on an incapacity fully to appreciate the counterintuitive structure of credit.

Unlike *The Secret History*, the *Memoirs* is inhabited by a significantly individuated persona. The Countess is apparently a lady-in-waiting privy to the Queen's unguarded moments as well as her policy deliberations. Her individuation is another reason that we accept her authorship. Her apparent access authenticates what she says. Through the Countess' eyes, the reader learns that the Queen was inconsolable over the protracted bloodshed, that "Her Majesty was very Heavy and Sad, and frequently in Tears by Her Self" (13). When the Queen despairs over her recalcitrant ministers, she is assured that "Men might be found, who . . . wou'd some Way or other, extricate Her out of this Difficulty, and put an end to the War" (14). The Countess admits that "this beginning gave Life to all the designs of those, who had so long waited to displace the Old Ministry, and to make an Impression upon Her Majesty . . . that some Way shou'd be found to deliver Her Mind from the Burthen of the War" (14–15). The Queen, however, is oblivious to the political degradation created by her obsession with ending the War. When sometime later she speaks before "some Persons of Eminence," she is so anxious to begin negotiations, that she takes upon herself to "protect all those, who acted in the bringing to pass so good a Work, with all her Power. That it could not be said of any one of them, that they had advis'd Her to it, for they all knew She oblig'd them to whatever was done, and would take it all upon Herself" (26, 27). She offers pardons to everyone involved in treating with France.

The Countess ties the Queen's anxiety for the Peace to a tearful, female emotionality, then links it with the Queen's solicitousness for her Ministers. It does not dawn on the Countess that the Queen's concern to "protect all those, who acted in the bringing to pass so good a Work," is not mere graciousness, but a use of prerogative to advance her cause. The Countess' silence may reflect her own graciousness, but it may also be obtuse, another reason why we tend to believe her and sniff at the Queen instead.

Yet notwithstanding the Queen's offer of a pardon, the Ministers' approach is cannier. They choose instead to become functionaries, lacking responsibility, rather than acting with responsiblity and so being *eligible* for a pardon:

[T]hey fortify'd themselves by the Assistance of the Queen on one Hand, and the Parliament on the other, doing nothing of themselves or by themselves . . . not to mention the Transacting every Thing in a regular Way in Council, where, by the Journals, or Books of their Proceedings, it stands recorded, that all the Transactions of the Peace were done, and acted in Publick, and in a manner not liable to the Censure of any Judicature whatsoever. (53-54)

Instituting the procedures of regularity to sanction a withdrawal from moral duty erases legal responsibility for a separate peace; but it throws into relief the moral dereliction of those who did not support the peace. The Countess makes this point in spite of herself, and it seems credible because it is unintended. The reader resents the Ministers' use of "the system" to disinscribe their opportunistic weakness, but resentment necessitates acceptance of facts that "convict" the Ministers of a nonjusticiable charge and preclude deeper inquiry. Since Defoe worked consistently to deter prosecution, his offering the Ministers up as weak (but canny) was a clever idea with which to finesse it. The apparent noncontrivance of the maneuver is its great strength, and also the basis of a credulous/credible persona who deflects potential pursuit of a "real" author.

Did it succeed? In the copy of the *Memoirs* owned by the University of Pennsylvania, an eighteenth-century reader has drawn a little hand pointing to a passage, and enclosed it in brackets. The Countess, always alert to the Queen's tearful, affecting speeches, describes her fantasies of "what Violence was us'd in several Parts of Her Kingdoms, to force Men into Service; that Men were drag'd by force out of the Arms and Embraces of their Wives and children, who were often left in a starving Condition for want of their labour" (24). I suggest that highlighting these words is an indelible gesture, both touching and scary, attesting to the power of Defoe's fiction. Whoever marked the text (even assuming a direct experience with impressment) conveys that he or she does not recognize the fiction, and is pausing at a passage that particularly persuades.

The two political fictions I have considered, written just a few years before *Robinson Crusoe*, are significant because they evince highly developed skills in evading authorial accountability, as well as Defoe's consciousness of the problem in generic terms. Defoe's strategies are consistent with those identifiable with credit texts, and I would argue that this accounts for their impact on readers. The conscious strategy of these fictions necessarily jeopardized a "rational" public sphere.[27] Indeed, if it is a commonplace that Defoe did not respect "fair" debate, and sought to influence politics *sub rosa*,[28] then I am suggesting that he deployed a system of elusive narrative fictions as a cover. By "system" I mean that the foregoing examples could be multiplied by a few dozen. The distinctive feature of these fictions is that in their deep structure, they are artifacts of the market, capitalizing on readers' willingness to imagine that discourse is not wholly imaginary.

TELLING IT LIKE IT MIGHT BE: DEFOE'S RELUCTANT FICTIONS

Defoe's "political fictions" threaten epistemology because they conscript the reader into their evasionary strategies. Though they warn against evasive authors, they appeal to a predisposition to evade such warnings. The reader thinks he can interpret the text. Defoe's "reluctant fictions," however, leave the reader anxious. On the one hand, they acknowledge their potential fictionality, as well as the fact that their provenance might legitimately be questioned. Indeed, they announce their status as commodities, artifacts of a complex print culture in which the apparatus of production distances author from work and allows interpolation. Yet on the other hand the texts offer proofs tending to rehabilitate themselves, asserting a verifiable provenance, a fidelity to historical events. The crux is that such proofs are themselves questionable, and destabilize the text still further. The text appears to deconstruct its own strategy, gratuitously generating demands to deny fictionality then responding with truth claims that provoke more such demands. The reader is caught in a whiplash, not knowing whether to distrust the text, having no means to find out. Whoever inscribed the text (perhaps several people) cannot be said to lie: the claims are suspended in Air-Money, too equivocal to satisfy hermeneutic desire one way or the other.

I shall argue that the reader's experience of "reluctant fiction" is continuous with his experience of "financial" texts in which truth claims are impenetrable. Like Defoe's "political fictions," his reluctant fictions prey on readers disciplined by the market, in this case to expect that texts will avow themselves neither as to provenance nor veracity. In particular, I argue that the Grub Street hermeneutic developed in *The Secret History of the Secret History*, diffusing authorship among a corporate body that creates and responds to demand, is reinscribed in *Robinson Crusoe*, and taken up (though not so elaborately) in *Moll Flanders* and *Roxana*. The market enters Defoe's reluctant fictions as a marginally more genteel version of Grub Street – it is "print culture" – editors, publishers and assorted intermediaries instead of a garretful of hacks. In *Moll* and *Roxana* the apparatus of the market is literally "dressed up" as an amendatory enterprise readying the text for consumption:

The pen employ'd in finishing [Moll's] Story, and making it what you now see it to be, has had no little Difficulty to put it into a Dress fit to be seen, and to make it speak language fit to be read . . .[29]

The History of this Beautiful Lady is to speak for itself: If it is not as Beautiful as the Lady herself is reported to be . . . the Relator says, it must be from the Defect of his Performance; dressing up the Story in worse Cloathes than the Lady, whose Words he speaks, prepar'd it for the World.[30]

By putting on a dress, print culture, like Grub Street, is gendered female, assimilated at the level of gender to a market in financial texts (embodied in Lady Credit) where authors are elusive and veracity obscured. The logic of that market – discouraging the reader from valuing the text, encouraging him to project a value – is translated through the medium of print culture into Defoe's novels. In both cases, the point is to make the reader take a risk, i.e. to buy the text.

Because I think there is conscious purpose to the vacillation in these texts between relative fidelity and infidelity to a textual "original," that in fact such indeterminacy is a marketplace trope by which authors remain in the market disclaiming cheats, I cannot agree with critics who consider such indeterminacy a kind of necessary accident. Citing Laura Curtis' rejection of "synthetic approaches that impose a theory a posteriori upon a novelist genuinely uncertain about his goals and techniques," Joseph Bartolomeo argues that he "shares this skepticism . . . Just as [Defoe's] novels extended and complicated conventional narrative practice, his critical comments – and the language in which he expressed them – incorporated conventional theories in a complex and ultimately enigmatic way."[31] While it is appropriate to situate the prefaces of Defoe's novels in a context of "conventional theories" of fiction, one cannot *not* situate these texts in the context of marketplace discourse, which Defoe produced and critiqued. Against this discourse – or rather, continuous with it – "the language in which he expressed" (or failed to express) a posture towards his own fiction takes on another valence. If it is "ultimately enigmatic," that is because marketplace language *is* enigmatic regarding the veracity of texts and accountability of identifiable authors. The "narrative practice" that Defoe recapitulates, discernible in the texts of credit, is already "complicated" by Air-Money ambivalence, already a calculated response goading readers into risky commitments.

Indeed, Defoe's prefaces assert the status of his texts as artifacts of the market, complaining about piracy in the second and third volumes of *Crusoe*, positioning *Moll* and *Roxana* relative to the carriage trade. If we read the prefaces in context, therefore, we must account for the context they direct us towards. I argue that Defoe consciously contrives to orient the reader towards the market, a site of indeterminacy. Represented in the prefaces as print culture, the market necessarily produces texts that are generically noncommittal, since manuscripts are subjected to ("dressed" by) multiple hands. By bringing to the surface incidents of production normally suppressed (as they were, supposedly, in *The Secret History*) Defoe insinuates that transparency is inconsistent with a print text tailored for mass circulation. The reader should expect discursive overlays, an inaccessible original and a dissipated authorial voice. In this regard, the market-oriented print text is deeply ironic: a palimpsest, manuscript upon manuscript (like fiction upon fiction) defaces and finally effaces originary discourse to an uncertain (but acknowledged) degree.[32] The material conditions of print, highlighted by Defoe, advance a strategy of deliberate indeterminacy even as they seem unavoidable – necessary to doing business.[33] This strategy appeals to readers conditioned by marketplace texts to expect the ambivalence of Air-Money promises, the multivalenced deferrals of credit instruments, the impacted palimpsests of the Funds. Print and credit, in other words, share a logic grounded in the market. Both produce (or are seen to, expected to produce) texts that dissipate the "original" and attenuate the "author." Defoe's invocation of print sets in motion logical cross-references, reinforcing the impenetrability of market-generated print texts, naturalizing the fancy "dress" that overcomes resistance by appealing to desire.

In light of the foregoing, I suggest that Defoe's prefatorial references to the print text as commodity authorize a literary/commercial rationale for his ideas of fiction.[34] David Burgin's comment on the artifact under contemporary capitalism applies equally to the self-consciously commercialized Defoean text: "[T]he market is 'behind' nothing, it is *in* everything. It is thus that in a society where the commodification of art has progressed apace with the aestheticisation of the commodity, there has evolved a universal rhetoric of the aesthetic in which commerce and inspiration, profit and poetry, may rapturously entwine."[35] We cannot ask purely "aesthetic" questions of a text where aesthetic and commercial concomitants are mutually inflected, and where the text announces this inflection. We cannot broach questions of genre theory citing only "conventional [genre] theories." To a significant degree, the relative veracity of a text offered to the market, the author's relative deinscription in editing and promotion, are proprietary data. One expects neither their disarticulation nor disclosure.[36]

By approaching Defoe's texts as self-acknowledged artifacts of the market that invite customary (frustrated) responses, I invert Lennard Davis' logic in *Factual Fictions*. Davis suggests that in *Crusoe*, Defoe gropes towards "a type of narrative both true and false," that in *Moll* he searches for "a way to say that the work is at once true and not true" (161, 163). However, the texts do not present themselves as true *and* false, but as discursive counters, products appealing to a desire for truth while withholding data to verify indicia of truth. Rather than attempting to occupy all generic positions, the texts leave them all vacant. If *Moll* invites readers to choose whether the text is true – "we must be content to leave the Reader to pass his own Opinion" (vii) – it also recapitulates marketplace discourse that readers identify with the suspension of generic avowal. It is not, as Davis suggests, that *Crusoe* and *Moll* are "ambivalent," holding out dual possibilities to the reader (163). They hold out neither possibility, since they are discursive formations into whose generic affiliation it is not proper to inquire. The paradox of these self-conscious artifacts, "wrought" by several hands and calculated to the market, is that they are naturalized within a literary/commercial paradigm, and elicit responses appropriate to discourse indigenous to the market. *Moll* is "chiefly recommended to those who know how to read it" (viii); my argument is that readers know *not* to "read" insofar as they would establish the text's fidelity/infidelity to truth, and hence (potentially) implicate the author in pretense. "Reading" a text in the market entails hermeneutic deferral.

If one accepts the "naturalness" of tropes that warn against too close an approach to generic integrity, then one must revisit arguments that Defoe tried – and failed – to rationalize a fictive intent within a regime of "naive empiricism" documenting Truth. In *The Origins of the English Novel*, McKeon cites categorical confusion as the crux in Defoe's failed discrimination of *Crusoe* from fiction:

> Defoe's attempts to formulate a coherent theory that will comfortably accommodate the false claim to historicity lead in circles . . . They are frustrating discussions because as Defoe works to vindicate the false claim, there is an inevitable slippage in the meaning of the terms that are central to his inquiry. Meanings shift in order to avoid confronting logical contradiction, for conviction must inevitably fall if "true history" is required to include false claims to true history. (122)

Defoe's "incoherence" is continuous with, and reproduces, the discursive "reality" of credit; it accurately represents categorical uncertainties in the narrative of Lady Credit. Within the paradigm of marketplace discourse, the *Crusoe* texts (as framed by the prefaces) *are* consistent (one might almost say True). They do not reach towards some stabilized genre alien to marketplace texts. The problem with "genre" criticism (Bartolomeo cites Defoe's "logical failure . . . muddle")[37] is that it tries to link cosmos and heterocosm into some rational relation ("true"/untrue), and therefore itself makes a category error. Were critics to situate Defoe's texts against a discursive paradigm where fiction/nonfiction remain suspended as categories, then the heterocosm of the text (as represented in the prefaces) would seem recognizable, strategically articulating the inarticulateness of texts that resist self-disclosure. The continuity of credit and print, configuring a market of generically impenetrable texts, defines the "cosmos" of Defoe's novels – they represent it, and constitute it.

The "preface" to the first volume of the *Crusoe* trilogy, *The Life and*

Strange Surprizing Adventures of Robinson Crusoe of York, Mariner . . . Written by Himself (1719) states:

> If ever the Story of any private Man's Adventures in the World were worth making Publick, and were acceptable when Publish'd, the Editor of this Account thinks this will be so . . .
>
> The Editor believes the thing to be a just History of Fact; neither is there any Appearance of Fiction in it; And however thinks, because all such things are dispatch'd, that the Improvement of it, as well as the Diversion, as to the Instruction of the Reader, will be the same; and as such, he thinks, without farther Compliment to the World, he does them a great Service in the Publication. (vii)

Crusoe's text, "Written by Himself," is recommended by an Editor, whose function is to appropriate authorial subjectivity into the corporate culture of print. Moreover, since the Editor is cited in the third person, one senses another potential presence – a publisher who may have penned the preface. Indeed, there is a publisher's introduction to the third volume. Thus even before the reader attempts the text, he learns that "Robinson Crusoe" is mediated, subject to (in league with?) agents identified with the market. Indeed, the Editor compliments his own "great Service" and encourages the text's consumption. In an environment of such self-conscious commercial discourse – where the Editor seems to have an interest "in the Publication" – it seems logical that the author's manuscript, even if true, was "edited" to increase sales. Little wonder that the Editor (through whomever inscribes his words) insinuates that authorial accountability is speculative. He "believes" that *Crusoe* is a "just History of Fact"; he doesn't know it. The text has no "Appearance of Fiction"; but the reader can judge appearance. Because the Editor cannot, or at least will not interrogate the text, the reader is estopped.[38] He also discourages any such effort because whether "Fact" or "Fiction," the text abounds in delight and instruction.[39] The reader is deflected from too close scrutiny of genre by a person who will not himself scrutinize, and who *ex officio* can preempt authorial intent. *Crusoe* therefore begins as a "reluctant fiction" by secondhandedly suggesting that it is "a Just History of Fact," even while the very person to whom this suggestion is attributed represents a function, indeed an establishment less interested in Fact than in its Appearance. This implication/counterimplication leaves the reader uncertain, but more particularly the formulation jibes with the logic of credit expounded by Defoe himself: there is always a fifty-fifty chance, but since the outcome is deferred and there is *no* present truth or lie, imagination must presently suffice. The text is an appeal to desire. It insulates Defoe from the imputation of lying, since neither Fact nor Fiction is represented; the reader acts upon his desire. In any case, the question of authorship – Crusoe's and therefore Defoe's – is attenuated by the multiplication of agents working on the text, directing it towards the market.[40]

The preface to *The Farther Adventures of Robinson Crusoe* (1719) reflects upon the first volume's commerciality:

The Success the former Part of this Work has met with in the World, has yet been no other than is acknowledg'd to be due to the surprising Variety of the Subject, and to the agreeable Manner of the Performance.[41]

Like the previous preface, this one is self-congratulatory, and notices that *Crusoe*'s "Manner of Performance" produced significant sales. In part, that "performance" recapitulated the text's own mode of production, linking it to market-oriented practices that block access to an "author" and encourage a type of reading content with Appearance. "Appearance" is a crucial phenomenon. It colonizes the surface and excludes transparency. In effect, *Farther Adventures* acknowledges that as a strategy, the text's self-reflexive commerciality worked, deflecting readers from subsurface phenomena: generic affiliation, the identity/integrity of the author. It is not "surprising," therefore, that the strategy continues.

The next paragraph argues that commercial envy is behind suggestions that *Crusoe* is a fiction:

All the Endeavors of envious People to reproach it with being a Romance, to search it for Errors in Geography, Inconsistency in the Relation, and Contradictions in the Fact, have proved abortive, and as impotent as malicious. (viii)

Such "Endeavors" can always be dismissed as "abortive" and "impotent," since the preface's author knows that Appearance cannot successfully be penetrated. If commercial envy characterizes critics who "reproach" the text, the incidents of commercial production insulate the text from an accurate assessment of its fidelity to Fact.

Yet this raises a further issue: if readers instructed to disregard marketplace sniping know that they cannot weigh it, and the author of the preface knows that they know it, why is the question of historicity raised? I would argue that while the text's impenetrability has already been established, the preface's *own* suggestion of fictionality can deepen the indeterminacy, rendering the reader even more likely to accept the alienation of the text from any coherent authorial intent:

> The just Application of every Incident, the religious and useful Inferences drawn from every Part, are so many Testimonies to the good Design of making it publick, and must legitimate all the Part that may be call'd Invention, or Parable in the Story. (viii)

Immediately after dismissing imputations of fiction, the text concedes that "useful Inferences" justify whatever "may be call'd Invention." While still deferring any outright admission (what may be "call'd" fiction, still may not be), the text drastically backs away from previous denials. The assertions are virtually self-cancelling, leaving neither Fact nor Fiction firmly in place. Like Lady Credit, like the impacted obligations of the Funds (each claiming their own internal logic, each cancelling the logic of the others), like *The Secret History of the Secret History*, the text reduces to a zero-sum. The reader does not choose among assertions, so much as he confronts nonassertion. I would argue that the juxtaposition of these paragraphs demonstrates the continuity of commercial printlogic and the logic of credit, each of which deflects the reader of marketplace texts from attempting to identify fiction.

The next paragraphs attack abridgements of *Crusoe* that followed publication. The concern is quintessentially commercial:

> By this [abridgement] they leave the Work naked of its brightest Ornaments; and if they would, at the same Time pretend, that the Author has supply'd the story out of his Invention, they take from it the Improvement, which alone recommends that Invention to wise and good Men.
>
> The Injury these Men do the Proprietor of this Work, is a Practice all honest Men abhor; and he believes he may challenge them to shew the Difference between that and Robbing on the Highway, or breaking open a House. (viii)[42]

The argument suggests that abridgement itself is a zero-sum game, since it treats the text as if it were Invention while depriving Invention of moral, didactic content. The abridgers are caught in their own trap, erasing any acceptable rationale for fiction based on its moral purport.[43] Yet if abridgers are self-defeating, they also threaten *Crusoe*, not only by robbing the Proprietor (i.e. publisher), but by suggesting that the Author (nominally Crusoe, by inference

Defoe) "supply'd the story out of his Invention." Under the logic that the prefaces are developing, this argument implicates the market in an ironic reversal of the market, so that commercial operations expose rather than occlude fictional praxis. Abridgement, though consistent with authorial alienation, preempts authors from parlaying submission to the market into a profitable, impenetrable accountability. It cuts through the wadding of print, leaving a bare shown-up author. Thus if abridgement steals sales by offering a cheaper alternative, and also undermines truth claims of the original, one may as well buy cheaper lies.

This riposte to abridgers reeks of protesting too much, since the text has already acknowledged its probable fictionality. If it is intended to muddle that acknowledgment by suggesting that *others* have "call'd" the text a fiction, then the protests cannot avoid being "call'd" jesuitical. Nevertheless, I suggest that the preface denounces abridgement because the practice foregrounds the commerciality of texts even more than Defoe wishes. It converts the impenetrability of print texts into a blatant admission that they are mere words with no possible integrity. It demystifies print culture too much.

The tirade against abridgement also introduces a third person concerned with the text as a commodity: the Proprietor. Under practices common at the time, the Proprietor/publisher would have purchased the author's copyright. Though he is ostensibly angry that abridgement is diluting profits, his threats reinforce Defoe's strategy, emphasizing that Author/Editor/Publisher constitute a concatenation of interests that disperses responsibility for the text. The Proprietor's indignation evinces the potency of the profit motive in shaping the text, which was no minor concern.[44] In 1716, Alexander Pope wrote a devastating attack on the notorious publisher Edmund Curll. Curll is made to say:

The Book of the Conduct of the Earl of N[ottingha]m, is as yet unpublished; as you are to have the profit of it, Mr. Pemberton, you are to run the Risque of the Resentments of all that Noble Family. Indeed I caused the Author to assert several Things in it as Facts, which are only idle Stories of the Town; because I thought it would make the Book sell.[45]

In Swift's *A Tale of A Tub*, the hack author is complicit in booksellers' efforts to promote sales, even through misrepresentation. He declares: "[W]hen a Customer comes for one of these [a copy of the *Tale*], and desires in confidence to know the Author; he will tell him privately, as a Friend, naming which ever of the Wits happen to be that Week in Vogue . . . This I mention, because I am wonderfully well acquainted with the present Relish of Courteous Readers."[46]

After *Farther Adventures* appeared, Charles Gildon issued his famous critique of *Crusoe, The Life and Strange Surprizing Adventures of Mr. D . . . De F . . . of London, Hosier* (1719). Gildon argued that *Crusoe* was Defoe's (not Crusoe's) fiction, and that it was insufficiently moral to be justified as fiction:

> I find that these Endeavors you seem to contemn as impotent, have yet had so great a Force upon yourself, as to make you more than tacitly confess, that your book is nothing but a Romance [citing the statement that a part "may be call'd Invention or parable," but that it is legitimated by its moral]. But when it is plain that there are no true, useful or just Inferences drawn from any of the Incidents . . . I think we may justly say, that the Design of the Publication of this Book was not sufficient to justify and make Truth of what you allow to be Fiction and Fable; what you mean by Legitimating, Invention, and Parable, I know not; unless you would have us think, that the manner of your telling a Lie will make it a Truth.[47]

Gildon attributes to Defoe a more straightforward concession than the text will bear. Nevertheless, he himself concedes a tension in the second preface ("the manner of your telling a Lie will make it a Truth") that strains against "tacitly" admitting that *Crusoe* is "but a Romance." Like Oldmixon, Gildon operates within a logic of linearity, and cannot analyze the *strategic* interest of impacted, mutually annihilating lines of argument that lead nowhere. He does not accuse Defoe of confusing the reader, but of "confess[ing]" the truth of his lie – Gildon's own misreading is responsible for his stumbling on the ruse. He bolsters his interpretation of the preface with extratextual evidence from the novel itself – contradictions such as Crusoe's swimming naked to the ship and stuffing his pockets – and in this latter sense poses the greater threat to Defoe. The whole *modus operandi* of marketplace texts relies on readers' forebearing to import data into the text. In answering Gildon, therefore, Defoe had to reaffirm the structural principles of his evasionary strategy, keeping the reader suspended in an irresolution that was airtight.

The preface to the third volume of the trilogy, *Serious Reflections During the Life and Surprising Adventures of Robinson Crusoe: With His Vision of the Angelick World* (1720), is perhaps the most infamous tissue of self-contradictions ever offered in defense of a text. Crusoe himself materializes in "Robinson Crusoe's Preface," denouncing critics who claim that *Crusoe* and *Farther Adventures* are "feign'd, that the Names are borrow'd, and that it is all a Romance" (A2r–A3v). Without cavilling, Crusoe inverts this claim, arguing "that their Objection is an Invention scandalous in Design, and false in Fact" (A3v). But if his riposte suggests that the "author," as opposed to intermediaries, addresses readers in a linear mode that discriminates Fact and Fable, the text quickly declines: Crusoe "affirm[s] that the Story, though Allegorical, is also Historical" (A3v) – not mere fiction, but not transparent either. Crusoe reinscribes Air-Money obscurities that surround his texts. His handlers learn how a *real* master complicates epistemology when Crusoe suggests his life's Story represents another's: "there is a Man alive, and well known too, the Actions of whose Life are the just Subject of these Volumes" (A3r–A3v). Crusoe's auto-biography is an allegory of someone else, but since the events are historical, it represents Crusoe. His text is a self-acknowledged hall of mirrors, a study in mutually inflecting personae. It occludes originary, stable sites of meaning, deflecting the reader towards "Deductions" inaccessible through direct apprehension of the text:

Without letting the Reader into a nearer Explication of the Matter, I proceed to let him know, that the happy Deductions I have employ'd myself to make from all the Circumstances of my Story, will abundantly make him amends for his not having the Emblem explained by the Original. (A4v)

The interpenetrating personae of the Story leave an epistemological blank, an Emblem whose Original – if there is any – is withheld. But since the logic of Crusoe's Original is actually impossible, not merely obscure, the blank seems to signify that the Story is a simulacrum, cut loose from an Original, more "original" than History will bear.

Yet how can a Story derived from "real Facts" (A4v), from incidents that are "all historical and true in Fact" (A4r), not be based on *someone*? The reader wavers. Crusoe ultimately reinscribes himself as the Original of a Story still fictive, but now seemingly about Crusoe, not "a Man alive, and well known too":

In a Word, there's not a Circumstance in the imaginary Story, but has its just Allusion to a real Story, and chimes Part for Part, and Step for Step with the inimitable life of Robinson Crusoe. (A5r)

Torn between a text that is a simulacrum, or a representation that insists upon – but defies – comprehensibilty, the reader eschews logical interrogation.[48] In this regard, *Crusoe* operates on the reader like a marketplace text, deferring generic affiliation. Its "Original" is the nonoriginary discourse of the market, reified in Crusoe.

Like Harley's emergence into *The Secret History of the Secret History*, Crusoe becomes a fiction upon a fiction, obscuring sites that generate meaning, that avow authorial intent.[49] The maneuver recapitulates the logic of the print/credit matrix, which through interpolation and displacement distends the distance between text and reader. Thus it is seemingly ironic that at the very beginning of the preface, Crusoe suggests that his own intentionality is the unifying factor among his texts:

As the Design of every Thing is said to be first in the Intention, and last in the Execution; so I come now to acknowledge to my Reader, That the present Work is not merely the Product of the first two Volumes, but the first two Volumes may rather be called the Product of this: The Fable is always made for the Moral, not the Moral for the Fable. (A2r)

One must pause for a moment over what seems conventional enough, to realize that discourse does not run backwards, that Defoe is actually mocking imputed intention (Gildon's imputations included). Crusoe's point is that one cannot know what a text intends, and that *post hoc* rationales (such as the very preface we are reading) will get us nowhere (in case we have not already figured that out).

Moll Flanders (1722) implicates "reluctant fiction" even more deeply in the Alphonse and Gaston deferrals of print.[50] The Preface begins by calling attention to the issue of fiction, then responding equivocally:

The World is so taken up of late with Novels and Romances, that it will be hard for a private History to be taken for Genuine, where the names and other Circumstances of the Person are concealed; and on this account we must be content to leave the Reader to pass his own Opinion on the ensuing Sheets, and take it just as he pleases. (vii)

Hermeneutic responsibility is the reader's. However, the categories suggested in the preface, "private" "History," offer no guidance to Moll's veracity. The editorial imposition so prominently touted, renders discourse in the text less particular to the "private" person who wrote it. It is now oriented towards the market: "the original of this Story is put into new Words," "put into a Dress fit to be seen." If the "original" was "History," it is now less so, since its new Dress is an overlay on the author's intent: "some of the vicious part of her Life, which could not be modestly told, is quite left out, and several other

Parts are very much shortened" (vii-viii). The reference to clothes was a popular trope with roots in biblical homiletics, but as Deborah Wyrick notes regarding *A Tale of A Tub*: "the clothes allegory centers not on garments as things but on garments as investitures of authority and transvestitures of will."[51] In the preface to *Moll*, clothes invest the editor with authority to transvest Moll, though the reader must determine the degree to which the exchange has occurred. As items that reveal and conceal, clothes become the perfect metaphor for the relation of print culture and mannequin text.

As further equivocation, "The Author is here supposed to be writing her own History" (vii), a supposition that may be incorrect as to author, genre, or both. In any case, editorial mediation dissolves "author" and "history" into ambivalent notions, frustrating inquiry into provenance and facticity irrespective of crafty syntax.

The "pen employ'd in finishing" Moll's story is increasingly prominent as the preface proceeds. It discloses the editorial strategy of the "pen" – not in this case a person, but a metonym for the impersonal market, concerned with defensible texts:

[T]he whole Relation is carefully garbled of all the Levity and Looseness that was in it: So it is applied, and with the utmost care to vertuous and religious Uses. None can without being guilty of manifest Injustice, cast any reproach upon it, or upon our Design in publishing it. (ix)

The "carefully garbled" text, turned over and sorted out, bears few marks of Moll's raffish tract.[52] Nevertheless, "vertuous" objectives are not allowed to occlude Moll's "Relation" insofar as it tends (ostensibly) towards a moral objective: "To give the History of a wicked Life repented of, necessarily requires that the wicked part should be made as wicked as the real History will bear" (viii). The text insists upon virtue but integrates the wicked; it is thoroughly garbled but invokes "real History." Such ambivalence destabilizes provenance and genre, even as it allows the reader to rationalize an anticipated thrill. The disclosure of its editorial strategy, ostensibly admitting the reader into the text's constitution, works ironically. It invites desire for the text, but disorganizes any effort to determine whether Moll is truthful or whether she even exists. Moll devolves into a function of discourse, coordinate with the "pen" through which she is rendered. Together they form a matrix that excludes a third-party author responsible for the text, for example Defoe.

Another author momentarily surfaces in a discarded text describing

Moll's last happy days: "but they are not told with the same Elegancy as those accounted for by herself" (xi). What "Elegancy"? what happened to a "Language more like one still in Newgate"? The very reason for editing Moll's text collapses into perversity. The preface comes full circle, constituting a cipher introducing a cipher. It is a bag of Air-Money.

Moll's own narrative exploits the market's capacity to diffuse responsibility for authorial production. Though not herself engaged with print culture, the first text she produces is inserted into a sector of the market vulnerable to an homologous logic. When she and her fortune-hunting suitor exchange texts, their apparent spontaneity is inflected by other texts – rumors floating in the marriage market, promoted by Moll and tending to ambiguate her own revelations of poverty. Thus when Moll tells the truth ("I'm Poor; Let's see how kind you'll prove"), there is rumor in the air suggesting that her claim may be "jest." Moll is banking on the common proclivity to credit Opinion, to regard extratextual data as a hermeneutic goldmine. The suitor obviously takes in Moll's literal text, but swayed by extratextual rumors, he hopes that a hyperliteral sense may be truer. He therefore plays along, writing "Be mine with all your Poverty." When Moll calls his bluff ("Yet secretly you hope I Lye"), it is because she understands how readers have been disciplined by the market to discredit texts (1, 80).

In the foregoing exchange, Moll's representation is no lie. However, she has been complicit in confusing her suitor's perception – allowing the market to proliferate fictions around her, relying on market culture to enhance their value as true. While she never explicitly endorsed the discourse around her, she seemed to acknowledge the market by ostensibly resenting it: "I pretended on all Occasions to doubt his Sincerity, and told him, perhaps he only courted me for my Fortune" (1, 79). By allowing discourse to inform her own text, Moll dislocates the source of misrepresentation, relying on her reader to interpret a text against itself where Opinion reinforces desire. By assimilating her text into discourse, insuring that its fictions will affect the reader but still not be traceable to herself, Moll escapes culpability:

He has fore closed all manner of Objection, seeing, whether he was in jest or in earnest, he had declar'd he took me without any regard to my Portion and, whether I was in jest or earnest, I had declar'd my self to be very Poor, so that, in a *Word*, I had him fast both ways; and tho' he might say afterwards he was cheated, yet he could never say that I cheated him. (1, 81)

Since Moll has not lied, and her suitor has acquiesced, the contract is enforceable. If he misunderstood, Moll is not the proximate cause of his misunderstanding. He might think he was cheated, but if not by Moll then by whom? By a "jest" in "earnest," Moll dissipates any objective determination of intent, leaving only the penumbra of negotiation – the market – in which to search for the cheat. If fault rests with anyone, then (subject to an I-told-you-so) it must be with the recipient of messages, who was susceptible to market practice and got lost in market noise.

The whole incident enacts the ambiguity of market-generated texts. Moll's fault cannot be measured, cannot even be attributed, because her text participates in an intertext. What should be an intimate transaction between author and reader, is inflected – infected – by marketplace currents that generate only a disembodied cheat. The suitor/reader is left with his own fault, producing his own faulty text. As we know from *Moll Flanders*, as an "author" she remains in the market to dissemble again; so does the author himself. Moll's success mirrors the strategy of Defoe. As Joseph Bartolomeo observes: "A reception-oriented aesthetic dominates the preface to *Moll Flanders*, with multiple references to types of readers and ways of reading ... Defoe, in the preface, has artfully left the question of literal truth up to the reader" (44–5). I would argue that a "reception-oriented aesthetic dominates" Moll's textual practice as well. She argues that such an aesthetic attaches to market-generated texts, which are products of discourse for which no single author can be accountable. *Moll Flanders'* reader, uncertain as to its genre, cannot blame the author of the preface for "leav[ing] the Reader to pass his own Opinion"; the print/credit matrix that informs apprehension leaves no other choice. He cannot blame the author (Moll? Defoe?) if the text is not "real History"; for the same reason, History is a text that we would not know if we saw it.

In 1724, Defoe wrote *Roxana*. Its preface is less complaisant towards print culture than is *Moll's*, casting the editorial process as potentially inept at bringing the text to market:

The History of this Beautiful Lady is to speak for itself; If it is not as Beautiful as the Lady herself is reported to be; if it is not as diverting as the Reader can desire, and much more than he can reasonably expect; and if all the most diverting Parts of it are not adapted to the Instruction and Improvement of the Reader, the Relator says, it must be from the defect of his Performance;

dressing up the Story in worse Cloathes than the Lady, whose Words he speaks, prepar'd it for the World. (viii)

If the present edition is possibly not as effective as the original, why not publish the original? Why not tout this edition as more effective – even if it isn't? I would argue that positing the paradoxical print text, one that is riskier than a direct transcription of the manuscript, suggests that print is overdetermined; its energy resists curbs. Manuscripts *will* be edited, perhaps by someone obtuse. The misfit intermediary, out of sympathy with the author's intent, insensitive to her style, disconnects text and provenance. His "Performance" is a history of print's audacity. Only incidentally is it "History" recorded by a subject. Indeed, defective performance may not even satisfy reader expectations. As the first paragraph of *Roxana*'s preface states, the degenerate print text is even more preemptive than a skilled edition: neither the author's nor the *reader*'s desires are reflected as it spins into its own discursive orbit. It is a cold, dis-integrated object so thoroughly without rationale that it baffles rational inquiry (cf. *The Secret History of the Secret History*). In this sense, print culture is presented as opposite its posture in *Moll*, where it is carefully rationalized, and the clothes it puts on flatter its subject – the text.

As in *Crusoe* and *Moll*, *Roxana*'s preface is written in the third person. Whoever inscribes the preface acknowledges that the text has replaced the subject's voice: Roxana does not speak, but is spoken for by a History – a re-relation of history – that "is to speak for itself." The solipsistic text, representing only its own processes, defines print culture as it is presented in *Roxana*; it is the hinge establishing an homology with the discourse of credit. As I shall argue in chapter 5, Roxana's narrative dramatizes the vulnerability of texts that aspire to such radical disengagement. The preface therefore proposes a paradigm that the Story threatens to deconstruct. Though the Relator stands in place of the "Lady, whose Words he speaks," he is only a feature in the text's middle distance, complicating its reception with his own possible misrelation.

The next paragraph suggests that he could not be trusted to account for the text, since his logic is as defective as his self-conscious diffidence implies:

He takes the Liberty to say, That this Story differs from most modern Performances of this Kind . . . I say, It differs from them in . . . That the

Foundation of This is laid in Truth of Fact; and so the Work is not a Story but a History. (vii)

He takes "the Liberty" to opine on the Story's truth, apparently aware that he is speaking without authority. His "defects" emerge in the unwarranted deduction that since the "Foundation . . . is laid in Truth," the entirety must not be "a Story but a History." Such illogic suggests that while the Relator thinks he "speaks" Roxana's "Words," he may not have followed her purport. It is telling, moreover, that the pronouns slip from third to first person. If the Relator is speaking, it would seem that his grasp on subjectivity is tenuous. Or is it that someone else immediately wrests the preface from him, too careless to be consistent? In either case, the reader is confronted with a radically unstable "relation": the Relator barely relates anything coherent, does not establish a relationship of trust with the reader, and possibly even with his colleagues. His colleagues (if there are any at this point) seem indifferent to producing a seamless text.

Other participants potentially emerge in the fourth paragraph, though the collective "we" may refer only to literate society in general. In any case, the writer(s) seem(s) unable to maintain the distinction between History or Story that the Relator/I was so keen to invoke:

It is not always necessary that the Names of Persons shou'd be discover'd, though the History may be many Ways useful; and if we shou'd be always oblig'd to name the Persons or not to relate the Story, the Consequence might be only this, That many a pleasant and delightful History wou'd be Buried in the Dark . . . (iv)

The ambivalent syntax, as well as the category slippage, convey a sense of lapsed rigor that redounds to the probable treatment of the manuscript.[53] At a further remove, it suggests that if the History *is* a Story, there may be no Roxana at all. We cannot be sure, however, since the inexactness and presumption that characterize the preface suggest there may be "garbled" History – a History verging on Story. There are multiple reasons for our not being able to find out.

When the Writer appears in the next paragraph, he is perhaps redundant in strategic terms, since the reader is already overloaded with personae. Moreover, he reduplicates the defective logic of the Relator/I, claiming that his knowledge of a small part of the events lends credence to the rest:

The Writer says, He was particularly acquainted with the Lady's First Husband, the Brewer, and with his Father; and also with his Bad Circumstances; and knows that the first Part of the Story is Truth.

This may, he hopes, be a Pledge for the Credit of the rest, tho' the Latter Part of her History lay Abroad, and cou'd not so well be vouch'd as the First; yet as she has told it herself, we have the less Reason to question the truth of that Part also. (viii)

Since the Writer does not divulge the nature of his "particular" acquaintance – he may have been the Brewer's drinking buddy or his creditor – the Writer's credibility will suffer as soon as the Brewer's fecklessness is disclosed. Moreover, how can he argue that Roxana is her own historian when the Relator already claims that office and now there is a Writer as well? A chronic disorganization affects this preface, suggesting that no one is in charge, that the protocols of print have escaped rational integration. The shift from Story (in one paragraph) to History (in the next) reverses the motion in the Relator's discourse, endorsing the sense of things falling apart, computing to a zero-sum. At a deeper level, where print meets credit in a matrix that baffles the reader in the market, the Story/History toss-up assimilates the discourse of the preface to the ambivalence of Lady Credit's narrative. The reader disciplined by marketplace textuality will react by abandoning any effort to pursue *Roxana*'s generic affinity, just as Roxana hopes that Susan will react.

The preface continues to contradict itself: in the face of the Relator's disavowals, the Writer notes that "all imaginable Care has been taken to keep clear of Indecencies and immodest Expressions" (viii). Moreover, though the Relator feared that the reader might neither enjoy nor profit from the text, all the personae jointly – and unequivocally – conclude that he will do both:

In the mean-time the Advantages of the present Work are so great, and the Virtuous Reader has room for so much Improvement, that we make no Question, the Story, however meanly told, will find a Passage to his best Hours, and be read both with Profit and Delight. (ix)

The text's appeal to the reader's desire is lost in what seems a last-minute cobbling together. We have every reason to assume it is disingenuous on the Relator's part, and that his acquiescence evinces a lack of authority (as well as a lack of credibility). The disorganization of the preface stands out in greater relief, as if it were constantly forgetful – or grossly negligent – of what has just been said. The attempt at composition is actually off-putting, jarring the reader into a reflex that, I have argued, is the customary reaction to marketplace texts. If in *Crusoe* and its progeny the reader could not follow the argument, throwing up his hands in surrender, here the reader seems to be in the midst of an argument, throwing up his hands in dismay. In both cases, however, the texts deploy the concomitants of print culture to baffle the reader. If he purchases the texts, it is not because he knows what he is purchasing but because he is perversely intrigued. I suggest that this is the essential strategy of marketplace texts – stocks, annuities, *Crusoe*, *Moll*, *Roxana*.

By situating Defoe's reluctant fictions within a print/credit matrix, I am suggesting that the confusion in these texts between historicity and fiction is overdetermined by the culture: if one writes fiction one does not acknowledge it, but neither does one risk detection by insisting that one is telling the truth. Evasion by confusion is inevitable. It is the only possible position of one seeking to cope with a cultural phenomenon – an animus towards fiction – while pursuing a personal predilection – a desire to inscribe fiction. Thus I take issue with McKeon's emphasis when he states: "the standard of historical truth, and the conviction of its rhetorical efficacy, are so powerful in Defoe's mind that he continues [for two decades] . . . to make and to justify the false claim to historicity, although with ambivalence and accompanied by a variety of uneasy extenuations" (120). Ambivalence and uneasiness are not secondary to a basic empiricist commitment. Rather, they are integral to a strategy that avoids making a commitment. Such avoidance is commonplace in texts whose epistemology is based in the market. Citing the occasional references to vice in Defoe's "edited" texts, McKeon argues that "it is only within the continuing fiction of an original and authentic document edited by another hand that his apparent documentary laxity can have any meaning" (122). But as I have suggested, the "documentary laxity" in Defoe's texts blurs the original document, even to the point where its existence becomes speculative. Both McKeon and I attribute gestures of "rhetorical efficacy" to Defoe, but where McKeon sees these as over-determined by "naive empiricism," I argue that they epitomize texts that defy empirical inquiry.

Defoe's texts, therefore, offer no appearance of conforming to Puritan concerns for epistemological clarity. Their "morality," acknowledged to be secondhand, is instrumental in a shiftiness that muddles – rather than mediates – God's creation. Such morality is in this sense ironic, a perverse appropriation of the term. Yet one cannot argue that any such apparent inversion of Puritan paradigms denominates Defoe as "immoral," or adequately explains his project. In my view, Defoe's evasiveness instantiates the *amoral* discourse of the market, where narrative is always potentially fictive hence always evasive. It does not mock religion because it is outside, though complementary to, a religious concept of the world. It is "overdetermined" by a secular discourse in which opacity inheres in textuality itself.

Yet if Defoean rhetoric is generated by the market as another impenetrable trope, how can one attribute to Defoe a strategic "intent," a motivation distinct from and not identifiable with "discourse?" I suggest that one should not try to separate the two. That is, while Defoe's texts deploy a strategy, and are "intentional" in a way that Deconstruction sniffs at, the intention recapitulates discursive phenomena embedded in culture that determine how texts shall seem. To be in the market selling fiction (or potential fiction) is to seek to evade accountability.[54] Thus if Defoe is writing texts that configure an evasionary market, the market as constituted by evasive texts is writing Defoe. The reciprocity between text and context (other texts) establishes the common discourse.

The irony of the evasive author is that as his agency is compromised, and he becomes another expression of marketplace discourse, he reproduces the very conditions – epistemological confusion – that the market abhors and that compromise his agency. Turning the irony back on the culture, however, Defoe's reluctant fictions demonstrate that if the culture opposes fiction it will be unable to punish it. The culture is increasingly baffled before fiction the more it is disallowed, and the more that its practitioners are driven to evasion. For the market-driven culture, fiction becomes like a Chinese finger trap: the harder you try to disengage, the tighter it gets. Defoe exploits the trap, suggesting that discourse is inescapable, that the more one tries to interpret a text, the more baffled one becomes.

As I suggested in the introduction, and have sought to demonstrate in this chapter, the homology between literary and financial texts does not reduce to simple causality. My approach has been to posit a simultaneity of literary and nonliterary phenomena and their ultimate dissolution into a "textual" crux. Literary and nonliterary texts play off one another, responding to and creating an epitome of uncertainty. As Stephen Greenblatt notes in "Fiction and Friction":

The relation I wish to establish between medical and theatrical practice is not one of cause and effect or source and literary realization. We are dealing rather with a shared code, a set of interlocking tropes and similitudes that function not only as objects but as the conditions of representation. (88)

I argue that while the market is a necessary condition enabling, even forcing literary tropes, such tropes *are* the market, just as much as those of credit.

CHAPTER 3

Credit and honesty in
"The Compleat English Tradesman"

CRITICAL AND GENERIC BACKGROUND

Critics do not intensively "read" *The Compleat English Tradesman* (1725–7) as they do Defoe's recognized "fictions." Its appeal to economic historians apparently perpetuates a notion that its discursive constructions are unchallenging.[1] Ironically, in view of his own treatment of the text as a *post hoc* primer for *Roxana*, Bram Dijkstra remarks that given "the largely inaccurate contention of certain Defoe scholars that he tended to contradict his own pronouncements ... and was always writing on both sides of a question ... many critics must have reasoned why bother to read ... the more than 800 pages [actually 990] of *The Compleat English Tradesman*."[2] But it is precisely *because* the text is thought to lack complexity and contradiction that critics shy away! Moreover, the crux in Dijkstra's remark is the term "read." Critics who have "bothered" relegate the text to "context" for Defoe's other work, citing its connection with Whig economics, or treating it as an example of didacticism that preceded "the rise of the novel." Such insensitivity may reflect the text's obvious, insistent practicality and concern for arcana such as bills and notes.[3] Curiously, critics might have been alerted to the text's relevance to fiction by Charles Lamb, who attacked it as a catalog of "the studied analysis of every mean art, every sneaking address, every trick and subterfuge (short of larceny) that is necessary in the tradesman's occupation."[4]

In any case, the consensus has restricted *The Compleat English Tradesman* to its most literal level, eliding culturally freighted discourse that deeply informs its meaning. Failure to "read" the text has prevented appreciation of its integral relation to Defoe's oeuvre, which – like the culture itself – concatenates emerging capitalism with ideas of fiction. I argue that one should read *The Compleat English Tradesman* as formulating a theory of practicable fiction within a market that would interrogate authors of potential fiction ("literary" or "financial"). It deploys marketplace discourse to theorize how fiction can remain in the market. Thus its apparent "economic" preoccupations, like those of Hutcheson but from an opposite point of view, recognize the fictive proclivity of market-generated texts. The difference is that it domesticates the homology between credit and fiction. The Tradesman's own credit, rather than the Nation's, provides a discourse through which credibility resists accountability. The text's concern, therefore, *is* with economics, but as it is valenced with epistemology. *The Compleat English Tradesman* articulates the shared, defiant epistemology of Defoean fiction and instruments of credit, apparent in the narrative of Lady Credit a generation before.

I shall also argue that the text does not just reflect *upon* a market discourse whose logic configures Defoe's other texts. As itself a production of the market, marketplace logic *inhabits The Compleat English Tradesman*, rendering it as elusive as *Crusoe*. The text's "didactic" pretensions, purporting to explain credit, also undermine a definition of credit, so that the reader encompasses neither credit nor the text. Didacticism issues in irony, demonstrating to the reader that knowledge in the market is contingent, texts impenetrable. In expounding a marketplace Honesty that devolves into unaccountable, subjective "intent," the text enacts its own theory, recapitulating the resistance of marketplace texts to interrogation. *The Compleat English Tradesman* is itself fictive in promising to "compleat" the Tradesman but refusing closure. But if like so many Defoean fictions, the text is self-reflexive, it reflects on texts beyond itself: Defoe's novelistic fictions, "compleat" by 1724. In breaking down the notion that market-generated texts represent phenomena with epistemological certainty, *Crusoe*, *Moll*, and *Roxana* can be held to no higher standard. Defoe succeeds to the position of Compleat English Tradesman, trading in fictions that cannot be held to account.

This "reading" of *The Compleat English Tradesman*, which challenges conventional approaches that isolate it within commercial discourse, views it as metatext, obsessed with textual trading. It *is* commercial in that it concerns the fictions of commerce. But it deploys tropes inherent in the fictions of commerce; it redounds to Defoe's own commerce in fiction; and demonstrates that each is a function of the other. To read it as *only* a positivistic tract is an Oldmixian mistake. The text is of a piece with the logic of Defoean fiction. In this sense I put it on a par with those texts.

More particularly, I challenge as simplistic a notion of "genre" that would pigeonhole "didactic" or "economic" texts supposedly lacking "literary" interest. To be couched in economic language and concerned with economic mores does not automatically prove that a text is transparent, that it fits a genre of ostensibly similar texts that exclude the complexities of "literature."[5] One need not postulate the demise of genre to observe, as Rick Altman does in another context, that "genre" has become a type of critical blinders:

> The constitution of a genre thus shortcircuits the "normal" sequence of interpretation. Text after text is generated from the same mold, thus highlighting certain textual relationships, repressing others, and eventually limiting the field of play of the interpretive community. The function of the interpretive community is usurped by the genre. . . .
>
> Rather than seeing genres as structures helping individual texts to produce meaning, we must see genres as restrictive, as complex methods of reducing the field of play of individual texts.[6]

In my view, *The Compleat English Tradesman* is inseparable from its context, its generic complexity registering the instability of surrounding discourse. The discourse of the market acknowledges the potential fictivity of credit; the text recapitulates credit-based tropes, deferring closure on its own promises. Yet because the text has been identified with a genre that excludes any such "field of play," criticism reproduces readings that reinforce such exclusions. I suggest that a greater understanding of the text requires that we stop reading it only as an economic treatise – even one concerned with states of mind. It should be seen as engaged with fictions in the market that configure its own strategies.

The issue of genre is central to assessing J. Paul Hunter's treatment of *The Compleat English Tradesman*. In *Before Novels*, Hunter attenuates the bald "economic" readings that characterize most criticism. However, in attempting to bring the text closer to novelistic discourse, he reinscribes a generic affiliation that excludes complex literary readings. That is, he situates the text in a "didactic" genre popular in the eighteenth century which, he argues, influenced the Novel's development. His purpose is not to rechristen such "didactic" texts as literary artifacts, but to delineate their instrumental relationship to "real" (novelistic) literature. Hunter concedes that such texts have theoretical features, but these (in his estimation) are moralistic and hortatory; they are not the amoral, elusive stratagems typical of marketplace fictions:

[I]t is not surprising that many of the everyday materials enjoyed by early eighteenth century readers – books and pamphlets that even in these anti-canonical times are still considered "background" or "subliterary" – have theoretical features similar to those in novels. Didactic materials of no literary pretension may, in fact, help us to a fuller understanding of aspects of early novels that modern readers have trouble with, for characteristics shared across generic and even "literary" lines show us important aspects of a cultural psyche that felt the need to influence behavior at any psychological cost. (226–227)

That is, texts in this genre "of no literary pretension" can be read *as* literary only as they display didactic techniques that filter into novels. I would argue, however, that rehabilitation of *The Compleat English Tradesman* into a precursor genre of the novel denies its engagement with more fundamental issues of fictionality, and therefore with epistemological concerns that were the obverse of didacticism, i.e. the concern that knowledge itself was unstable.

In his preface, Defoe announces that "The Title of this Work is an Index to its Performance. It is a collection of useful instructions for a young Tradesman" (iii). This is a fascinating beginning, suggesting a transparency between representation ("The Title") and fulfillment in a text (*The Compleat English Tradesman*), between promise and Performance. Yet the whole text enacts misrepresentation and failed promises, wavering in its definition of honesty, dramatizing "the certain ruin ... of trading upon borrow'd credit" (ix). The text insists that a disjunction between language and intent is the norm:

CUSTOM indeed has driven us beyond the limits of our morals in many things, which trade makes necessary, and which we cannot now avoid; so that if we must pretend to go back to the literal sense of the command, if our yea must be yea, and our nay nay; if no man must go beyond, or defraud his neighbor; if our conversation must be without covetousness, and the like, why then it is impossible for tradesmen to be Christians, and we must unhinge all business, act upon new principles of trade, and go on by new rules: in short, we must shut up shop, and leave off trade, and so in many things we must leave off living; for as conversation is call'd life, we must leave off to converse . . . (I, 234–235)

This passage, reflecting the text's engagement with credit, reflects on the text itself as a commodity, discomfiting the reader with the prospect that the preface may have been an "acceptable" lie. Hunter's recruitment of the text into a simple didacticism does not account for – does not permit – the conflictual overlay introduced by the text's commodity status. Indeed, the discursive consequences of commodification are glaringly apparent in the text's comments on its marketing strategy. When the supplement to volume 1 was issued, it claimed to be outside the market:

And the Editor (himself a Tradesman,) is so considering of his fellow shop-keepers, and so far from encroaching upon them in this Supplement, that he gives notice to all the friends of this undertaking, that to all those who have bought the book this Supplement shall be deliver'd gratis. By which they will be fully convinc'd he makes no gain of the encrease. (1, supplement, 2)

But the supplement maintained interest in volume 2 – issued shortly thereafter for a price – and *its* preface disclosed that "It was easy to see at the Close of the first Volume of this Work, that the Subject was not exhausted . . ."

I am arguing that "didactic" texts can – and that *The Compleat English Tradesman* does – raise issues of textual interpretability associated with literary (and marketplace!) artifacts. I therefore disagree with Hunter's view that such texts are not hospitable to readings that expose their contradictions and unsettle the very possibility of didacticism:

When didactic issues are approached at all in present day criticism or theory, authorial designs are treated as at best a nuisance, at worst a fake. The values found in such writings are assumed to be displaced ones, with readers surreptitiously finding morsels of forbidden fruit among tables laden with dull didactic gruel. If such a description were accurate, then eighteenth-century texts would be almost universally the most perverse of all written materials, utter failures as communication, seriously problematic as art. Whatever one thinks of such principles as a general strategy for reading, applied to a whole mode (didacticism) and a whole cultural epoch (the English eighteenth century), the refusal to honor face value at all has the effect of dismissing as irrelevant a full quarter of the English literary tradition. (227)

Hunter does not consider the paradox of "authorial designs" that contradict didactic ends. Hence one does not have to be a deconstructionist to locate "displaced" values, internal subversions of linear intent that baffle the ostensibly positivist, "naive empiricist" purport of didacticism. I am arguing that *The Compleat English Tradesman*, identified by Hunter as an example of didacticism, is such a paradoxical text, "designed" to teach that market-generated texts are ultimately baffling.

My reading does not refuse "face value," but suggests that on its face the text is bivalent. If it purports to teach economic morality, it demonstrates the instability of moral knowledge (what constitutes Honesty). Hunter's approach unduly privileges the one over the other, eliding a face value of contradiction in "the brash dogmatism of the species . . . its very refusal to admit the possibility of doubt" (242). Hunter positions the text so that it suffers from the discursive limitations of a limited genre, the Guide, which "provided for particular occupations and conditions of life" (252). As a result, critics might be tempted to overlook anomalies in such a text that would suggest entirely new "readings."

There is a certain irony in Hunter's rescuing *The Compleat English Tradesman* from an upstart Whig commercialism, situating it in the more genteel mode of precursor to the novel. In effect, he wipes away commercialism too cleanly, suggesting that the market produced such firmly didactic texts – tracts and novels – that its own imprint, its own strategic elusiveness disappeared. As I have suggested, the preface to *Serious Reflections* relates fable and moral as part of a strategy that baffles linear reading. Moreover, print culture is invoked by Defoe in *The Secret History of the Secret History* and in his novels because its operations conflict with textual transparency. Such texts, playing on cultural fear that textuality was an unstable situs of Truth, acknowledge that the didactic project is valenced with the epistemological uncertainty of the market. Hunter's suggestion that we read the texts of this period with a positivist bias is therefore incongruent with at least *some* texts' strategies. While Hunter argues that "didactic rhetoric prized the trust it placed in readers to choose rationally when choices were explained clearly" (231), *The Compleat English Tradesman* continually represents language misrepresenting, and finally resists rational apprehension in its own wavering arguments.

In the following discussion, I situate it against its nearest analogue (always cited with it), Richard Steele's *The Trades-man's Calling* (1684).[7] In the next chapter, I situate the text within the context of accounting manuals, definitely "subliterary" by Hunter's standards, but evincing the culture's concern for transparent texts.[8]

ANXIOUS CAPITALISM

Defoe's text is not a narrative, but the scheme for a narrative. It begins with the Tradesman's apprenticeship, follows his career through bankruptcy and partnership, and concludes with advice to leave trade after accumulating £20,000. Its 990 pages constitute the most comprehensive anatomy of shopkeeping ever written, probably in any language. The thread running through such chapters as "Of the ordinary Occasions of the Ruin of Tradesmen," "Of Fine Shops, and Fine Shews," "Of the Tradesman keeping his Books, and casting up his Shop," is the fear of exceeding limits, venturing with and losing capital, yielding personal agency to an impersonal market:

[T]he bill is payable on such a day, and that day is at hand, and perhaps [the Tradesman] has more bills running upon him, at the same time; the prospect is frightful, and he is in the utmost perplexity about it: His credit, which he knows is the basis of his whole prosperity, is at stake, and in the utmost danger; if his credit is gone, he is gone; he has, as is said before, launched out too far . . . what shall he do? (I, supplement, 6)

In *The Compleat English Tradesman* the scene of credit is "perplexity," the absence of clear direction. Given the "frightful" risks of credit-based trade, the text excoriates rumor-mongering ("Of Tradesmen ruining one another by Rumour and Clamour, by Scandal and Reproach"), decries common frauds ("Of the customary Frauds of Trade, which honest Men allow themselves to practice, and pretend to justify"), demands Honesty. Yet the explication of Honesty – how credit is valued, improved, lost – finally entails the text in epistemological collapse.

In volume 2, Defoe speaks to the mature Tradesman. He enumerates the personal qualities required for success ("he need not be a Scholar, yet should not be a Dunce," chapter 2), how the Tradesman should guard against disaster ("Of what are the particular Dangers, to which a rich over-grown Tradesman may be liable, what he has to fear, and how he may avoid a Miscarriage"), how he should resist narcissism ("Of the Tradesman being Purse-proud; the Folly and Scandal of it; and how justly ridiculous it renders him in the World"). He argues that Tradesmen can always tumble into ruin until safely retired; disparages litigiousness; condemns sharp, monopolistic practices that exclude young tradesmen.[9] In terms almost biblical, Defoe exhorts the Tradesman to be charitable towards those who miscarry, and to die as well as he has lived – disputes settled, debts paid, his affairs humanely wound up.[10]

In addition to hundreds of pages of advice, there is a virtual encyclopedia of commodities, a Mandevillian reprise ("Of the Luxury and Extravagancies of the Age becoming Virtues in Commerce, and how they propagate the Trade and Manufactures of the whole Nation"), and an unsentimental assessment of trading ethics that jars with the boosterism of previous chapters ("Of such Tradesmen, who by the necessary Consequences of their Business, are oblig'd to be accessory to the Propagation of Vice, and the Increase of Wickedness of the Times; and that all the Immorality of the Age is not occasion'd by Ale-Houses and Taverns"). But to describe such a text by its "contents" is misleading. What fascinates is the text's irresolution, a "face value" conscientious didacticism engaged dialectically with moral/epistemological uncertainty.

Throughout the text, the Tradesman is in danger of failing to distinguish fictive from real. He is warned against "fine shops and fine shews" that tie up capital which should be invested in linens and silk:

[B]ut let me tell you, the reputation of having a great stock is ill purchas'd, when half your stock is laid out to make the world believe it; that is, in short, reducing yourself to a small stock to have the world believe you have a great one; in which by the way, you do no less than barter the real stock for the imaginary, and give away your stock to keep the name of it only. (1, 262)

The Compleat English Tradesman imports the language, the concepts of public credit into the shop. Like purchasers of South Sea stock, the Tradesman imagines that his "stock" is "real." Attempting to build a "reputation" on "imaginary" phenomena, he risks ironic reversal, a "name" that dissipates his assets. The Tradesman's enterprise continues by maintaining a balance between fictive and real, provoking desire in the market while not suffering collapse. The negotiation of fiction and reality epitomizes the market-place operative.

Caught in fictions of his own devising, he is also prey to those of others:

To say I am Broke, or in danger of breaking, is to break me: and tho' sometimes the malicious occasion is discovered, and the author detected and exposed; yet how seldom is it so? and how much oftener are ill reports rais'd to ruin and run down a Tradesman, and the credit of his shop? and like an arrow that flies in the dark, it wounds unseen. (1, 191)

The "credit of his shop" is subject to a remote, undetected "author," displaced onto a market unaccountable for its fictive productions. The Tradesman is configured within a metropolitan market; its operations conduce to misnaming those with good names while conferring anonymity on those who "ruin and run down." The definitive quality of this market is its inclination to shift figurations among players, allocating fiction without reference to source. The market is impersonal, impenetrable, alienating the self from its own agency (except insofar as the self is complicit, producing fictions that redound to its own "ruin").

In *The Compleat English Tradesman* it is virtually impossible to escape seduction by fiction. It goads the creditor/reader towards *un*willing suspension of disbelief as reality crumbles by default:

Tho' I know the clamour of rumour was raised maliciously, and from a secret envy at the prosperity of the man; yet if I deal with him, it will in spite of all my abhorrence of the thing, in spite of all my willingness to do justice, I say it will have some little impression upon me, it will be some shock to my confidence in the man; and though I know the Devil is a Liar . . . and carried on this scandal upon the Tradesman, yet there is a secret lurking doubt (about him), which hangs upon me concerning him; the Devil is a Liar, but he may happen to speak the truth just then, he may chance to be right, and I know not what there may be in it, and whether there may be anything or no, but I will have a little care, &c.

Thus insensibly and involuntarily, nay, in spite of friendship, good wishes, and even resolution to the contrary, 'tis almost impossible to prevent our being shockt by rumour, and we receive an impression whether we will or not. (I, 192)

The Tradesman's credit is a text for examining the reader's relation to potential fiction. His credit is destabilized because potential fiction destabilizes the *reader's* apprehension. The reader is caught by Air-Money; he suspects fiction but cannot resist its appeal as potential truth. His "intent" to read without bias, to locate intrinsic value in the text, is "insensibly and involuntarily" preempted. Hence the *reader* is constructed by the market, and he constructs another in a chain reaction binding together market indigenes in a mutual loss of agency. The source of such mutual degradation is displaced onto rumor, the market, "the Devil." As a result the act of reading is fraught with ambiguity, yielding anxiety and self-doubt even as doubt is cast upon the text itself.

Defoe constantly situates the obliquity of marketplace discourse in the susceptibility of readers to misread. The threat of potential fiction is so pervasive that fiction can be constructed even from the absence of discourse. Thus where a tradesman would not speak at all about his peers, his very reticence is read as condemnation even though he denies it (I, 204–208). These stories suggest that signs in the market are radically unquantifiable, that they trap subject and object, debtor and creditor, text and reader in a dialectic of unresolved estimations that are frequently categorically wrong. *The Compleat English Tradesman* enforces this notion, demonstrating that a text is refracted through a congeries of opinion that alienates text and author, leaving only the reader as the source of potentially fictive discourse. Even where the Tradesman produces his own fictions, it is because he mis*reads* them as true. Reduced to its essentials, *The Compleat English Tradesman* depicts the construction of a market in the play of perception and misperception, always suggesting that one's own misreading is one's own fault.

Most critics have noticed the text's concern to promote the dignity of trade and tradesmen, and to demonstrate the necessity of trade to Britain's prosperity ("Of the Dignity of trade in England, more than in other Countries," "Of the Inland Trade in England, its Magnitude, and the Great Advantage it is to the Nation in general," "Of whom we are to understand by the Tradesmen of England, and in whose Hands the vast Inland Commerce of this Nation is carried on . . ."). In this regard, the text is consistent with economic nationalism apparent as early as the *Review*. What is distinctive – and announced in the title of *The Compleat English Tradesman* – is the dual, reciprocal focus on Nation and individual. The text is among the first theoretical works of macroeconomics, including Defoe's, to incorporate (indeed to emphasize) a microeconomic focus, and consider a Tradesman as a measure of national prosperity. This link to the individual, and to economic formations that affect his psyche, is crucial. It permits the text to engage with credit as a condition of reading. During the Bubble's aftermath, such an approach reflected on the indeterminacy of market-generated texts and on the chronic bafflement of readers. *The Compleat English Tradesman* develops this discourse within the sphere of private traders. It demonstrates that the market, this time configured through the exchange of bills, notes, and ious, is a site of potential, impenetrable fiction unhinged from responsible authority.

To the (considerable) degree that *The Compleat English Tradesman* systematically portrays mental as a consequence of mercantile processes, it is unprecedented. Its insight is that the mind is formed by economic formations. While this is a post-Marxian commonplace, the virtual absence of such discourse before Defoe is a measure of the text's significance. Though the connection between epistemology and credit-based economics emerged during the financial crisis of the early eighteenth century, Defoe gives this discourse a local habitation and a name, anchoring it in the psyche of the Tradesman.[11]

The text begins in the premise that the world has changed: "What then must be the reason that the Tradesmen cannot live on their trades, cannot keep open their shops, cannot maintain themselves and families, as well as they could before? Something extraordinary must be the case" (I, vi). The new costliness of trade is the effect of show. The individual is disciplined by the gaze of others who command the market: "Custom and the manner of all the Tradesmen round them command a difference, and he that will not do as others do, is esteemed as no body among them, and thus the Tradesman is doom'd to Ruin by the fate of the times" (vii). The community of tradesmen constituting the market encroaches upon self-definition; one's agency is derivative, responding to an internalized public decorum.

The Tradesman warned away from "fine shops and fine shews" is advised that his standing among fellow tradesmen depends on show. In a similar conflict, the text portrays the community that preempts the Tradesman's agency as – simultaneously – a source of his survival:

All these things [news, business techniques] will naturally occur to him in his conversing among his fellow-tradesmen; a settled little society of trading people, who understand business . . . here he learns the trading sciences; here he comes to learn the arcana, speak the language, understand the meaning of every thing, of which before he learnt only the beginning . . . (I, 41)

Tradesmen share a seemingly Edenic language where words represent reality. In *The Compleat English Tradesman*, therefore, the Tradesman is directed towards an ambivalent, liminal world which demands "Performance" within a natural setting ostensibly free of fiction. Such liminality leaves the Tradesman "incompleat." His agency, ultimately sublimated in the market, is replaced by what might be called "capacity." This degree of empowerment encourages the Tradesman's participation in the market.

The preface argues that the Tradesman's conflicted position is a conundrum of credit:

In short, there is a fate upon a Tradesman, either he must yield to the snare of the times, or be the jest of the times; the young Tradesman cannot resist it; he must live as others do, or lose the credit of living, and be run down as if he were Broke: In a word, he must spend more than he can afford to spend, and so be undone, or not spend it, and so be undone.

If he lives as others do, he Breaks, because he spends more than he gets; if he does not, he Breaks too, because he loses his credit, and that is to lose his trade; what must he do? (viii)

In a commercial universe, a persona is a function of market demand, which it totally expresses. Since the Tradesman is forced to adopt a persona he cannot sustain, his misrepresentation can be "credited" to creditor/readers whose demands he acknowledges. In its very opening remarks, *The Compleat English Tradesman* resonates with *The Secret History of the Secret History*: in both texts, authors alienated from subjectivity by a market economy are rendered nonauthorial. Grub Street and the High Street intersect. Defoe rationalizes the market in the author's favor. If credit is anxiety-provoking, necessitating personae discontinuous with the self, the self is unaccountable for its self-presentation. Across his oeuvre, Defoe elaborates and insinuates a logic whereby the self-as-persona, i.e. as text, is an alienated production demanded by a market of readers.

This is not to suggest that Defoe disparages transparency – he continually demands it. Rather it is to demonstrate that *The Compleat English Tradesman* destabilizes such demands so that they seem difficult to achieve. Two diametrically opposed strictures stand as an emblem of this conflict:

TRADE is not a Ball, where people appear in Masque, and act a part to make sport; where they strive to seem what they really are not, and to think themselves best drest when they are least known; but tis a plain visible scene of honest life, shewn best in its native appearance, without disguise. (I, 117)

he must be all soft and smooth; nay, if his real temper be all fiery and hot, he must shew none of it in his shop; he must be a perfect *complete hypocrite*, if he will be a *complete tradesman*. (I, 94, original emphasis)

Where is "didacticism," i.e. straightforward moral discourse? The bivalence of credit configures the Tradesman's irresolution *and* the self-presentation of *The Compleat English Tradesman*. Each is a marketplace text that defers resolution.

The text's anxiety with respect to credit ambiguates its obvious promotion of trade. This tension distinguishes it from didactic literature whose "brash dogmatism . . . is instructive in its very refusal to admit the possibility of doubt."[12] While the text argues that "credit is the foundation, on which the trade of England is made so considerable" (I, 335), it is wary of personal engagement with credit, dramatizing the Tradesman's psychological exposure within a matrix of credit relations. For the Tradesman who has "launched out too far" and seeks help from a scrivener:

there is Death in the pot; 'tis all but like a patient in a violent disease, taking a strong opiate to dose his senses, and aswage the immediate Torment; for they perform no cure, but their strength being expended the pains return with more violence than ever, and the opiate must not only be renew'd but encreas'd, nay perhaps doubl'd in quantity, till at last it becomes mortal it self, and he is kill'd by the very medicine which he apply'd to the cure. (I, supplement, 8)

The final collapse of the Tradesman's credit in bankruptcy occasions an extended conceit on mortality:

[F]or the circumstances of it are attended with so many mortifications, and so many shocking things, contrary to all the views and expectations that a Tradesman can begin the world with, that he cannot think of it, but as we do of the grave, with a chilness upon the blood, and a tremor in the spirits. Breaking is the death of a Tradesman; he is mortally stabb'd, or, as we may say, shot thro' the head in his trading capacity; his shop is shut up, as it is when a man is buried; his credit, the life and blood of his trade, is stagnated . . . his certificate is a kind of performing the obsequies of the dead, and praying him out of purgatory. (I, 69–70)

While credit is "the life and blood of his trade," it also precipitates the Tradesman into psychological death throes. This concern with the psychic impact of credit distinguishes the text from traditional didactic literature. Such literature regularly cited the potential catastrophes of trade, but did not dwell on the anxieties provoked by a credit economy. By interpreting catastrophe in credit-based terms, *The Compleat English Tradesman* converts the moral/economic suasion of traditional tracts into epistemological/psychological phenomena registered in the psyche of the Tradesman. Its approach, which transforms the didactic mode, measures the distance between a preacher – Richard Steele – and a novelist. More particularly, it enables a discourse that is not univalent, but "perplexed" like the Tradesman, like credit itself. The incidents of credit overwhelm the moral–religious overtones of traditional Guides, which linger only in metaphor as the "certificate" becomes "a kind of" performance praying the Tradesman "out of purgatory."[13] The textuality of credit predominates, asserted in the certificate that marks the Tradesman as living only in memory.

Undeniably, if *The Compleat English Tradesman* were read selectively it might be called "How To Succeed In Business By Trying Very Hard." Defoe provides standard guidebook fare, recommending that "nothing but what are to be called the necessary duties of life, are to intervene, and even those are to be limited so, as not to be prejudicial to business" (I, 49).[14] He counsels the Plain Style, "that in which a man speaking to five hundred people, of all common and various capacities, Ideots and Lunaticks excepted, should be understood by them all, in the same manner with one another, and in the same sense which the speaker intended to be understood" (I, 26). Yet if the text features a certain asceticism and rationality, the interpolation of credit overwhelms such counsel – asceticism devolves into alienation, rationality into calculation. Hence I cannot accept Hunter's genre-driven argument that the text, like Steele's *The Trades-man's Calling*, is transparently ideological:

> Defoe's volumes two generations later show how much more complicated the concerns of a London tradesman had become. . . . But for all its factuality and practicality, Defoe's advice is seldom value-free, and a major part of his concern is to guide tradesmen ethically . . . His guide is more "secular" in spirit than Steele's – and the 1720's are generally less religious than the 1680s – but the difference is subtle, and both these Guides for trade are deeply and pervasively didactic. Together they suggest how Guides and other didactic literature of the late seventeenth and early eighteenth century were changing and yet were basically staying the same.[15]

The difference between the texts is not merely qualitative, reflecting Defoe's greater "factuality and practicality." It is a difference in kind. Defoe renders an existential anxiety consequent on the uncertainty of credit. God offers no help. While Steele acknowledged the uncertainties of trade, he situated the tradesman within a moral economy regulated by Divine will:

> For when a Man hath with his utmost Skill proceeded so and so in his lawful Calling, he should never torment himself with unnecessary Fears of the Event, either of that Affair in particular, or of his Welfare in general: No, you are in your way, you have the Providence and the Promise of a wise and good God engaged with you: Your Fears will not prevent your Disasters, but rather provoke God to inflict them: And the Passion of Fear was seated in Man's Heart only to prevent Evils, not to encrease them: and therefore, as it is a very great Folly to entertain or cherish them about Contingencies, when we have done our best; so it is the Triumph of Wisdom to check and extinguish them. (64)

For Steele, anxiety over trade is an affront to God. One's "calling" mediates a relation to God, and it is that relation – not the sum of relations in an impersonal market – that constructs the tradesman.[16] In *The Compleat English Tradesman*, however, one is a node in a network, "perplexed" in attempting to maintain credit, "perplexed" because one has lost it. The Tradesman struggling with a congeries of relations, the object of "what shall he do?," is opposite one under the "Promise of a wise and good God" counselled to allay his fears.

The nature of promises is at the heart of the texts' divergence. While Defoe conceives of promises "conditional in the very nature of them," Steele argues that promises bind inexorably unless conditions are specifically attached:

You should be careful before you promise anything, you should be cautious in them; that what you promise be lawful and possible, or else you sin in the very making such Promises. . . .

If you answer, That your Purpose went along with your Promise, but that unexpected Accidents prevented your Performance; other work of more haste or profit came in; you had unforeseen Diversions, &c. I reply: Your Promises then ought to be conditional, and such as he who imployeth you will admit of, or else you wrong him to advantage your self, or to gratify another. (99, 101)

Steele premises a moral order in the universe; Defoe argues that promises, the basis of credit, are implicated in a potential for disorder that needs no explanation.[17] The factor differentiating these two positions is credit, in which fiction is always potentially emergent. In *The Compleat English Tradesman*, epistemological issues overtake and complicate morality. It contemplates a market where representation is perpetually uncertain. In *The Trades-man's Calling* representation is univalent ("Let your Words be a true Copy of your Meaning" [155]). Steele never discusses the complications of credit except for a warning not to give surety and a caution against overtrading. The contingencies to which he refers were familiar to the Merchant of Venice.

In the passage on "CUSTOM" cited earlier, Defoe argued that "if our conversation must be without covetousness, and the like, why then it is impossible for tradesmen to be Christians, and we must unhinge all business . . . for as conversation is call'd life, we must leave off to converse" (234–235). Like Defoe's statement on promises, it seems almost a direct reply to Steele, who had argued that:

This Veracity is so commodious, yea so necessary among Men; that all Civil Society is dissolv'd without it. For all Transactions and Commerce between Man and Man, do lean upon the Fundamental Point; That one man may believe another; now if men do not *constantly* speak the Truth, how can they be believ'd? Thus all human Conversation is shaken. (141–142, original emphasis)

In Steele, epistemological crisis is the result of sin; it can be avoided by not sinning, i.e. not lying. Knowledge and virtue are coordinate: "the Scripture is direct for speaking Truth" (140). Within a sphere of virtue, communication functions; knowledge is knowable, and in that sense stable. What is beyond our knowledge is in God's hands and not the proper subject of our fears. Defoe's interpolation of credit into a commercial universe presumes (and inculcates!) the contingency of phenomena. The "Fundamental Point" in *The Compleat English Tradesman* is that the Plain Style is coordinate with "covetousness," with the looming potential fictiveness of credit, so that belief is more a matter of will than assurance. A man may speak with apparent plainness yet *not* "speak the Truth." The opacity of plainness is the paradox of credit. Thus to compare Steele and Defoe by arguing that both articulate a Protestant moralizing tradition is to uncomplicate Defoe. Defoe's recognition that fiction *in potentia* is intrinsic to credit-based commerce, his sense that one negotiates a self while producing fiction and being produced as fiction, marks a watershed between his view of commerce and that of Steele. Credit's subversion of moralizing precepts in *The Compleat English Tradesman* renders it discontinuous with Steele's text in that the act of reading it *produces* anxiety. This anxiety is based on doubts about transparency and comprehensibility that challenge Steele's assurances of order. Steele's epistemology does not contemplate a text like *The Compleat English Tradesman* since it only marginally contemplates credit.

In the chapter "Of the Tradesman's Writing Letters," Defoe demonstrates a right way of communicating, but acknowledges that textuality is routinely confusing. Even apart from "covetousness" and customary "trading-lies," language is so rarely well-crafted that its latent ambiguities destabilize a text, multiplying in direct proportion to attempts to decipher it. Reading closely is therefore ironic. The irony of the chapter is that its apparent purport – to encourage clarity – is undermined by demonstrating that clarity is elusive. The reader's construal of a text will ultimately rewrite it, producing a maze of potential meanings that seem equally plausible. Thus even as Defoe urges the Plain Style, his urgings jar with an elaborate (and one expects gleeful) display of the quotidian miscommunication that discredits most texts. Reading the chapter is an eerie reprise of attempting to read Defoe's prefaces; it rationalizes that experience, suggesting that texts in the market are in general unyielding. My point is not that Defoe is "undidactic" – undeniably he urges clarity –

but that he goes to exceptional lengths to demonstrate the other side of clarity, and to suggest that it is predominant. He suggests that within the context of credit, where dealings are at a distance, the potential for readerly error increases.

Contriving a letter that seems conventional enough, Defoe states:

I pretend to say there is nothing at all in this letter, tho' appearing to have the face of a considerable dealer, but what may be taken any way pro or con. The Hambro factor may be a ship, or a horse, be bound to Hambro, or London. What shall be dispatch'd may be one thing, or any thing, or every thing in a former letter. No ships since the 11th may be, no ships come in, or no ships gone out. The London fleet being in roads, it may be London fleet from Hull to London, or from London to Hull, both being often at sea together. The roads may be Yarmouth roads or Grimsby, or indeed anywhere. (I, 20)

Citing another letter, he states:

Here is the order to send a cargo, with a please to send; so the factor may let it alone if he does not please. The order is 150 chest Seville; 'tis supposed he means oranges, but it may be 150 chests of oil, or any thing. Lisbon white may be wine, or any thing else, tho' 'tis suppose'd to be wine. (I, 21)

As Defoe pressures his texts to disclose meaning, they become Sorcerers' Apprentices, proliferating meaning until there is chaos. Each "meaning" is potentially fictive, imagined by a reader unable to locate authorial intent. The scene reveals the capacity of language to respond to pressure by baffling apprehension. While opacity is the author's fault, the greater "fault" is in a language too full of potency to be subdued into univalence, especially (and ironically) by an astute, persistent reader. The search for transparency is another Chinese finger trap, ensnaring the most diligent. Embedded in the logic of the trap is the notion that readers must take a chance on one "meaning" or another; keep multiplying "meanings" and *then* take a chance; or discard the text, which desire for a payoff does not permit.

Using the example of a clothier, Defoe suggests that miscommunication in the context of credit has ramifying consequences. It not only aborts the subject transaction, but diminishes the credit available in future. Readers are conditioned to treat all the author's texts as skeptically:

[W]hen orders are darkly given, they are doubtfully observ'd; and when the goods come to town, the Merchant dislikes them, the Warehouseman shuffles 'em back upon the Clothier, to lie for his account, pretending they are not made for his order; the Clothier is discourag'd, and for want of his money discredited, and all their correspondence is confusion, and ends in loss both of money and credit. (1, 25)

The burned – or burnt out – reader, "discourag'd" by textual opacity, resists future dealings with this author, as does the trading community. But if the condition of textuality is that it generally breaks down into multiple possible meanings, one cannot resist all the "dark" authors. Defoe's logic naturalizes opacity. Though it denounces opacity, it leaves no option but to continually (if grudgingly) reconstitute trade from failed credit. Trade remains suspended in pervasive skepticism, pervasive "doubtful observance." Since it is unfeasible to trade at a distance with cash, credit may be shaky but trade will proceed. I am arguing that *within* an ideal of transparent texts, Defoe's logic – stressing the lapsed ideal – rationalizes distant authors and readers into uncomfortable accommodation. Credit-based texts, prey to their imperfect medium, resisting the pressure of too close reading, discredit their authors but still mediate trade. Defoe, like "The Right Honourable the Countess of —," makes one point by seeming to argue another, conscripting the reader into a logic that seems to register by default.

One of the text's most stunning instances of failed communication is its encounter with "politeness," which is broached as an inexorable marketplace trope. The "polite" transaction scripts the Tradesman; divergence between polite persona and actual self is a necessity of doing business. The Tradesman's polite toleration of the customer exhibits the anxiety/exculpation matrix typical of the Tradesman's need to maintain his credit by maintaining a painful persona. As an incident of maintaining it, language becomes a medium of non-volitional fictivity, trade a site of repression:

A Tradesman behind his counter must have no flesh and blood about him; no passions, no resentment; he must never be angry, no not so much as seem to be. . . .

[T]he man that stands behind the counter must be all courtesy, civility, and good manners; he must not be affronted, or any way moved by any manner of usage, whether owing to casualty or design; if he sees himself ill-used he must wink, and not see it. . . .

[W]hat impertinences, what taunts, shouts and ridiculous things, he must bear in his Trade, and must not shew the least return, or the least signal of disgust: he must have no passions, no fire in his temper; he must be all soft and smooth; nay, if his real temper be all fiery and hot, he must shew none of it in his shop; he must be a perfect *complete hypocrite*, if he will be a *complete tradesman*. (1, 85–94)

Politeness in trade is overdetermining. It requires self-misrepresentation so stringent that no insult can ruffle the Tradesman's "courtesy, civility, good manners." The complete tradesman, a complete irony, lacks agency. He is a function of market protocol. Defoe tells the story of a tradesman full of rage, going upstairs, beating his head against the wall, kicking his children, returning to the shop calm but a "soul-less animal" (1, 95). "Civility and good manners" are valenced with incivility. The Tradesman's calm becomes a version of the market's discursive impenetrability; he is transparent only for the brief moment he is literally beyond the market. Within the market, he is a fiction anxious over self-revelation; but as an extension of the market, he is inculpable for the fiction he projects.

Beginning in the late seventeenth century, "politeness" described a form of conversation, of "commerce" between genteel persons.[18] The term "commerce" applied to interpersonal as well as financial transactions. As financial commerce grew towards the end of the seventeenth century, with its own self-conscious laudatory discourse, interpersonal transaction was modeled on commercial practice. Polite "commerce" implied negotiation, a give-and-take wherein (as in trade) the self both expands and compromises to obtain a payoff – in the case of conversation, approval and sympathy.[19] While on one level such conversation seemed motivated by altruism, on another it could be a type of theatre.[20] In that case, both participants constructed themselves to satisfy the gaze of the other, in that sense derogating from their intrinsic natures.[21] Since an equality of social position is presumed, so is a reciprocity of demand. If the revelation of self must be repressed, it is repressed on both sides, and both sides expect a commensurate "payoff." Defoe, however, intervenes in polite conversation at the site where it becomes ironic, where form persists to *mock* function. The Tradesman, treating the customer as genteel even if she is not, dramatizes himself so as to ingratiate, but with no expectation of mutuality. In a context of discursive asymmetry, the negotiation is reduced (from the Tradesman's point of view) to all "give." Politeness denatures the Tradesman into a complete performance, a mask with no one behind it to make any demands. No matter how imperious or inane, the customer can require a flawless performance, giving nothing of herself (except perhaps some cash or a promise – or she may just walk out). Like the Grub Street hack, the Tradesman loses his subjectivity to the market. Deploying its language, he speaks himself out of existence.

The Tradesman's plight reveals the implicit connection between politeness and credit. If "commerce" is the initial model for politeness, credit takes it a step further, drawing conversation away from the negotiation typical of traditional commerce towards the one-sided manipulation of jobber/Chymists. As if to demonstrate the power of credit to remodel discourse, some pages later Defoe hypothesizes playing the scene in reverse. A Mercer and a Lady accuse each other of unremitting lies concerning the quality of the merchandise. Musing, Defoe observes:

> yet what is all the shop-dialect less or more than this? The meaning is plain; 'tis nothing but *you lie*, and *you lie*; downright *Billingsgate*, wrap'd up in silk and sattin, and deliver'd dres'd finely up in better cloathes, than perhaps it might come dress'd in, between a Carman and a Porter. (I, 254)

The point is that the market regulates discourse. The mercer – who sells "silk and sattin" – delivers language "wrap'd" in the very materials that define his trade. Like *Moll*'s Editor and *Roxana*'s Relator, the mercer dresses language, delivering it as if refracted at an extreme angle from the original intent. Both mercer and Lady, producing "shop-dialect" appropriate for the market, sublimate meaning in protocol. The text suggests that real, honest pronouncements, "you lie, and you lie," are so impossible to contemplate that it is comical even to conjure the possibility. It indulges in *obvious* fiction about such an alternative. Its repeated suggestions of the market's co-optation of speech reinforce the notion that in the market, the "intent" of the person with anything for sale is irremediably deflected.[22]

One of the most famous scenes in *The Compleat English Tradesman* is that in which a husband tries to hide his impending "break" while the wife painfully forces a disclosure. The long dialogue dramatizes the pressure engendered by the credit-based market to maintain a state of obliquity. When the husband, after skulking around for days, assures the wife that there is "no danger . . . at least not yet" (138), she responds:

> your way of speaking is ambiguous and doubtful; I entreat you *be plain and free with me*, what is at the bottom of it? why won't you tell me? what have I done, that I am not to be trusted with a thing that so nearly concerns me? (I, 138, original emphasis)

The wife reacts as an unsatisfied reader, demanding that the husband's Air-Money text be clarified. She demands a Husband, speaking "plain and free," not an Author speaking through his marketplace persona. To the wife, the husband's retreat from spousal confidence into author(ity) is signalled by his retreat from transparency into the discourse of credit, capable of precipitating divergent narratives. She does not accept this position, and determines that if she is to rescue him from (what she surmises to be) his shaky credit, she must require that he replace the language of credit with more credible speech.

While the husband's strategy is to keep up appearances as long as possible, the wife offers an alternative – retrenchment in their style of living, honest admission of precariousness, and the chance to forestall an actual break. Her offer tests the husband's capacity to present himself straightforwardly in a market where "not to live as others do," not to seem creditable, sinks credit. The language, the deportment of credit affects even his domestic arrangements; credit is so powerful a yoke that he willingly endures immense anxiety rather than foregoing the persona required to maintain credit: he "appear'd all the time to be pensive and sad . . . only now and then [the wife] heard him fetch a deep sigh, and at another time say *he wish'd he was dead*, and the like expressions" (136). The dialogue between husband and wife is itself caught in the bivalence of credit, at once a "moment of truth" in which the husband doffs his persona and acknowledges the potential fictivity of his text, and also an insinuation, suggesting that the discourse of credit requires opacity so that credit can subsist.

The foregoing examples dramatize the capacity of credit to disintegrate the self and displace the production of language onto the market. In the next section, I consider the same movement but at a further remove: the Tradesman's credit is constructed through transactions that force him to qualify absolute statements, or that demand certainty, leaving him no choice but to make unqualified statements that may prove false. In the first instance, wheedling customers pressure tradesmen, who must sell for whatever they can get irrespective of the announced price. In the second instance, creditors require an absolute commitment to pay. The Tradesman, prohibited from qualifying his promise, simply satisfies a demand for a fiction-that-there-is-no-fiction. If that is the only way to survive in a market wary of fiction, how can one be culpable? In both cases, "fiction" is the product of negotiation that the Tradesman loses (but in a moral sense wins). Indeed, if qualification is demanded on the one hand or banned on the other, so that one's performance is relative only to another's intent, then there may be no such thing as liability for fiction, since the consumer has pre-empted the Tradesman's agency. Fiction in this category is neither aspiringly invisible nor reluctant; it just dissolves as a moral/epistemological crux. The underlying logic of such "dissolving fiction" is the same as for that discussed in the previous section, however, in that in both cases culpability for fiction is attenuated by displacement.

DISSOLVING FICTIONS

In the chapter "Of Honesty in Dealing: and (1.) Of telling unavoidable Trading Lies," the text differentiates marketplace discourse from ordinary "conversation": "There is some difference between an *honest man* and an *honest Tradesman*" (1, 226). "Honest" is qualified by "Tradesman," a speaker implicated in credit and therefore ambiguously credible. The assertion that a tradesman "must not only intend or mean honestly or justly, but he must do so" is therefore not absolute, as its face value suggests. Behind it is the instability of the market. One wonders what substance remains to "Honest," since Defoe observes that "there are some latitudes, like poetical licenses in other cases, which a Tradesman is and must be allow'd" (1, 226). Is the Tradesman assimilated to the Sidneian poet, who cannot lie because he does not aspire to truth? Defoe appears to suggest that aspiration towards truth is a moot point, since the nature of the Tradesman's transactions deflect him towards the "licenses" of nonrepresentational discourse.

The text provides a fascinating example of how pressure from the buyer forces the Tradesman into abdicating "intent." The issue arises with respect to "asking more than he [the Tradesman] will take" (227), and precipitates an extended rationale for announcing one price, charging another, but still not being guilty of a lie:

INDEED, it is the buyers that make this custom necessary; for they, especially those that buy for immediate use, will first pretend positively to tie themselves up to a limited price, and bid them a little and a little more, 'till they come so near the seller's price, that they, the sellers, cannot find in their hearts to refuse it, and then they are tempted to take it, notwithstanding their first words to the contrary: It is common indeed for the Tradesman to say, *I cannot abate any thing*, when yet they do and can afford it; but the

Tradesman should indeed not be understood strictly and literally to his words, but as he means it, viz. that he cannot reasonably abate; and there he may be in earnest, viz. that he cannot make a reasonable profit of his goods, if he is obliged to abate, and so the meaning is honest, that he cannot abate; and yet rather than not take your money, he may at last resolve to do it, in hopes of getting a better price for the remainder, or being willing to abate his ordinary gain, rather than disoblige the customer; or being perhaps afraid he should not sell off the quantity; and many such reasons may be given, why he submits to sell at a lower price than he really intended, or can afford to do, and yet he cannot be said to be dishonest, or to lie, in saying at first he cannot, or could not abate. (1, 227–228)

Like the implied conditionality of promises, the apparent certainty of a price "should indeed not be understood strictly and literally," since it is subject to a rule of marketplace "reason," i.e. the need to make a profit. The Tradesman's intent is imputational, a conjecture upon the amount of profit he considers reasonable; it is not, nor should it be expected to be, transparent in his words. Moreover, even assuming an intent conditioned by profit, and at that level absolute, the Tradesman may still qualify his price and not "be said to be dishonest, or to lie." This is because he "submits" to sell at "a lower price than he really intended," forced by a haggling customer into representing one state of affairs (that he cannot abate) and accepting another. "[R]ather than disoblige the customer," the Tradesman disobliges himself, rationalizing his position by projecting future price adjustments ("getting a better price for the remainder") that will recoup his loss.

The passage presents two notions that exculpate the Tradesman. The first is that his "intent" is not articulated literally, but is enmeshed in a hermeneutic of the market ("as he means it, that he cannot reasonably abate"). The customer is responsible for determining what is meant based on his knowledge of market practice. Were he to bring absolutist principles to bear, he would be ineffective.[23] At a deeper level, intent is portrayed as subjective, a private matter not fully available to objective assessment. How can one be "said" to lie if one's "intent" is a deduction by another, who in fact cannot ever be certain what one "meant." The operative word in Defoe's analysis, "he cannot be *said* to . . . lie," is crucial, since whether or not the Tradesman *does* lie – in some absolute sense comparing intent to action – he cannot openly be denominated a liar. Defoe's initial dictum, "he must not only intend or mean honestly and justly, but he must do so," becomes a standard with no practical application (except to the extent that the Tradesman wishes to torment himself with the knowledge of his own falsehood, which he is unlikely to do based on all the available rationalizations).

The second exculpatory notion is that buyers "make this custom [of abating] necessary." By their pressure, the Tradesman is forced to destabilize his representations; he "submits." Noncorrelation between intent and performance cannot be ascribed to the Tradesman, who depends on the customer to move his goods. As in the case where the patron succumbs to rumor *against* his will since "the Devil is a Liar, but he may happen to speak the truth just then," so – rather than blaming the Tradesman – "if indeed there is a sin, the sin is the buyer's; at least he puts himself in the Devil's stead, and makes himself both tempter and accuser" (I, 229).

The Compleat English Tradesman inculcates a notion that sellers cannot be held liable for apparent fictions, since representation is conditioned by an hermeneutic that abolishes the absolute knowability of intent, as well as the seller's practical responsibility for his representations. Representations are contingent constructions. The seller responds to implicit protocols of the market; buyers rewrite the seller's position into a mere negotiable offer. The rationale of credit mediates the transaction between buyer and seller; the buyer cannot reasonably expect epistemological clarity, or attribute to opacity an intent to lie. Representation that does not correlate with a reality disclosed by negotiation – itself a type of narrative – represents the "true" state of the credit-based market. In that sense fiction may be "said" to be "apparent" but not "real."

The text applies a similar logic with regard to promises. While Defoe considers promises conditional in their very nature, and claims that explicit conditionality would gloss God's own authority, he nonetheless suggests that creditors require absolute promises that misrepresent the conditional ability of debtors to pay:

BUT to this [demand for conditionality] I answer, the importunity of the person, who demands the payment, will not permit it; nothing short of a positive promise will satisfy; they never believe the person intends to perform, if he makes the least reserve or condition in his promise, tho' at the same time they know, that even the nature of the promise and the reason of the promise strongly implies the condition; I say the importunity of the creditor occasions the breach, which he approaches the debtor with the immorality of. (I, 234)

Fiction is coerced, or rather it is a necessary condition of remaining in the market. Indeed, because it is coerced, "fiction" may not be fictive at all, but an inevitable discursive construction reflecting the power of creditors to intimidate debtors.[24] In the metaphysics of *The Compleat English Tradesman*, fiction dissolves. Not merely does liability dissolve, but the phenomenon itself, diffusing into a negotiation (a negation) that forces discourse into one-sided contracts. Tradesmen must "submit" to buyers; creditors demand "nothing short of a positive promise"; the author's representations accurately correspond to another's will.

Defoe argues further that the creditor's coerciveness forces fiction to proliferate more fiction, irrespective of the Tradesman's intent:

[M]en in trade, I say, are under this unhappy necessity, they are forced to make them [unconditioned promises], and they are forced to break them; the violent pressing and dunning, and perhaps threatning too, when the poor shop-keeper cannot comply with his demand, forces him to promise; in short the importunate creditor will not otherwise be put off, and the poor shop-keeper almost worried, and perhaps a little terrified to [*sic*], and afraid of him, is glad to do anything to pacify him, and this extorts a promise, which when the time comes, he is no more able to perform than he was before; and this multiplies promises, and consequently breaches, so much of which are to be placed to the account of force, that I must acknowledge though the debtor is to blame, the creditor is too far concern'd in the crime to be excused. (1, 235)

In multiplying promises, Defoe attributes a certain "blame" to the Tradesman. Nevertheless, the overwhelming force of the argument is that multiple, galloping fictions such as Crusoe's appearance in *Serious Reflections* or the outrageous assertions of *The Secret History of the Secret History*, are responses to the demands for certainty of credit-based culture. The "crime" of multiplying fictions is aggravated by the purported victim; in any court of law, the question of self-defense would arise. The debtor's culpability would be reduced by the seriousness of the provocation (in this case "violent"). In Defoe's logic, the offense (an "unhappy necessity") would be little more than token.

The demand for certainty in an ambivalent market dominated by credit, produces fiction which fictively abolishes ambivalence. Defoe's logic suggests that unwillingness to accept the involvement of credit with potential fiction (which may not be "fiction" if it is unintended) ironically produces deliberate fiction, which sets off yet another cycle of anxiety and fiction. If creditor/readers want to believe that credit is univalent, and will not engage with discursive opacity, they demand a fiction-that-there-is-no-fiction, attempting to wrench promises into certainty. The debtor/author willing to acknowledge the potentiality of fiction (by extenuating his commitment) is compromised; co-opted by a creditor/reader; forced into misrepresenting reality with "certainty." In the context of this rationale, the unsettling prefaces of *Crusoe, Moll,* and *Roxana* can be justified as inevitable, responding to (though still not satisfying) demands for "nothing short of a positive promise" of truth; evincing readers' fear that the author never "intends to perform"; ultimately, embodying credit's suspension of any outcome. Defoe's argument excludes the possibility that the preface of *Crusoe,* for example, could explain that irrespective of readers' skepticism, the "appearance" of truth will not be vouched for by anyone, even by a distant Editor. In *The Compleat English Tradesman* potential fiction is the market's discursive reality. That reality is reflected in Defoe's fictions.

One of the text's "perplexed" features, endemic to the discourse of credit that defines it, is that Defoe seems to argue on both sides of the issue of Honesty. Lying is inevitable; tradesmen can survive without it. The following passage seems to run counter to the import of previous scenes:

Let [Tradesmen] confine themselves to truth, and say what they will: But it cannot be done; a talking rattling mercer or draper, or milliner, beyond his counter, would be worth nothing if he should confine himself to that mean silly thing called *Truth*; they must Lie, it is in support of their business, and some think they cannot live without it: but I deny that part, and recommend it, I mean, to the tradesmen I am speaking of, to consider what a scandal it is upon trade, to pretend to say that a Tradesman cannot live without lying; the contrary to which may be made to appear in almost every article. (I, 251–252)

Indeed, it runs counter to the argument that immediately follows:

much of it [lying] is owing to the buyers, they begin the work, and give the occasion. It was the saying of a very good shop-man once upon this occasion, That their customers would not be pleased without Lying . . . The buyer telling us, adds he, that every thing is worse than it is, forces us, in justifying its true value, to tell them it is better than it is. (I, 252)

How does one read a text that doubles back upon itself, suggesting that customers and creditors force tradesmen into lying while suggesting that tradesmen can survive without it? In the foregoing passages, tradesmen themselves offer evidence countering Defoe's argument against lying. Defoe even depicts the chagrin of a tradesman who, unable to accept his rationale that promises are conditional, is still forced to lie:

NOR was it any satisfaction to him to say, that it was owing to the like breach of promise in the shop-keepers, and gentlemen, and people whom he dealt with, who ow'd him money, and who made no conscience of promising and disappointing him, and thereby drove him to the necessity of breaking his own promises; for this did not satisfy his mind in the breaches of his word, though they really drove him to the necessity of it. (1, 236)

The passages reproduce the sense of ambiguity produced at the outset, when warnings against show jostled with claims that credit requires it. One "reads" such a text not by trying to reconcile its contradictions, but by accepting them as part of a design. The design recapitulates the tropes of credit, maintaining the reader in a state of unsettlement. Like the Tradesman at whom the text is directed, the reader fails to resolve what an "honest Tradesman" is. More particularly, his experience inscribes the notion that the text in the market does not disclose its meaning; the more one pressures it – reading to interpret – the more resistant it becomes. In *The Compleat English Tradesman*, the author's "intent" flaunts its elusiveness.

When the text is read against Defoe's novels, it delineates their provenance as marketplace texts, rationalizing the tropes of credit with which the novels' own strategies engage. It demonstrates that potential fiction is always a possibility, but that "fiction" is not a culpable category. It may not even be a cognizable category. I would argue, therefore, that even though *The Compleat English Tradesman* never mentions the novels, it is in dialogue with them, establishing the grounds for their author's inculpability.

ENDORSING: THE ULTIMATE FICTION

Defoe's rationale for the dissolution of fiction may be explained in part as a reaction against the consequences of acknowledging a fictional text. *The Compleat English Tradesman* develops an extended cautionary discourse with respect to writing Bills, attaching one's name to a text that, no matter how many times it is alienated and discounted, ultimately returns to fix one as the party responsible for fiction. As Defoe explains, Bills of Exchange or Promissory Notes (and their domestic equivalent, inland bills) are due on a date certain with a three-day grace period. They are "sacred in trade," and "nothing can be of more moment to a Tradesman, than to pay them always punctually and honourably" (1, 357).[25] Bills are the extreme instance of imposing certainty on a credit-based instrument as potentially fictional as Air-Money.

The difference is that one's name is attached. If the potential fiction materializes, one's responsibility is not dispersed; one is identified and held accountable for breaking a "sacred" promise. Moreover, because bills are "certain," they serve almost as money, passing from hand to hand upon endorsement. Should the obligation not be satisfied when due, the last holder passes it back down the chain of endorsers, demanding cash, with the result that the original obligor's credit is blackened even with total strangers. One's fictions become notorious, no longer a private affair between debtor and creditor. They become automatically self-multiplying.

With a bill, it is not the creditor's demand for certainty that forces a desperate lie. Since payment is always uncertain, the fiction of "certainty" inheres in the instrument, which admits no ambivalence. Indeed, the bill perpetuates a vulnerable promise without (at the time of commitment) revealing how far it may go. It ramifies potential fiction. If a promise fails, the bill reasserts it to a string of angry endorsers, though the debtor/author only promised once. The bill embodies the momentum of an autonomous, ironic market, depriving the debtor/author of control (as to his reputation) as it inscribes him in responsibility. In this sense it enacts his commercial subservience, his inability to negotiate credit without the market itself entailing consequences beyond his agency. The only means of remaining in the market is to withhold one's name wherever possible. *The Compleat English Tradesman* constructs the necessity, indeed the fairness of this strategy. It suggests that signing one's name to an assertion that market-based texts are certain, leads to ignominy. One is caught in marketplace discourse with no chance to extenuate. How could one expect *Crusoe, Moll, Roxana* to make such commitments? Their qualifications, the print culture mediation that dissipates authorial exposure, must be tolerated regarding texts in the market.

The first chapter of the Supplement to volume 1 opens with a "distress'd Tradesman" drowning in "an ocean of business" (1, supplement, 3). In Defoe's narrative, the Tradesman's bills return to haunt him:

bills are drawn on him from the country, payable at the precise time that his debts are due, for the countrymen cannot stay for their money; these bills are accepted, that he cannot avoid, and his credit is at stake, and in the utmost state of depression if they are not paid; for, as I observed, if the Tradesman does not pay his bills currently when they are accepted and become due, he not only weakens his credit with his Creditor, or Employer who draws, but with the whole town. Bills run from one Tradesman to another, then to the Goldsmith, or to the Bank, and are endors'd from hand to hand, and every one of these hears of it if the Tradesman delays payment . . . . (I, supplement, 3-4)

The Tradesman-as-discourse is not unlike Defoe, whose name had been "hackney'd about the Street by Hawkers, and about the Coffee Houses by the Politicians." But how many times can one Appeal to Honour and Justice? Can one write a *Secret History of the Secret History* of a bill whose signature acknowledges one's authorship? Bills implicate the self inextricably in the creation of culpable fiction. In Defoe's rendering, there is a horror attached to bills in their refusal of extenuation. Their autonomy reflects the "injustice" of a market operating behind one's back, pouncing with absolute right. Defoe notes that the Tradesman "has taken too great credit while his credit was good, and given too great credit to those whose credit was not so good . . . But the difference lies here, when their payments are due they can trespass upon their credit, and put him off with words instead of money" (I, supplement, 3-4). He draws the distinction between ordinary credit, which can be wheedled and ignored, and iron-fisted instruments of "certainty" that prohibit linguistic intervention.

In response to his own claims, the Tradesman receives "words"; he cannot pass on "words" to the creditor with a claim against him. The bill stops the circulation of "words"; its premise is on its face; it implies acquiescence. In its preemption of discourse, the bill epitomizes the noncommunication instituted by credit – the politeness that silenced the Tradesman, the distance between husband and wife. By forestalling discursive elaboration, the bill is all *too* "readable," shifting power even further towards a creditor/reader who can implicate the debtor in fiction. It renders that power absolute, greater even than just being able to *demand* unconditional performance. Even if the debtor decides to resist a remote creditor's demand for payment by declaring bankruptcy, the first creditor will still have implicated him in a galloping fictionality by negotiating the bill to *his* creditor (who can multiply fiction again). This exacerbation of the asymmetry of the market reduces the debtor to the worst possible situation – at once a hack, responsible for proliferating fiction in a market over which he has no control, and a hack with a name, so that his responsibility can be identified.

The paradox of the bill is that as it travels through the market it links together total strangers; yet in the end they turn back upon each other with complete self-interest. In substituting for language, the bill performs a function opposite to that of language, connecting people only so that they can disconnect and even become hostile. *The Compleat English Tradesman* portrays a market in which natural, normal modes of communication have become attenuated. By extension, it opens a space for compensating strategies that restore the discursive balance, allowing authors to remain in the market without making airtight commitments to representational "truth." Creditor/ readers who insist on such representations are demonized; instruments that institutionalize such insistence are demonized.

In the next chapter, "Of Discounting and Endorsing Bills, and the scandalous Practice of passing Promissory Notes, on purpose to borrow money by Discount," Defoe examines the desperate Trades-man's endorsing bills over to a usurious discounter. He becomes liable not only for payment on the bill (which may in fact be worthless), but for the interest as well. As the Tradesman continues passing and repassing bills in this fashion, attempting to cover himself by endorsing and borrowing at discount, the interest mounts. Finally, the house of cards crashes as he has less and less money to cover more and more liabilities. Endorsing becomes even more treacherous when desperate tradesmen begin endorsing bills for each other. One's debtor, as a way of postponing his debt, may endorse and so become one's creditor as well:

if he cannot get a particular friend to endorse the Bill for him, or a debtor, then he comes into a fatal confederacy with another Tradesman in like circumstances with himself, and he having endors'd for the weaver, the weaver does the like for him, and so they change endorsements; blending in a word, not their credit only, but even their fortunes together, till at last he finds himself insensibly involv'd, and 'tis ten to one but a disaster follows, nay, and 'tis much if they do not fall together.

It is not easy to reckon up the complication of mischiefs, which this joyning together to endorse Bills, brings upon a trader, for it is in a word . . . a striking hands with a stranger. (I, supplement, 26–27)

The Bill becomes a paradox: "certain" in its representations, but contingent, meshing the credit of "strangers." Endorsement becomes a Möbius strip of paradox: the Tradesman's credit is constructed by others, but he is responsible for theirs. If their credit fails, and their liabilities cannot be covered, they will be unable to cover his, and his credit will fail as well. Endorsing creates a community of desperation, the ultimate subversion of the linguistic community postulated by Defoe as the Tradesman's ideal. In this community, the only possible speech concerns demand for and acquiescence in further endorsements. The endorsed *text* is itself an evasion, posturing in the market as "certain," becoming more and more uncertain as each endorsement implicates another contingency. Thus if the conventional bill impales the author – and successive readers – on the uncertainty of the market, such uncertainties generate accommodations that discredit certainty itself. *The Compleat English Tradesman* does not stop at demonstrating the unconscionable imbalance of power against debtors; it demonstrates how such imbalance drives them to create texts that exacerbate the uncertainty of the market. The demand for certainty is counterproductive. Best allow a certain qualification and be content.

When the Tradesman begins "joyning together" with others:

> he is certain that all the rest are Bankrupts, as he is sure they are men; they could not engage in the manner they do else, for they will endorse for any sum and never dispute the securities, but either if they endorse for you, you must do the like for them, or if they endorse they have a part of the money for their own occasions, only giving a note to pay so much again when the endorst Bill comes to be paid; and this brings me to the next and most fatal article of Discount, and that is passing Bills for one another; this is done in a club, I have known ten or twelve tradesmen form a club together for coining money, as they very well call'd it. (1, supplement, 27)

The "club" is a fiction factory similar to that described in *The Secret History of the Secret History*, "coining money" that depreciates towards the counterfeit: "when one fail'd, he shook all the rest, so that few of them could stand it after him, and not one of these above a year, or thereabouts" (28). The club epitomizes a market where texts pretending to be certain are enmeshed in processes that make them presumptively impenetrable, even if their face value is clear. It dislocates indicia of the likelihood of performance *from* the discrete text *to* a complex of unseen accommodations (in the club's case, among "Bankrupts" whose only proprietorship is of texts that distract the market). The names on the text instantiate the noise of financial culture.

Defoe's treatment of endorsing is a broad attack on the certainty of texts. It suggests that *demands* for certainty leave debtor/authors no chance but to evade certainty wherever possible, and to resist signing their names. But it also suggests, consistent with the epistemology of

The Compleat English Tradesman, that certainty is a mirage. The marketplace text pretending to be certain is (like Air-Money) fiction waiting to happen. It is merely a means for catching authors caught in the processes of an uncertain market. If readers of *Crusoe*, *Moll*, and *Roxana* were to expect such texts to be unqualifiedly certain, readers would be committing a category mistake.

THE NEGOTIATIONS OF FICTION AND TRUTH: THE TEXT AS A THEORY OF FICTION

As I have suggested, *The Compleat English Tradesman* is quintessentially a text of the credit-based market, promoting Honesty – purporting to define it – while evincing the blur between Honesty and Lies that sustains marketable (unaccountable) fiction. In this regard the text recapitulates the irresolution of Defoe's oeuvre, reinscribing the confusion of market-generated texts even as it claims to deliver the Tradesman from that confusion. The text's "failure," which is its rhetorical success, measures its engagement with credit. It responds to demands for certainty while inculcating a defense against certainty, i.e. the coalescence of fiction and truth. It exculpates fiction by submerging its integrity as a category; *a fortiori* it exculpates the author of fiction, whose agency it also diffuses. *The Compleat English Tradesman* is Defoe's ultimate ideological incursion into the market of ideas about fiction, subverting it audaciously.

In the chapter "Of Credit in Trade, and how a Tradesman ought to value and improve it: How easily lost, and how hard it is to be recover'd," Defoe lays down the rule that:

[T]wo things raise credit in trade, and I may say they are the only things required: there are some necessary addenda, but these are the fundamentals:

1. INDUSTRY.
2. HONESTY.

I have dwelt upon the first; the last I have but few words to say to, but they will be very significant; indeed that head requires no comment, no explanations or enlargements; nothing can support Credit, be it publick or private, but Honesty; a punctual dealing, a general probity in every transaction; he that once breaks thro' his honesty, violates his credit; once denominate a man a knave, and you need not forbid any man to trust him. (1, 345–346)

But the text does not define Honesty. Instead, by offering a theory of honesty grounded in epistemological uncertainty, the text authorizes at the level of theory – of failed theory – the slippage in Defoe's texts towards indeterminacy, towards an elision of the distinction between Truth and Lies.

A central feature of the text's epistemology, carried over from the discourse of public credit, is that intent cannot be objectively measured. There is a disjunction, for example, between what a tradesman intends and how others perceive him. Hence Defoe advises tradesmen not to commit themselves regarding the character of other tradesmen. At the same time, he suggests that silence will be construed as "intended" dispraise, despite the effort to be neutral. (What is the "intent" of this conflicted advice?) Likewise, as the discourse of Promises makes clear, one cannot project performance from intent, since every promise is refracted through God's will as well as through a mesh of secondary phenomena (e.g. other promises). It is therefore crucial that intent – which cannot be verified, and is always potentially at odds with perception and performance – is central to the text's logic of Honesty. By isolating Honesty in intent, which cannot be measured and can always be rationalized, the text can insist on Honesty while (with epistemological irresolution) submerging it in unverifiable subjectivity.

Chapter 1 of Volume 2 is entitled "Of HONESTY in Trade; how rare to be found; how necessary for the promoting of Commerce; what Scandal the Tradesmen generally lie under about it; and what the Meaning of it is; and how to be understood; with a Word or two to distinguish the Kinds of it." The title suggests rigorous didacticism, based on an hermeneutical project explicating "Meaning," directing how that should be "understood," distinguishing "Kinds." Yet the chapter retreats from its announced goals. Its argument with respect to intent begins by invoking the discontinuity between Honesty and reputation:

To be honest, therefore, and to have the Reputation of it, as I said above, are two Things, and vastly different from one another: There may be, and I know there are, a great many Tradesmen that are nicely honest, intentionally so, even to perfection; for Intentional Honesty may be perfect, whatever actual Honesty may be. (II, part I, 38)

According to this formula, there is a sort of metaphysical Honesty that *may not be perceived and may not be expressed in performance*, but can still be "perfect." Such perfection must be hypothetical, since without external indicia one can never know another's intent. Defoe's assertion, "I know there are" such Honest men, is dis-Honest, a logical, epistemological impossibility.

Yet this metaphysical honesty should be a man's measure: "To desire to be honest, is Honesty" (II, part 1, 43). The crux is that we cannot measure another's desire (which is "intent" minus a degree of volition). Defoe ostensibly attempts to attach "desire" to some objective correlative: if a man desires to be honest, he "will not fail to endeavor, by all possible Means, to act honestly in every Thing he does; if not, he will give but very slender Testimony of the Sincerity of his honest Wishes" (II, part 1, 43). But this conflicts with Defoe's premise that "intent" – the less active precursor of "endeavor" – is often not realized in Testimony, i.e. in some verifiable action yielding "Reputation." Moreover, anyone can assert that his "endeavor" has borne no fruit. At best, the text contradicts itself. At worst, it leads back to unknowable intent.

The argument respecting intent becomes even more perplexed since Defoe has castigated the Tradesman's willingness to harm his creditors by lying to himself, running down his reserves by denying he is going to break: "I'll never drown while I can swim; I'll never fall while I can stand" (1, 73).[26] If honesty is measured by intent/endeavor rather than performance; if a man can be expected to lie about an intent that cannot be verified; if he will lie to *himself* so that "intent"is a contradiction, then the measurable boundaries between fiction and reality collapse, leaving every man to place them where he will. Crusoe, to cite one example, places them rather eccentrically. Moreover, Defoe's dictum that the Tradesman "must not only intend or mean honestly, but must do so," demonstrated how fragile – how easily rationalized – intent may be.

The argument respecting intent is particularly confusing because it seems contrary to the operations of credit. The text argues that men lose credit because of how they are perceived – when their promises fail, so does their credit; when the Devil plants a rumor, it takes hold (in this last case, notwithstanding the perceiver's intent). When a man's performance is creditable, the world responds: "NOTHING but probity will support credit; just and fair, and honourable dealings give credit" (1, 348). Since credit is based on what creditors see, unseen intention has no application. The issue is not merely whether one has "lied" in Steele's sense ("a Lie is a falsifying the Truth with an Intention to decieve" [152]), but how one establishes an objective measure of Honesty for purposes of attributing credit. By delivering a measure that is no measure, the text fails of its promise to guide the Tradesman through the world of credit as that world is portrayed in the text. Had the Tradesman read *An Appeal to Honour and Justice* (where Defoe pleads the intent of his pamphlets), he would not be sanguine about founding his credit on claims of intent.

But if intent is asserted as the basis of Honesty, it permits a perpetual falling away from Perfection with no *loss* of Honesty. Defoe cites the Golden Rule (*"Do* unto others . . ."), but his ultimate standard remains anchored in intent:

> I cannot doubt in the least but that there are many Tradesmen that, abating human Infirmity, may say, That they have endeavor'd after such a Perfection; who if they fall, rise again; if they slip, are the first to reproach themselves with it; repent, and re-assume their upright Conduct; the general Tenor of whose Lives is to be honest, and to do fair Things. And this is what we may be allow'd to call *an honest Man*, for as to Perfection, we are not looking for it in Life; 'tis enough if it be found in the intention and Desire: Sincerity of Desire is Christian Perfection. (II, part 1, 43)

Just as Defoe turned the tables on Steele by arguing that it is Christian *not* to require conditionality on promises, he does so again, arguing that to *desire* perfection is Christian, thereby negating a mandatory Golden Rule.[27] If it is "honest" to *wish* to be honest – to *be* more-or-less-honest – then honesty is some liminal ground between Truth and Lies, between "endeavor" and consistent performance. It is not necessarily "dishonesty" – though it might be, since we cannot measure desire – but it *is* the type of confused performance delivered by Crusoe. How can we be sure what he intends? Under such a standard, it is enough that Crusoe wishes to be honest. It is enough that the Editor of *Moll* wishes he could say that Moll is a fiction, but must hedge in light of demands for truth. The liminality he delivers fits precisely with Perfection-as-less-than-perfection. Moreover, we cannot penetrate his "desire."

The Tradesman who disagreed with Defoe measured himself by a standard of Honesty that did not recognize "intent": breaking his word was grounds for reproach, though he had given it in good faith. The Tradesman's standard is communal and hence public (as is the Golden Rule). Defoe, however, privatizes the standard for measuring honesty, since only the individual can measure his own intent (assuming he does not lie to himself). Dis-Honesty becomes a matter of discretion, not subject to public supervision, let alone public sanction. Thus the logic of Dissolving Fictions is approached from the rear: instead of denying the existence of fiction or at any rate its culpability, public authority is denied the capacity to measure and hence to punish fiction. Under this rationale, *The Shortest Way With the Dissenters* could not have been punished when it was exposed. *The Compleat English Tradesman*'s erosion of its discourse on communality, evident in the chapters on Endorsing, accelerates with the privatization of intent.

To insist upon Honesty but to define it into contradiction, indefiniteness, and subjectivity, silences the critique of fiction because Truth and Lies collapse as separable categories. This not only rationalizes, but institutionalizes the logic of credit as the measure of the real. It preempts any ideological apparatus attempting to scrutinize artifacts displaying such logic. Defoean fiction, insisting upon honesty but (like credit) always falling into ambiguity, is inscribed as natural, the Way of the World.

As a final turn, the text complicates intent even further, arguing that there are no standards at all between Buyer and Seller. Even if the Tradesman wanted to internalize acceptable, community-generated standards, he could not:

> Nor are the Bounds and Limits of Honesty strictly settled betwixt the Buyer and the Seller. How far the former may recommend his Goods; how far the latter may decry and disparage them; how far the Seller (Tradesman) may set them off with flourishes and Rhetorick; and what Art he may use to persuade the Customer to buy; and how far the Customer may strive and struggle with the Tradesman, by running down the Goodness of the Goods, and lessening the Value of them, in order to bring him to abate.
>
> The limits between these two, I say, are not settled with respect to their Honesty or Dishonesty; and so it remains a Difficulty, how far the Tradesman is to be censur'd on that Account. (II, part 1, 44–45)

The Customer and the Tradesman can "strive and struggle," but if no standards govern their exchange, "Dishonesty" dribbles away with the "Difficulty" of censure. If intent is not held to community standards; if such standards are themselves "not settled'; and if Perfection "is found in the Intention," then it is perfectly honest (so to speak) to intend whatever can be rationalized. In this context, Honesty becomes a vague, subjective, circular evasion.

The text's argument, at once insisting upon but dismantling honesty, regressing into an infinitely ambiguous intent, represents the ultimate refinement of Defoe's strategy to remain unaccountable for fiction. It deprives the creditor/reader of any authority to censure the text, completely reversing the extreme concentration of power in creditors (e.g. as respects endorsement of bills). It is a form of revenge for the hostility towards fiction and the demand for certainty. It is a complete enforcement of credit-based epistemology: texts are inherently opaque. Their authors cannot be "said" to lie.

In *Defoe and Casuistry*, George Starr discusses the notion of "intent," noting that casuistic logic held an evil intent to be as culpable as an evil act, even if the act is never committed; a good intent, however, can absolve even a bad act.[28] However, in *The Compleat English Tradesman* Defoe's emphasis on intent hardly jibes with casuistry. If intent is mired in self-conflicted subjectivity; if it can never be measured by any cognizable standard, accessible to the subject, then it cannot be invoked as the basis for determining culpability. In this sense, *The Compleat English Tradesman* evades casuist doctrine (as it would apply to Honesty) voiding any inquiry based on intent. In one of his most brilliant pamphlets, *A New Test of the Sence of the Nation* (1710), Defoe argues that it is now understood that swearing allegiance has no meaning; one cannot be guilty of lying because pro forma linguistic formations are without signification. That is, convention unhinges action and intent. *A New Test* is avowedly satiric, but it formulates in reverse the phenomenon that *The Compleat English Tradesman* tries to institute: intent and action are discontinuous. *A New Test* argues that intent will not be inferred from action, and that action is primary; *The Compleat English Tradesman* argues that intent is primary, but cannot be inferred from action. In both cases the deliberate lie becomes moot.

In *Crime and Defoe*, Lincoln Faller argues that:

> Defoe was never quite able to argue his way out of the "scandal" that trade was inherently dishonest and so comparable with theft. However much he tried to make it seem a heroic and worthy endeavor – *The Compleat English Tradesman* with all its confused, ungainly, even tortured arguments is a monument to this effort – he could never quite erase its bad name. (141)

Faller cites the text's "tortured, inconclusive arguments," Charles Lamb's letter suggesting it was "difficult to say what [Defoe's] intention was in writing it," and Thomas Meier's puzzled concern over Defoe's "tendency to weaken his own position" (141, n.4). My argument accommodates the text's contradictions by suggesting that it is a mistake to attempt to reconcile them into linear "heroic and worthy endeavor." By interpolating credit into his text at the level of its own logic, Defoe produces a text that reinscribes – as a norm – the *non*-linearity of credit. The reader cannot press the text to reveal meanings that it cannot reveal, since its point is to deter the reader from linear pursuit of meaning. "Meaning" is in the deferral of meaning, in the marketplace strategy that rationalizes Defoean fiction.

CHAPTER 4

Fictions of stability

REALITY AS ARTIFICE

Defoe's exculpatory strategy in *The Compleat English Tradesman* hinges on the apparent chronic disjunction in marketplace texts between volition and performance: no text could be presumed to manifest personal agency, and thereby to constitute a willed representation of the self. Yet if *The Compleat English Tradesman* posits the radical uncertainty of representation, it must still account for, and ideally destabilize, discursive formations that purport to render credit free of ambiguity. Such formations threaten the epistemological posture of the market exploited by Defoe, i.e. that texts which represent the market are generically uncertain and their authorship dispersed. Only if nontransparency is attributable to all texts involved with credit, will readers forego attempts to determine genre and locate accountable authors. The existence of texts claiming both certainty *and* an involvement with credit is therefore an urgent preoccupation of *The Compleat English Tradesman*.

Texts that claim absolute transparency subsist as highly wrought artifacts, the perfect expression of volition in performance, where the "intent" is complete self-revelation. The author renders himself with candor and signs his name. This certified clarity, emphatically distilled from the surrounding phenomenal flux, renders such texts fictive – their abstract stability misrepresents the real. The crucial factor is that such texts never acknowledge their abstraction, and do not conceive of themselves as fiction. Purporting to be univalent, certain, and absolutely true, such texts are Fictions of Stability.

However, if one imagines Truth as an abstraction of reality, then fictions of stability are "true." In contradistinction to the credit/fiction homology, Truth (so represented) is isolable and quantifiable, detachable from potential fiction. The competing narrative potentials of credit-based texts are broken apart, each given a distinctly marked path that precludes perceptual confusion. The processes of the market are stabilized, leaving fiction a separate, discernible category. Unlike bills, which *impose* certainty merely by denying uncertainty, fictions of stability *reorganize* the world; certainty and uncertainty are discriminated, represented as different logical systems. Truth emerges as stable, distinct, representable. Not only does art claim to represent reality, it makes claims *about* reality that make it representable. Fictions of stability reflect an optimism that mutually disorganizing phenomena can be dis-integrated; that the world can be reinterpreted and reintegrated so that such phenomena continue to exist, but in mutual exclusivity.

While bills assert authority to represent "reality" on a certain date, they do not acknowledge counterpressures that can subvert that authority. Fictions of stability, however, account for the potential confusion of certainty and uncertainty but explicitly (so they claim) sort out the confusion. To inscribe fictions of stability is inculpable, since such texts presume that phenomena purporting to be certain *will* be.

The fiction of stability addressed in *The Compleat English Tradesman* is accounting. Texts produced by accounting claim to be "readable": credit-based phenomena *can* be represented; a single, discrete author *is* responsible for a text; he is subject to rules that expel uncertainty. Accounting, therefore, threatens the logic of unaccountability attributed to the epistemology of the market. I shall argue that *The Compleat English Tradesman* combats accounting, reintegrating it with the *modus operandi* of credit. The text's accounting lessons destabilize the certainty of accounting. They demonstrate (once again) that the text's "didacticism" may be "read" as serving an ulterior purpose, i.e. that of rehabilitating generic uncertainty and authorial unaccountability. Accounting texts in *The Compleat English Tradesman* are not "untrue," but like the Tradesman's bills and notes, mere shaky representations of potential payoffs. My point is that by reintegrating credit and accounting within a single paradigm – the epistemologically opaque market – Defoe develops a theory of "unaccountable" commercial texts spanning both credit and its monitory apparatus.

ACCOUNTING

History and Theory

In *The Gentleman Accomptant: Or, An Essay to Unfold the Mystery of Accompts* (London, 1715), Roger North described the processes of accounting as "an Act of the Mind, intent upon the Nature and the Truth of Things" (9). Like art, its production requires "the Solitude of a Compting-House, or the Retirement from all Manner of Interruption . . . [R]ather than leave Defect, Impropriety, Doubts, or Ambiguity of Expression, whereby the very Truth is obfuscated, the Accomptant is not to grutch his pains" (23). The conviction that Mind acts on the world to describe it, and that the world is amenable to such description, is basic to accounting. It is reflected in North's obvious reference to the ideology of empiricism espoused by the Royal Society: "Accompts are kept in a certain Method . . . which method is so comprehensive and perfect, as makes it worthy to be put among the Sciences, and to be understood by all Virtuosi" (1). In *A New Treatise of Arithmetic and Book-keeping* (Edinburgh, 1718), Alexander Malcolm makes the same point, arguing that accounting evinces the ability of the mind to dispel disorder, to refine phenomena into intelligible categories:

As Regularity and Order are the Product of Reason, they serve to distinguish the Rational, from the irrational World: Reason is not only the Glory of our Nature, but to exercise it with utmost Advantage, is certainly the Interest of our Being; its Functions are not confined to one Sort of Actions, they extend to every Thing transacted among Men, in so much, that wherever we find the Effect of Counsel, Contrivance and Design, there we acknowledge Reason. (113)

The premises of accounting directly challenge the ambivalence of marketplace texts. In their eighteenth-century articulation, they evince an empiricist current that privileges sense perception and presumes that rational and irrational can be segregated.[1]

Accounting ("double entry bookkeeping") arose in the commercial city-states of fourteenth-century Italy, enabling merchants to determine the financial status of ongoing, diverse enterprises too large for daily supervision. Such enterprises were conducted through foreign agents, were subject to complex rates of exchange, and depended on credit. The need arose to rationalize all these transactions under a single proprietorship, while being able to analyze any class of transactions (as to goods, trading partners, status of amounts owed and owing). The first printed text on double entry was published in 1494 by a Milanese monk, Fra Luca Pacioli.[2] The technique spread to England by virtue of contacts among English merchants with Italian and Dutch traders, and by 1543 the first text in English appeared.[3] During the seventeenth century a vast number of treatises on the subject were in circulation, each promoting double entry in general and their own pedagogy in particular.[4] By 1718, Malcolm acknowledged "the great . . . Cloud of authors in my Way" (preface). Since Defoe adopts much of his predecessors' apparatus, such as sample accounts, as well as much of their standard rhetoric, such as warning against the perils of ignoring accounts, he must have examined such texts and probably learned his accounting from them.[5]

The remarkable feature of these texts is their consistency. They present a system that was fully evolved by the time of Pacioli, differing only over minor theoretical matters and in pedagogical modes.[6] However, my concern is not with the formal intricacies of accounting, but with the structural basis for its extraordinary claims to truth and stability. Alexander Malcolm poses the issue precisely:

> Now, Words or Writing, are the Picture or Representation of a Thing, and in the present Case, I conceive the Merchants Books of Accompts, which being a Thing subject to Alterations, according to the various Additions, Subtractions, and other Changes, the Course of his Negotiations brings it to, to have always the true Picture, it must suffer the same Changes with the Original, i.e. since every Transaction by the Merchant, or his Doers, makes some Alteration, if not in the Value, at least in the Posture of his Affairs: Therefore; a faithful record ought to be made of every Thing that any way concerns a Man's Business. (124)

The characteristic mode of accounting is its assertion that a "true Picture" in "Words or Writing" can accommodate "Changes" in one's affairs; it elides any epistemological challenge that would disrupt true pictures.[7] It assumes that a "faithful record" can be maintained in absolute representational clarity as each "faithful record" is assimilated into the whole. The accounting text is in dynamic equilibrium, conceptually opposite the radical disequilibrium of credit texts, where truth or fiction may precipitate with equal (un)certainty. Accounting is univalent, always reliable. Malcolm defines it in terms that emphasize its perpetual accuracy as "[t]he Art of recording the Transactions of a Man's Affairs, in such exact and regular Order, that at any Time he may know the true and just State of any Particular Part of his Affairs, or of the whole, with the greatest Ease and Dispatch" (114).

The salient feature of accounting is that in its ultimate articulation in the ledger, it produces an antinarrative. At every point in the continuing notation of one's affairs in that text, closure – that is, complete disclosure – is implicit. Openness to revision is always coincident with an amenability in the text to collapsing the sequence into an extended discursive present. There is no suspense, no necessity to "read" through data to locate the outcome. The outcome is always already there, the end is emergent at every point, waiting to be ascertained "with the greatest Ease and Dispatch." This perpetual availability of definitive knowledge, and constant purported correspondence between text and world, assures absolute, certain Truth. The author's intent is revealed. In its antinarrative figuration, accounting is the opposite of credit-based texts, whose promises to pay precipitate a narrative suspense in which genre itself (Truth or Fiction) is suspended. Roger North articulates the sense that the accounting text is accurate to the moment as if it had actually been inscribed in that moment:

For the Dr. and Cr. [debtor and creditor method of accounting] is pure and perfect right Reason, and contains the whole Material Truth and Justice of all Dealing, and nothing else . . . And all this is in a perpetual State; so as every Question that can be proposed concerning any Dealing, is answered almost as readily as demanded; and so no person can be injured, who takes his Accompt upon the stating of the Books, so far as it runs: And in all Times, even in After-Ages, the Transactions thus duly accompted, will be understood as well, as if the same had been inquisited at the very Instant of the Writing. (3)

This "perpetual State" of true (dis)closure is achieved through the conversion of temporal notation into an extensive spatial relationship among interrelated, always changing (but ultimately stabilized) accounts.

To appreciate this conversion, and Defoe's assault on it, it is necessary to understand prescribed accounting technique. The first step was to inscribe each transaction in a "waste book" under a specific date: A sold B two yards of cloth. There might be ten transactions that day, some in which the tradesman himself buys cloth, some involving purchase and sale of other commodities, some on credit and some for cash. Already one has a plethora of customers and suppliers, varying lines of business (e.g. cloth and nails), different modes of payment. How does one keep track of "accounts" with debtors and creditors, of the profitability of different commodities, and of one's business as a whole? There has to be a way of unifying these transactions. The next step is to transcribe the transaction into a journal, so that each appears as a relationship between debtor and creditor: B is debtor to A for two yards of cloth. At this point the statement is analytical, but it is still one unit. The next and crucial step is to transfer each journal entry into the ledger *at least twice.* Accounts are opened, each with a debtor and creditor side. For each entry under each account (on one side or the other), there must be a reciprocal entry in another account (again, on one side or the other) cross-referenced in each case to its origin in the journal. Thus under B's "account" in the ledger would appear under the debtor side: two shillings, the price of two yards of cloth. Under A's Accounts Receivable would appear: two shillings, the price of two yards of cloth sold to B. If B had sold A a commodity, the notations would be reversed, with A's liability noted in Accounts Payable. As payments came in and went out, the reciprocal accounts would be adjusted, so that all debtor entries and all creditor entries would *always* be equal and opposite each other. One might also open accounts to measure how well cloth was doing in comparison to nails. Ultimately, the results of all transactions would be carried to an account for profit and loss. Once the ledger was posted (ideally every night), one could measure B's performance (assuming the proprietor to be A) merely by balancing his particular account, so that it might appear that he is ten shillings in arrears, but on purchases so far this year of £100. One could measure the profitability of cloth, and bring all one's accounts down to determine enterprise profit and loss.

What begins with sequential notation is ultimately apprehended as if synchronic, with a sector for each account. As entries are posted, each account remains an ostensibly exact representation of the phenomenon within its purview. Moreover, the system contains its own self-checking mechanism, which insures against misrepresentation: because each transaction is entered as *both* a debit and credit, all the debits and all the credits will balance if added separately (a process known as "trial balance"). If they do not, then the ledger can be checked against the journal, and if need be against the waste book, until error is found. Narrative remains suppressed, except to the degree required to achieve transparency in an antinarrative iteration, the ledger.

North cites the integrity of the whole, epitomized in its continual balance:

The Art of Regular Accompting depends wholly upon this Supposition, viz. That every thing negociated comes out of something, and goes into something, having (as they say of Motion) its *terminus a quo and ad quem*. But Increase or Decrease of the Whole, or any Part in the Transition, there is a common Receptacle, or Place, which receives or furnisheth exactly the same. So that however spaciously the Books are branched out, there is conserved a perpetual Par, or Balance of the Whole. (8)

North's language invokes a restrained organicism, a steady-state reliability "conserved" in organized, internally consistent space. He uses the example of shifting contents from one drawer of a "Scritoire" to another, which "Alterations make no Disorder, but the Repertory of the whole is continually compleat" (17). Most importantly, he emphasizes that intertextuality is the key to representational perfection:

As the Accompts depend on one another, so all the Books and Papers belonging to the Business, are connected in the Accompt by References; for the Ledger calls on the Journal, That on the Waste-Book, That on the Subsidiary Books of all sorts . . . And an Alphabet of the Names, or Titles of the Accompts, always attends the Ledger; by Help of which you have ready Recourse to any Accompt there; and then you have the Thread that guides thro' all: which Disposition, as to Consultation or Searches, is to all Intents perfect. (31)

The point is that the entire system is designed for the "perfect" retrieval of marketplace reality, with an internal discipline that enforces accuracy, certainty. By writing first in the waste book, transcribing to the journal and posting to the ledger, there are multiple restatements that curtail the possibility of a hasty, careless, or fraudulent posting with no backup text to provide correction. Not only can fiction be caught, but right use of the system discourages perpetration of lies. Truth inheres in following the system:

And that other way [posting directly to the ledger] is also open to Frauds, as may be practiced at any time, by writing what you please in the Books; for perhaps there is not occasion to write a Line in an Accompt for three or four Years together; and in the last year you may write with a Date two Years before; and what shall shew the falsity?

If the parcel be entered in the Day, it is justified to be done at the Time, by the continual, daily, and perhaps hourly Entries, that are made before and after it. So that an After-cheat, not designed, when the Books were carried on day by day, can afterwards foist nothing into the Books that is false, to give a Colour to it. (31)[8]

Virtually all accounting texts discuss the prevention and cure of errors. North says flatly, "Errors are to be adjusted to Truth in the Books" (39). The ultimate point of avoiding Error is that not only do accounts *display* one's affairs, they regulate the self – the author – who is the agent of inscription and whose affairs are the subject of the text. As North says, "Accompting is a great Means of keeping out of Debt" (41). Since the exact status of one's affairs is always available, it is possible to "reform [one's] measures of living" in case one's affairs go slack (7). Far from positing a remote, disseminated author with no authority, accounting produces an author intimately engaged with the text, striving to ensure its honesty and responding to its cautions.

Accounting's claims to represent Truth require that truth be a distinct discursive category, and that accounting texts be able to segregate fiction and truth. In other words, such texts *must be* the exact discursive opposite of credit as it is described in *The Compleat English Tradesman*. How is this accomplished, since accounting itself describes transactions *mediated* by credit? In *A New Treatise*, Malcolm speaks of "Imaginary" accounts (122). In *Principles of Book-keeping, explain'd*, Alexander Macghie speaks of "fictitious accounts."[9] Such terms sound paradoxical within a discourse of militant transparency, but they make sense: events that must be represented (because they are historical), but cannot be accommodated by accounting's representational conventions (because their outcome is uncertain), are given accounts of their own. The convention remains uncompromised in rendering Truth. "Imaginary," "fictitious" events are reified as separate accounts *consistent* with the discursive project. The discourse of credit, in which "truth" and "fiction" are indeterminate, is superseded by a logic that maintains both categories in the same discursive space (the ledger), but as distinct.

Malcolm explains that in order to separate determinate from indeterminate, "some Accompts be used, which, for Distinction, I call Imaginary":

Suppose I send Goods as Tobacco to Sea, consigned to my Factor at Amsterdam, the Creditor Side of the Accompt of Tobacco, must be made to show, how it is dispos'd of; a Creditor requires a Debtor, but there is no

Person or Thing come in their Place to be made Debtor; for I cannot Charge my Factor, till he advises me they are come to his Hand, therefore I erect an Accompt in my Leger by the Title of Voyage to Amsterdam, &c. which I charge, or make Debtor for the whole Cargo, and so it will stand till I am advised that they are Lost, or come safe to my Factor, and then the Accompt Voyage is discharged, i.e. made Creditor, to my Factor Debtor. (122–123)

The system requires creation of a "fiction," an imagined entity separated from real entities (real accounts representing transpired phenomena), referring to a transaction whose outcome is uncertai and therefore unrepresentable as a conventional debit or credit. Fiction *signifies* indeterminacy, and is segregated from determinate accounts. Malcolm describes a similar scheme where a debt is "due only upon Condition of a certain Event" (123), and Macghie requires a "fictitious" account when one receives but does not deliver in return (9–10). Thus the possibility of alternative outcomes is not permitted to ambiguate the project of ascertaining the exact state of one's affairs. One knows when and in what particulars the text is uncertain, since contingency is not represented in the same discursive continuum with settled (in that sense real) phenomena; it is identified with fictivity.

The mode of production of accounting texts prohibits them from exhibiting the ambiguity, for example, of the preface to *Serious Reflections*. Accounts are not engaged with print culture, and are therefore off limits to Editors, Publishers, and other personae with authority to supervise (to revise?) texts unaccountably. The author is never forced to compromise his agency for reasons relating to market demand (which requires that Moll's text be scoured, and which forces the Tradesman to promise unconditionally). Rather, the author's agency is asserted, and if he observes accounting protocol, his honesty is a prima facie fact.[10] In *Idea Rationaria, or the perfect accomptant* (1683), Robert Colinson argues that accounting induces reader confidence in the authorial persona:

If he be unfortunate it satisfies the world of his just dealing, and is the fairest and best Apologie for his innocence and honesty to the World, and contributes exceedingly to the satisfaction of all his friends and well-wishers, and to the Confutation and silencing of all his malevolent and detracting Enemies, and often proves the great cause to bring him a most favorable Composition with his Creditors: whereas these that are ignorant of it, in such a Condition are censured by all, when they have nothing to show but bare words to vindicate themselves.[11]

The accounting text is credible to reader/creditors because it opens itself to investigation, confuting "malevolent and detracting Enemies." In *The Compleat English Tradesman*, credit texts that cannot bear investigation resist protocols that would permit, invite investigation. Against this disparity, Defoe has to discredit accounting's claims to clarify credit relations.

Defoe's accounting

In *The Compleat English Tradesman*, the accounting text is fragile. While it may defend the Tradesman against lax debtors and opportunistic creditors, it potentially produces irony, readily reinscribing the confusion it is intended to dispel. Defoe argues that "That Tradesman, who keeps no books, may depend upon it, he will e're long keep no trade, unless he resolves also to give no credit" (I, 268). He then suggests, however, that:

> He that does not keep his books exactly, and so as that he may depend on them for charging his Debtors, had better keep no books at all . . .; for as books well kept makes business easy and certain, so books neglected turn all into confusion, and leave the Tradesman in a wood, which he can never get out of without damage and loss. (I, 271)

Defoe's logic leads to paranoia. Inexact books are worse than no books; it is impossible to eschew books unless one gives no credit; yet "He that gives no trust . . . is not yet born, or if there was any such, they are all dead" (I, 268). In other words, if your books are inexact, you are out of business. The texts supposed to safeguard the Tradesman can provoke his undoing.

Defoe suggests that the inept text proliferates hostile fictions around it:

> [I]f ever his dealers know that his books are ill-kept they play upon him, and impose horrid forgeries and falsities upon him; whatever he omits they catch at, and leave it out; whatever they put upon him, he is bound to yield to; so that in short, as books well kept are the security of the Tradesman's estate, and the ascertaining of his debts, so books ill kept will assist every knavish customer or chapman to cheat and deceive him. (I, 271)

The inexact text is vulnerable, yielding to "forgeries" that reconstruct the author as discreditable. No longer constrained by an abstracting protocol, the text is open to marketplace noise, to opinion and irony. The vulnerability of the Tradesman's texts distinguishes them from those described by Colinson, North, and Malcolm, who emphasize that well-kept texts resist "After-cheats." Defoe's version of accounting, which provides "the security of the Tradesman's estate" if well-inscribed, easily pitches into reverse.

The Compleat English Tradesman ambiguates the accounting evangelism so prominent in Defoe's predecessors. The difference is one of emphasis, of raising doubts. The point is not to discredit accounting, but to affiliate it with credit, so that commercial textuality becomes uncertain even in expository iterations. The impact lies not in any send-up of accounting, but in the blunting of its knife-edged perfection.

The market can be depicted as particularly oppressive since accounting procedures that Defoe recommends are technically unrefined. There is no analysis of the transaction into debtor and creditor as in a formal journal entry. More significantly, transactions are recorded only once in the ledger, under the debtor's account, rather than at least twice and potentially under multiple accounts. As a result, the theoretical justification of classic double entry falls away: the ledger cannot be rationalized, cannot be "balanced" by applying the rule that for every debtor in one account there is a creditor in another. Errors are more likely to intrude, and a trial balance cannot be struck to determine whether a mistake has crept in.

Defoe's directions to the Tradesman for eradicating error suggest that accounting texts are inherently uncertain. Defoe proposes that accounts be wrenched into transparency by main force, by physically counting one's cash. Prior tracts describe a method that is self-correcting, indigenous to a regime of self-enclosed textuality. In order to "ballance" the cash book with the cash on hand, thereby achieving transparency, the Tradesman takes an inventory:

What I call ballancing his Cash-book, is, first, the casting up, daily, or weekly, or monthly, his receipts and payments, and then seeing what money is left in hand, or, as the usual expression of the Tradesman is, what money is in cash, secondly, the examining his money, telling it over, and seeing how much he has in his chest or bags, and then seeing if it agrees with the ballance of his book, that what *is* and what *should be*, correspond. (1, 276–277)

Defoe's notion of "ballance" is different from that of classic accounting. In classical theory, balance does not refer to what is *actually* in the cash chest, determined by physical counting, but to an agreement among discursive categories from which one can derive – deductively – the state of one's cash. Classical accounting is autotelic, relying on the perfection of a self-referring ledger, annotated by subsidiary texts within a self-referring regime. Defoe's accounting is transgressive, denying the perfection of textuality, moving the ground of affirmation from Text to World. While Defoe states his theory in terms that resemble double entry ("What is" in the cash chest and "what should be" in the cash book "correspond"), he interposes a physicality that denies the immediate (if notional) "correspondence" of classical theory. Textuality loses any automatic presumption of veracity (though of course it *may* be true). While Defoe's method is likelier to yield an accurate "picture" than double entry, provided the Tradesman actually applies himself to the task, his approach makes concessions to the fragility of the text that double entry does not. The text becomes contingent, a secondary notation of "what is," rather than a self-sufficient iteration constituting "what is." Since the Defoean text must always be confirmed extratextually, it hovers between "what is" and "what should be" with an incalculable margin of Error.

In a curious paradox, it is the very textual solipsism of classic double entry, the mirror images of the ledger reflecting the subsidiary images of anterior texts, which allows the system (in theory) to reflect commercial Truth, since fictional After-cheats are hard to disguise. The serenity of an encompassing, self-assured textuality differs from the anxiety projected onto the Tradesman, who as reader/accountant must anxiously interact with texts of contingent efficacy:

The keeping a cash-book is one of the nicest parts of a Tradesman's business, because there is always the bag and the book to be brought together, and if they do not exactly speak the same language, even to a farthing, there must be some omission; and how big or how little that omission may be, who knows? or how shall it be known, but by casting and re-casting up, telling, and telling over and over again the money? (I, 279)

By mandating a continual "casting and re-casting," Defoe denies the text's abstraction from the world, its ability to absorb flux and remain "true" independent of any intervention (other than mere notation). The text is "true" only until the next transaction.[12] It ceases to be a site for the generation of truth. The anxiety of reading credit texts is reintroduced.

At the empirical level, Defoe refocuses the reflecting mirrors of double entry into a *mise-en-abyme*, where "what is" and "what should be" become unsettled dependent variables. Since the text loses its (purported) absolute integrity, one cannot be certain whether one's

Books need reform or one's cash is deficient or unfairly in excess. In the most astounding irony, the first page of sample accounts in *The Compleat English Tradesman* displays a glaring arithmetical mistake: in a long column of figures, sixpence and sixpence are added to make sixpence (1, supplement, 46). The error infects pages and pages of subsequent accounts, with no internal method (trial balance) sending the Tradesman back to check his math. The Tradesman "telling" his cash might think he collected sixpence too much, and wonder who overpaid. If he does not "tell" his cash, he will think he has less than he does – when he discovers the error, the text will stand exposed. Though I do not suggest that Defoe "planted" this error, I am suggesting that it reifies the fragility of the accounting text modelled in *The Compleat English Tradesman*.

By eviscerating double entry, Defoe permits the uncertainty of credit to flow back into a text that would ideally keep it out. As a result, the confusion of credit occupies both the Tradesman's accounts and the account of accounting in *The Compleat English Tradesman*. Defoe destabilizes the project of commercial culture to fix commercial phenomena into readable form. His reformulation of that project is itself unfixed; the exposition of marketplace certainty ends in the bathos of schoolboy mistake. Accounting, ostensibly a refuge from the impenetrability of texts, comes to exemplify it, becoming just another emblem of an ironic market.

Of all the major accounting tracts of the period, only Defoe's does not offer a proximate version of double entry.[13] He offers instead a version that *can* be transparent, but that just as likely may not be owing to human error and the flux of the real. The bottom line is that *The Compleat English Tradesman* advances a notion that texts intended to monitor credit need to be monitored as well. This dialectic between text and world reduces the veracity of accounting texts to coincidence. In answer to the question of whether an accounting text *is* true ("how shall it be known?"), Defoe directs the reader back to the world with its own contingencies.

It is crucial that while Defoe destabilizes the accounting text, he suggests that the Tradesman should be responsible for keeping abreast of his position relative to creditors. Yet even in so quintessential a matter, Defoe does not *require* textual perfection. "What is" and "what should be" become matters of approximation, of the slippage of the text towards some subjective standard established by the Tradesman:

Certainly Honesty obliges every man, when he sees, that his stock is gone, that he is below the level, and eating into the estates of other men, to put a stop to it in time, while something is left. It has been a fault, without doubt, to break in upon other mens estates at all; but perhaps a plea may be made for this, (viz.) that it was ignorantly done, and they did not think they were run so far, as to be worse than nothing . . . but I must add that can hardly happen without his fault, because he ought to be always acquainting himself with his Books, stating his expences and his profits, and casting things up frequently, at least in his head, so always to know whether he goes backward or forward. (I, 74)

The phrase, "at least in his head," deprives the text of objective verifiability. It becomes the Tradesman's private bellwether, rather than a public document that anyone can construe. This undermines the world's ability to measure the Tradesman's "Honesty." While Defoe insists that "Honesty obliges every man" to consider his creditors, and recognize the "backward or forward" direction of his accounts, how can someone reading those accounts know what the Tradesman knew "in his head"? The Tradesman might claim that he thought payments were coming due for transactions not yet entered, or that he made a tough calculation subject to an oversight. Thus the passage jibes with Defoe's excursus on Honesty as consistent with a subjective, unmeasurable "intent." Defoe seems to urge consideration for creditors and to "fault" the inattentive Tradesman, but then he positions "fault" beyond verifiability. Defoe does not demand that the text be perfectly maintained, as do North, Malcolm, and the classical accountants. He frightens the Tradesman with the consequences of an inexact text, but when it comes to defining Honesty in relation to a text, Defoe hedges. The text is allowed to remain an imperfect signifier of "intent," while the Tradesman can claim to be Honest.

The fragile accounting text becomes the source of a freakish piracy in the chapter "Of the Tradesman letting his Wife be acquainted with his Business." An apprentice asserts himself, prejudicing a wife and family of a deceased Tradesman who kept his books "in his head":

The only relief [the widow] has, is her husband's Books, and she is happy in that, but just in proportion to the care he took in keeping them; even when she finds the names of debtors, she knows not who they are, or where they dwell, who are good, and who are bad; the only remedy she has here is, if her husband had e're a servant, or apprentice, who was so near out of his time as to be acquainted with the customers, and with the books; and then she is forced to be beholden to him to settle the accounts for her, and endeavor to get in the debts; in return for which she is forced to give him his Time and

Freedom, let him go into the trade, make him master of all the Business, set him up in the world, and it may be, at last, with all her pride, lets the boy creep to bed with her; and when her friends upbraid her with it, that she should marry her 'prentice boy, when it may be she was old enough to be his mother: Her answer is, "Why, what could I do? I must have been ruin'd else? I had nothing but what lay abroad in debts, scatter'd about in the world, and no body but he knew how to get them in: What could I do? If I had not done it, I must have been a Beggar." And so it may be she is at last too, if the boy of a husband proves a Brute to her, as many do, and as in such unequal matches indeed most people do. (1, 288–289)

The accounts facilitate the apprentice's self-aggrandizement because they are arcane. The husband's enterprise, constituted in the circulating, disembodied capital of credit, and evinced in the "husband's Books," falls to the servant by dint of an ability to interpret the Books. The servant's financial knowledge is a bootstrap into carnal knowledge, and then into marriage with the Wife. The marriage breaches a proprietary system that excludes servants from sexual and financial prerogatives; it exposes a vulnerable system, hinged on a set of fragile texts that embody its operations. The credit economy, supported by and reduced to the textuality of financial accounts, does not take into account (so to speak) the potential opacity of crucial texts. At the very point where proprietorship is determined, where one party or another succeeds to capital, the opaque text precipitates an unwarranted outcome. The text is not public, not even a "text" so much as a sketch, and can only be interpreted with extratextual data. While accounting can reflect commercial truth, its vulnerability has the capacity to disorganize economic relations.

This is not to suggest that *The Compleat English Tradesman* does not contemplate the transparent accounting text. For example, when the Tradesman realizes that he must "break," he tells his creditors that "he is willing to shew them his books, and give up every farthing into their hands, that they might see he acted as an honest man to them" (1, 175). Upon showing that he has made "a faithful and just account of every thing," his creditors accept an offer of fifteen shillings on the Pound, since "who but a parcel of hot-headed men would reject such a man?" (1, 176). *The Compleat English Tradesman* vacillates, demonstrating that accounting texts may or may not be readable; they may be readable only to those who can decipher them; the Tradesman's honesty may or may not be derived from the state of his texts. In their ambivalence, they are like the texts of credit, which ostensibly they monitor.

In the market, fictions of stability react against the instability of fiction, its tendency to resist discrete categorization. *The Compleat English Tradesman* destabilizes fictions of stability, interpolating an element of ambivalence into the texts of accounting. Such partial dismantling of accounting participates in a larger project: dismantling the measurability of Honesty, which I have argued is Defoe's essential concern. This concern establishes the shape of *The Compleat English Tradesman*. The text offers to define Honesty, but the offer is deferred, ultimately lost in a definition of intent that is circular and measurable (if at all) only subjectively. *The Compleat English Tradesman* enacts textual incapacity to deliver as promised and to represent phenomena that constitute credit. Yet except where Defoe concedes that a point is "unsettled," the text does not self-consciously acknowledge that the reader will decide the text's value by trying to "settle" unsettlement. It operates within a marketplace ideology that attempts to maintain desire for a text notwithstanding its lack of generic commitment.

A Journal of the Plague Year (1722) resembles *The Compleat English Tradesman* in that like its successor, it reflects upon the resistance of unresolved phenomena to entextualization. The difference is in the degree of self-consciousness it displays. *A Journal* acknowledges its incapacity to represent the plague. It challenges fictions of stability by asserting that they collapse. It asserts that as a text, it does not aspire to *be* such a fiction. In this regard it is central to Defoe's theorization of inculpable fiction. By insisting that fictions of stability do not perfectly render reality (and refusing the option), it demonstrates that "fiction" constitutes itself by presuming to correspond rigorously to the extratextual. The "true" text does not presume such rigor, and indeed points to areas of its own reticence: "I could give a great many such Stories . . . which in the long Course of that dismal Year, I met with, that is heard of, and which are very certain to be true, or very near Truth; that is to say no, true in the General, for no Man could at such a Time, learn all the Particulars."[14] Authorial honesty is constituted in acknowledging that one's text does not render "all the Particulars" of the real when "at such a Time" (i.e. epistemological uncertainty) certainty plays no part in the real. The paradox of honest discourse "at such a Time" is that it premises incongruity between a text and phenomena. It recognizes that "real" uncertainty is compromised by texts claiming to be certain. In this regard, *A Journal* reinscribes marketplace tropes. Credit abolishes certainty, producing uncertain texts; it ambiguates Fiction and Truth, so that the deferral of certainty is the only "true" representation of the real. The "author" of *A Journal of the Plague Year*, H. F., rejects fictions of stability, announcing that "at such a [hazy] Time," honesty requires ambivalence.

A Journal is Defoe's most explicit statement that discursive truth is constructed in part by discursive abstention. To require certainty – the undiminished presence of reality, rendered in a text – is to ask that an author produce fiction. Since H. F. is outside the market, under no pressure to produce certainty and able to confront the limits of discourse, he is an ideal(ized) author. He can dismiss the fictivity of excessive substantiation. At the same time, H. F.'s immersion in a plague scene that fluctuates as much as phenomena in the market, allows his responses to reflect on the wider population of authors. He inscribes a model text, aspiring to a "truth" consistent with the limits of textuality in an uncertain milieu. He is not so much a still point outside the market, as he is *inside* a larger compass of discourse. What applies to the texts of plague applies to any text produced "at such a Time": it cannot satisfy demands for complete disclosure. Defoean fictions must gesture towards such demands because they *are* based in the market. *A Journal* (that is, the "journal" inscribed by H. F., not the *Journal* produced by Defoe) is not subject to these demands, and is the type of text an author could write were his "truth" unalloyed with the fiction of pretending towards a completer – certain – truth. At one level, *A Journal*, like Defoe's other pretended memoirs, purports to be "true," i.e. nonfiction. At another valence, it is about a type of honesty that need not pretend to entire Truth. At this level, it comments on the demands of the market and postulates the shape of textuality as if it could ignore them. It justifies the epistemological uncertainty of texts in the market, such as Defoe's own.

As I suggested in chapter 1, credit was frequently described in terms of plague. In *A Journal of the Plague Year*, the plague is a figuration of credit: ramifying, unavoidable, preying on imagination. Both are versions of comprehensive uncertainty.[15] In the early 1720s, the credit crisis and the threat of plague virtually coincide. The plague at which *A Journal* was directed (by analogy with the 1660s, the subject of the text) was poised to cross the Channel (as had the model for the South Sea scheme) soon after the Bubble burst. The plague, credit, and *A Journal* become mutually informing narratives, raising questions about the sufficiency of representation. Credit and plague are discursively open-ended, never fully resolved; *A Journal* represents the discursive condition of irresolution "truthfully," providing an account which participates in that condition through discursive noncommitment.

The text develops a discourse of noncommitment through the continual deferral of H. F.'s narrative:

The Truth is, the Case of poor Servants was very dismal, as I shall have occasion to mention again by and by. (28)

The Story of those three Men, if the Reader will be content to have me give it in their own Persons, without taking upon me to either vouch the Particulars, or answer for any Mistakes, I shall give as directly as I can ... I say all this previous to the History, having yet, for the present, much more to say before I quit my own part. (52)

For when we came to see the Crouds and Throngs of People, which appear'd on the Sabbath Days at the Churches, and especially in those parts of the Town where the Plague was abated, or where it was not yet come to its height, it was amazing. But I shall speak again of this again presently. (163)

Such deferrals enact the responses of discourse "at such a Time," when linear, resolute narrative is presumptuous, erroneously betraying the resistance of phenomena to entextualization. The plague's demand for textual postponement is brilliantly cameoed in H. F.'s encounter with women stealing hats from his brother's warehouse. After threatening to lock the hat thieves in and fetch the Lord Mayor's Officers, H. F. recognizes:

[I]t would necessarily oblige me to go much about, to have several People come to me, and I go to several, whose Circumstances of Health, I knew nothing of; and that even at this Time the Plague was so high, as that there dy'd 4000 a Week; so that in showing my Resentment, or even in seeking Justice for my Brother's Goods, I might lose my own Life; so I contented my self, with taking the Names and Places where some of them lived, who were really Inhabitants in the Neighborhood; and threatning that my Brother should call them to an Account for it, when he returned to his Habitation. (74)

Plague reduces H. F. to inscribing a partial list ("where some of them lived") unlikely to be useful once the thieves disperse, and to offering a deferred threat that cannot be pursued within the compass of his narrative (the Plague Year) since H. F.'s brother is committed to retreat until the plague is abated. The imperfect roster, coupled with a threat whose outcome cannot be reported, evince at the level of text (the list) and metatext (*A Journal*) plague's counterpressure against entextualization.

As the foregoing incident demonstrates, plague shares with credit a capacity to expose the limits of inquiry:

> Now it seems [a certain man with a sensitive wound] found his Wound would smart many Times when he was in Company with such, who thought themselves to be sound, and who appear'd so to one another; but he would presently rise up, and say publickly, Friends, here is some Body in the Room that has the Plague, and so would immediately break up the Company. This was indeed a faithful Monitor to all People, that the Plague is not to be avoided by those that converse promiscuously in a Town infected, and People have it when they know it not, and that they likewise give it to others when they know not that they have it themselves; and in this Case, shutting up the WELL or removing the SICK will not do it, unless they can go back and shut up all those that the Sick had convers'd with, even before they knew themselves to be sick, and none knows how far to carry that back, or when to stop; for none knows when, or where, or how they may have received the Infection, or from whom. (151–152)

The positive identification of carriers ("some Body in the room has the Plague") is approximate, and H. F. observes that it is impossible to reason backwards towards some isolable cohort of the sick. The man with the wound cannot produce a definitive text (e.g. "He has the plague"), nor can H. F. conceive of a particular person's disclosing a specific genealogy of disease. Rather, each is presumed tainted by an entire community of unidentifiable potential carriers, as were post-Bubble traders: "[N]o one at this time knows whom to trust for a Remittance of Money, or Goods. It's impossible to remedy this Evil, while one merchant goes off after another. Traders are so linked with one another, that unless a man knew his Correspondent's Affairs better than his own, he could not know how to venture upon dealing with him."[16] Credit and plague are alike in "linking" mutually referring selves, each of which potentially reflects all relations in an undefined, ramifying community. Individuals cannot be "read" since they cannot be abstracted from this network, itself vague and in flux. Like credit, plague baffles attempts to define an origin or terminus, prohibiting discourse that assumes its own closure.

The chronically tentative texts of plague and credit are opposite those of accounting, where the interrelationship of inscribed sites establishes the provenance of every inscription and constitutes a fully articulated representation: "As the Accompts depend on one another, so all the Books and Papers belonging to the Business, are connected in the Accompt by References . . . then you have the Thread that guides thro' all; which Disposition, as to Consultation or Searches, is to all Intents perfect" (North, 31). Accounting assumes that each "account" is a comprehensive measure of reality, that no matter how intensified the database, each datum will be accounted for, constituting the history of a particular person or commodity up to the moment. Credit and plague deny the accessibility of history, and insofar as comprehension of the present depends upon history, the present becomes inaccessible as well. Plague imports into narrative, and into the narrative of *A Journal of the Plague Year*, a radical uncertainty regarding its history, status, and prospects. It recapitulates at the level of disease discursive phenomena of the market that permit extenuation and suspension of outcome.

At their most basic, credit and plague constitute a coextensive regime of irrepressible language production that outruns attempts at restraint:

[I]f our conversation must be without covetousness, and the like, why then it is impossible for tradesmen to be Christians . . . we must shut up shop, and leave off trade, and so in many things we must leave off living; for as conversation is call'd life, we must leave off to converse.[17]

[T]he Plague is not to be avoided by those that converse promiscuously in a Town infected.

In both cases, "conversation" is the vehicle of corruption – in the one case producing "table lies, salutation lies, and trading-lies," in the other bubonic plague.[18] The impossibilities of shutting up houses and shutting up shop are coordinate. They configure a discursive environment where it is impossible to "shut up" conversation; where trade and disease spread by conversation; and in which relationship, rather than the isolated individual, is the culpable vector. Natural human resistance to isolation ("conversation is call'd life") supports the mutuality of risk. The basis of the Lie/the Plague in irrepressible language production restricts the possibility of producing texts that encompass (and hence circumscribe) the play of risk. The man whose leg smarted at the approach of an infected person "conversed freely"; he kept an antidote, but H. F. admits that "how far it may be depended on I know not" (151). H. F.'s text eschews certainty because he cannot tell with whom the man spoke, whether he contracted the disease or gave it to others. The relational nature of plague conditions the discursive limits of the text just as unlimited discourse conditions the reach of the plague.

H. F. acknowledges the ineffability of plague phenomena, hence the incapacity of language to provide transparent readings of them:

This may serve a little to describe the dreadful Condition of that Day [looking into the pit], tho' it is impossible to say any Thing that is able to give a true Idea of it to those who did not see it, other than this, that it was indeed *very, very, very* dreadful, and such as no Tongue can express. (53–54)

"Tongue" implies *any* language, the whole of Babel, but also resonates with the anatomy of the speaker, suggesting that humans would shrink from naming such "very, very, very dreadful" sights. Truth exists, therefore, in conveying the unresolved dialectic between outsize phenomena and the generic limitations of language, citing as well one's own very human resistance to recalling unspeakable scenes.[19] "[I]t is impossible to describe the Variety of Postures, in which the Passions of the poor people would Express themselves" (69). "The Confusion among the People, especially within the City at that time, was inexpressible" (142). Such formulaic recitations, in a "journal" written (in the first instance) for one's personal edification, suggest a profound disjunction between phenomena and the medium of representation, as well as between phenomena and the will to reimmerse oneself in sensory overload.[20] Even where signifiers seem adequate to the signified, texts seem belated, obsolete reminders of phenomenal flux:

by the time that the Houses were known to be infected, most of the Persons infected would be stone dead, and the rest run away for Fear of being shut up; so that it was to very small Purpose, to call them infected Houses and shut them up; the Infection having ravaged, and taken its Leave of the House, before it was really known, that the Family was in any way touch'd. (133)

One cannot "call" these sites "infected Houses," since it is pointless to bring them into discourse. The shutting up of houses is a type of fiction of stability, exposed as unable to remain a current representation of a phenomenon that continually escapes (en)closure.

The failure of quarantine resonates with the unstoppable flight of discrediting rumor in *The Compleat English Tradesman*. Both evince the underlying logic of "conversation," all momentum and no origin:

If then the blow is thus insensibly striking – if the arrow flies thus unseen, and cannot be discovered – to what purpose are all the schemes for shutting up or removing the sick people? (213)

[T]ho' sometimes the malicious occasion is discovered, and the author detected and exposed; yet how seldom is it so? and how much oftner are ill reports rais'd to ruin and run down a Tradesman . . . and like an arrow that flies in the dark, it wounds unseen. (I, 191)

The unseen flying arrow, which in the case of rumour *is* conversation, leaves no trace of its trajectory; infection comes to light only after the arrow "wounds." The metaphoric exchange between plague and credit, compacting both the vulnerability of the flesh and the unpredictability of the market into the logic of conversation, suggests that at the level of logic both phenomena coalesce. It is impossible to resurrect events, to put them into a comprehensible compass. The "author" of events (of pernicious wounding conversation) eludes the author who would attempt it. Texts are "true" to the extent that they reproduce the logic of a vague, elusive market. *The Compleat English Tradesman* reproduces such logic by enacting it, baffling the reader, inculcating without ever announcing that texts in the market are opaque. *A Journal of the Plague Year* acknowledges its own limitations, grounding them in the nature of plague, of language, and ultimately the human condition.

H. F.'s resistance to authorial "authority" is evinced in his unwillingness to endorse vile "reports":

[I]t was reported, that the Buriers were so wicked as to strip [the dead] in the Cart, and carry them quite naked to the Ground: But as I can not easily credit any thing so vile among Christians, and at a Time so fill'd with Terrors, as that was, I can only relate it and leave it undetermined. (55)

Typically, H. F. qualifies a report simultaneously with its relation, the mounting horror of an event jostling with a rhetoric of noncommitment – "it seems," "it was suggested," "I suppose," it "cou'd not be certain":

Another Cart, it seems, found in the great Pit in Finsbury Fields, the Driver being Dead, or having been gone and abandon'd it, and the Horses running too near it, the Cart fell in and drew the Horses in also: It was suggested that the Driver was thrown in with it, and that the Cart fell upon him, by Reason of his Whip was seen to be in the Pit among the Bodies; but that, I suppose, cou'd not be certain. (143)

In H. F.'s account, the cart, the horses, the whip in the pit, literally pile on top of each other. The sequence of how they came there – the cart's trajectory, the horses' motion, the driver's fate – is lost, splayed into alternative narratives indicated by "or" and "but." The passage is a discursive correlative of the pit, into which the facts (whatever they are) have disappeared. Because he is uncertain, H. F. is paradoxically accurate in describing plague, which like an arrow that flies unseen "cannot be discovered." The uncertainty of the plague – why it struck, whom it will strike, when – is reflected in H. F.'s reticent, qualified account, which delivers "truth" by way of the absence of closure. H. F. discursively reproduces the *modus operandi* of the plague, and in that sense is Honest. That he did not substantially revise his account for publication, allowing it to stand with all its recursions, qualifications, and silence, signifies H. F. as (literally) lacking any of the "designs" cited in the prefaces to *Crusoe*, *Moll*, and *Roxana*.[21]

The text's most compelling demonstration of the disjunction between plague and attempts at textual embodiment involves the Bills of Mortality, themselves the most conspicuous texts in *A Journal*. By acknowledging the Bills' inadequate description of deaths from plague, the journal conveys the plague's ability to escape confinement – in houses, in texts. The closest simulacrum to accounting texts, the Bills likewise do not acknowledge their statistical fragility. Yet H. F. makes a point of it, noting how the process of compiling numbers degenerates as death takes a toll on the compilers themselves:

I have Reason to be assur'd, [the Bills] never gave a full Account, by many thousands; the Confusion being such, and the Carts working in the Dark, when they carried the Dead, that in some Places no account at all was kept, but they work'd on.

Now when, I say, that the Parish Officers did not give a full Account . . . let any one but consider how Men could be exact in such a Time of dreadful Distress, and when many of them were taken sick themselves, and perhaps died in the very Time when their Accounts were to be given in.

Indeed the Work was not of a Nature to allow them Leisure, to take an exact Tale of the dead Bodies, which were all huddled together in the Dark into a Pit. (82–83)

Like H. F.'s own account of the death cart, the parish officers' disappears "into a Pit" that stifles inquiry. As Defoe does in *Crusoe*,

Moll, and *Roxana*, H. F. brings to the surface the Bills' mode of production, which obviously affects their accuracy but which would normally be suppressed. In *A Journal*, however (unlike Defoe in the other novels) H. F. leaves no doubt that the mode of production renders accurate accounting impossible. Plague flows into the Bills' fabric even more conspicuously than credit sinks accounting in *The Compleat English Tradesman*. The distance between the Bills' pretentious certainty (much like that of inland bills), and H. F.'s own persistent qualification (which includes exposure of the Bills) measures H. F.'s Honesty.

The Bills epitomize textual insufficiency, and require constant reinterpretation: ". . . though the Bills said but 68 [died] of the Plague; every body said there had been 100 at least, calculating it from the usual Number of Funerals" (10). ". . . the Misery of those that gave Suck, was in Proportion as great [as those dead with child]. Our Bills of Mortality cou'd give but little light in this" (97). "I might reckon up more, who, within the compass of my Knowledge or Observation, really drowned themselves in that Year, than are put down in the Bill" (132). The Bills claim to provide a total, albeit abstract version of the plague, but by attempting to abstract experience their totalizing project fails. *A Journal* does not abstract, but leaves lacunae, and in so doing renders the totality of an experience whose impact was essentially incalculable. Paul Alkon has suggested that H. F.'s "explicit disclaimers" and "omission of any attempt to describe" phenomena, involve readers "in some effort to imagine additional details."[22] Yet if readers indulge any such inclination, writing their own text, they transgress the nature of plague, producing a fiction of stability with too much detail to be True. The definitive text, during "such a Time," *is* the open text, acknowledging that definitiveness is impossible. The reader is forced into a mode of retreat. Unless he has extra-textual "Knowledge or Observation," he must accept the (open) text as the limit case.[23]

A Journal validates itself, much like *Crusoe*, *Moll*, and *Roxana*, outside a regime of explicit fidelity to events. When relating the story of the three men who survive by living off the land, H. F. argues: "Their Story has a Moral in every Part of it . . . and if there was no other End in recording it, I think this a very just one, whether my Account be exactly according to Fact or no" (100). This is more than the Bills can do by claiming absolute certainty. Indeed, H. F. suggests that behind the Bills' seeming (dis)closure lay a manipulating impulse, ironically linked to fraud on the community and resistance to the shutting up of houses. In effect, the Bills are stockjobbed, their numbers rearranged to baffle the creditor/reader:

People were very loth at first to have the Neighbors believe their Houses were infected, so they gave Money to procure, or otherwise procur'd the dead Persons to be return'd as dying of other Distempers . . . as will be seen by the vast Encrease of the Numbers plac'd in the Weekly Bills under other Articles of Diseases. (161)

At this point in the narrative, H. F. comes as close as possible to identifying the bills with marketplace textuality, identifying texts in the market (were there any doubt) as inherently manipulable and suspect. The discourse of plague and the discourse of credit, which participate in metaphoric exchange throughout the period and indeed in *A Journal* itself, *cease* to be metaphoric equivalents, and at the level of textuality become equivalent in fact. Though H. F. does not dwell on this convergence, it is a stunning moment in the text, exposing a Defoean project to situate *A Journal* within a discourse of marketplace texts, and to discredit such of those texts making claims to certainty.

By destabilizing fictions of stability, H. F. is a foil to his own commercial culture. A substantial merchant familiar with accounting, he nonetheless interrogates its conventions, eschewing any pretension that texts abstract reality into art. His imperfect articulacy is a gambit, detracting from his "authority" but finally discrediting discursive formations that establish such authority. In the end, authority is reconstituted in another, if more modest mode – not in the grandiose certainty of bills of exchange, bills of mortality, and double entry bookkeeping, but in the recusal of an author who perceives discursive limits. H. F. poses the question of how far representation *can* be certain, and extricates his own ego from the answer. His Honesty is elevated to an existential concern.

H. F.'s ultimate ascription of the plague to supernatural forces ("it was evidently from the secret invisible Hand of him, that had first sent this Disease" [191]), anchors the text in a mode of referentiality that by definition defies definition. Its resistance to the commonplaces of language is curiously ironic – plague is spread by "conversation." But in a trope of existential terror, plague advances wordlessly: "[D]eath now began not, as we may say, to hover over everyone's Head only, but to look into their Houses, and Chambers, and stare into their

Faces" (33). Plague produces a type of antidiscourse, a scene of urban apocalypse where communication is displaced, not only by phenomena resistant to language, but by violent acts that preempt language altogether.[24] H. F. describes the brutal incident of a woman embraced by a man who "told her he had the Plague, and why should not she have it as well as he" (128). It is followed by the attempted incursion into a house of one who announces, "I have got the Sickness, and shall die to morrow Night" (129). It is hard to know whether such persons are deranged or vindictive; H. F. finesses rumors that victims are intent on infecting the well, and suggests that both the diseased and the healthy complain against each other. If the question remains unresolved, neither does H. F. permit himself the comfort of denial. He remains open to data that could be resolved (if resolution were possible) into a hideous truth. He lives suspended in uncertainty, the very opposite of an accounting mentality, where one is always in sight of closure.

A Journal is an experiment in living without fictions of stability. It suggests that one *can* accommodate to uncertainty, indeed one must, since the only alternative "in such a Time" is hysteria. The plague-world is the world of credit before one narrative or another precipitates. H. F.'s ability to survive suspended in uncertainty evinces a kind of dogged sanity.[25] It models a type of right reading/writing in a credit/plague episteme. As such, it is a brilliant rationalization of Defoean fiction, picking up where Crusoe left off in *Serious Reflections*, instructing potential readers of Defoe's later texts. Yet if it argues the paradox that the text in the market is forthcoming precisely because it is not, such an argument is a Defoean fantasy, proper to an author – H. F. – unconstrained by market demands for certainty. It is as if the Tradesman had refused the creditor's demand for payment on a fixed date, since he feared no reprisals. Such a posture is hardly sustainable.

Arguably, *A Journal of the Plague Year* is Defoe's deepest ideological fiction, an effort to sway public opinion in favor of the government's quarantine measures.[26] In a positivistic sense, it probably is. Yet it is also the most overtly self-reflexive of all of Defoe's texts, and I suggest that at its most highly motivated level, it is an ideological fiction about the project of fiction itself. If it is propaganda, it is propaganda for Defoe. By presenting a character – a tradesman! – who rejects fictions of stability, Defoe invites readers to do so. The crux, of course, is that Defoe cannot issue such an invitation in his own name. He is tied to a market that demands certainty, and a *real* tradesman – such as Defoe – cannot ignore the market. Had he written *A Journal* in his own name, it would have been an apparent fiction.

A Journal, therefore, is speculative, coming as close as Defoe ever does to advocating (albeit vicariously) avowed uncertainty. In *Roxana*, Defoe examines the posture of the author of fiction, but the market is inescapable, and the author must navigate its demands.

CHAPTER 5

Lady Credit's reprise: "Roxana"

THE READER IN THE TEXT

The Compleat English Tradesman suggests that fiction cannot be identified a priori – potential fiction is a risk of marketplace texts. The prefaces of *Crusoe*, *Moll*, and *Roxana*, flaunting an affiliation with print- (and hence market-) culture, reinscribe the generic elusiveness of commercial texts, deferring interrogation of the protagonist/authors. "Promiscuously conversing" with other texts in the market, Defoe's narrative fictions construct "fiction" as a generalized perceptual crux, neither confined nor mediated by a genre that localizes and avows fictionality. As such, Defoe's fictions resist formalist, exclusively aesthetic analyses that assign them to a genre: the novel. They emerge into focus only contingently, as nodes in a textual/contextual matrix that elaborates marketplace "fiction." Thus it is anachronistic to suggest that because the final episodes of *Roxana* describe a plotted trajectory, anticipating narrative closure, the text displays impulses adumbrating the "novel." Such dehistoricizing of form casts *Roxana* as an autonomous aesthetic object, remote from tropes in the market that (through seductive "appearance") suspend (dis)closure and enable generic evasion. In this chapter I argue that *Roxana*, which formalists cite as inviting readers to accept it as fiction, dramatizes the opposite motion: a terror that fiction may be exposed. *Roxana* explores the limits of authorial capacity to sustain generic uncertainty, hence evade accountability.

In this heuristic mode, *Roxana* (or rather Roxana) is an ironic reprise of Lady Credit, the tour de force narrative phenomenon who defies (dis)closure. As the primary projection of Defoe's discourse of generic evasion, Lady Credit is poised to inhabit Defoe's most ambitious generic evasions, the narrative fictions that concatenate with rise and fall in the speculative market. Indeed, I argue that she is deployed as the whore she becomes when the Bubble bursts, once again (in the person of Roxana) registering Defoe's relationship to fictions that inhabit the market without avowing fictionality. Like Lady Credit, Roxana is a Lady/Mistress (*The Fortunate Mistress . . . the Lady Roxana*) with a past. As a whore, a commodity, she expands her wealth fabulously. Tutored by England's foremost, controversial financier, Robert Clayton, Roxana becomes a construction of the market, like Lady Credit an extension of its discourse. Even the modulations of her name evoke the unstable market evinced in Lady Credit's career as royal mistress/tradesman's wife. "Mademoiselle de Beleau, afterwards call'd The Countess of Wintelsheim . . . Being the Person known by the Name of the Lady Roxana," shifts from French to German to an Anglicization that elides a "real" name, ironically the same as her cast-off daughter's, Susan. Also like Lady Credit, Roxana resists domestication, for a long time refusing to marry the Dutch Merchant so as to preserve financial independence.

Roxana's affinity with Lady Credit comes under pressure in the last third of *Roxana*, when she decides to disown her narrative, adopt a Quaker's persona, and pretend that the past never happened – with her maid Amy, to "transform ourselves into a new Shape" (II, 13). The difficulty is that unlike Lady Credit, who kept the Whigs off-guard, Roxana encounters a reader who is astute, who believes that textuality is finite, that readers can exit the text to test its veracity. Roxana's elaborate persona is threatened by Susan, the discarded daughter obsessed with establishing Roxana's maternity. Susan excavates the past, piecing together the person beneath the persona. The counterpoint between Susan and Roxana, a chessgame in narrative, is riveting. Lady Credit's casual reassumptions of virtue, her assault on linearity and hence on history, cannot be easily reproduced in a "real" woman. Roxana agonizes over "whether I was to be expos'd or not expos'd" (II, 105). Amy vows to murder Susan. She apparently keeps her word.

Within the context of Roxana's struggle to evade history, Susan emerges as the nightmare reader. Undeterred by militant nonlinearity in a narrative subject, Susan is determined to read for coherence, to refabricate Roxana *as* History, not Story, without regard to Roxana's evasions or the cost of such a project. She refuses to be bound by the decorum of uncertainty produced and embodied by Lady Credit. Why? If Roxana is the post-Bubble expression of Lady Credit, the latest female incarnation of the elusive marketplace text, then Susan is the post-Bubble reader. *Conceived* post-Bubble, she is burned by Air-Money texts, determined to uncover their veiled perpetrators and to hold them to account. She neither crumples in bafflement nor drifts towards "appearance," but assimilates extratextual discourse to establish a provenance, test a text's authority. Her approach (epistemological, physical) is maddening because it bends to no constraint. It disregards a decorum of reading that accepts textuality as the limit case, controlled by an author configured by a market in which ladylikeness is "recovered." In light of the discourse surrounding the Bubble, Susan is the Annuitant embittered, the Orphan turned sour, the disabused Defoe of *A Brief Debate Upon the Dissolving of the Late Parliament*. She and Roxana are each other's text and context.[1]

Thus if Lady Credit is the new woman in the market, circulating on her own terms while regenerating an original virtue, then Roxana aspires to that condition; if Defoe is engaged with Roxana as he is with Lady Credit, then (through Roxana's engagement with Susan) Defoe is addressing self-reflexively the narrative consequences of personae that *can* be detected; if readers (such as Susan) will maneuver around personae, detecting the reality behind the fiction, then fiction in the market – notably Defoe's – can be "expos'd." Crusoe, The Right Honourable the Countess of —, Roxana, would fall before unruly readers, sharing the fate of Lady Credit in her post-Bubble disgrace.

Viewed as opposite "takes" on a single project – authorial evasiveness – Roxana and Lady Credit emerge as sites in which Defoe, configuring the discourse of the market through a woman's capacity to sustain open-ended narrative, reflects on his own capacity to sustain generic indeterminacy. In Defoe's frame of reference, Lady Credit succeeds monumentally, eluding the powerful Whigs. Even after Defoe acknowledges her shiftiness, discourse a decade later registers surprise. Roxana is the reverse: conceived post-Bubble, she registers a certain decline in Defoe's discursive assurance. Her text takes up the case of a reader who refuses indeterminacy; refuses to accept textuality as the limit case; who penetrates Roxana's persona despite frantic efforts to elude her. As a projection of marketplace disorder, Roxana's ordeal with Susan exposes the vulnerability of texts to (dis)closure when readers look a "Trojan Horse" in the mouth.

The ironic reemergence of Lady Credit in the person of Roxana, demonstrates that Defoe's concern with the viability of marketplace fiction is trans-generic, indeed it develops outside the bounds of genre. In both cases, Defoe conceives the project of marketplace fiction in terms that implicate a woman's sexual deportment, displacing his honesty as Author onto the gendered "honesty" of the female body. Through such displacement, Lady Credit, Roxana, and Defoe configure a single problematic: the sustainability of generic elusiveness in marketplace narratives. When we approach Roxana as a component of Defoe's obsession with marketplace fiction, *Roxana* evades readings that suppress a marketplace discourse, itself evasive, which the text appropriates.

As a marketplace text reflecting on marketplace texts, *Roxana* is the mirror image of *A Journal of the Plague Year*. It represents Defoe's dogged return to a regime where uncertain texts respond to demands for certainty. *A Journal* postulates readers in an economy of plague – credulous, bubbled by mountebanks, "buying" what the market offers. "At such a Time" authorial (dis)closure is impossible. Indeed, certainty equates with dissembling, and becomes a badge of fiction. Roxana, however, fears disclosure because certainty *is* possible. The history of a text escapes its author's jurisdiction. Unlike *A Journal*, then, *Roxana* confronts the obsessively close reader, determined to construct a text's generic affiliation. Whereas *A Journal* fantasizes authority unsubjected to demands for certainty, *Roxana* contemplates a discontented reader, able to overcome *un*certainty. Susan, like Boyer, Oldmixon, and Gildon, can blow a convenient cover, but because she is neither professional nor political she is the deeper threat. She enlarges (magnifies, liberates) the average reader, motivated solely by a will to know. She is the amateur policing the market, her own Gresham's Law expelling the pros that would police her.

The distance between *A Journal* and *Roxana*, between fuddled readers and those producing transparency, constitutes the normative Defoean scene: obscure representation and potential clarification are mutually suspended. To negotiate this scene, one strategy – Defoe's, optimally any author's – expands fictionality, further obscuring intent. The opposite strategy – Susan's, optimally any reader's – introduces extratextual data, intending to expose intent. The persistence of such readerly threat (to fictions that survive through generic instability) renders fiction's elusiveness vulnerable. It shifts the balance of power between author and reader, and by driving towards closure it undermines strategies of deferral and ambivalence endemic to the market.

My argument against attributing acknowledged fictionality to

Roxana reflects the text's contrapuntal resonance with such strategies. *Roxana* rearticulates ironically a market discourse that inhabits Defoe's oeuvre in its earliest stages.[2] The text is therefore embedded in the logic of the market; like the market it is obsessed with, committed to generic evasion; its irony is in broaching the uncertainty of generic uncertainty. However, if *Roxana* is a vehicle for ironic reinscription of the market, it cannot wilfully signal its own fictionality, thereby disinscribing the tension that constitutes the basis of its irony. Susan is the source of *Roxana*'s ironic tension, raising the possibility of generic disclosure that is wholly involuntary. Accordingly, I focus on Susan to meet claims that she is the agent of a plotted trajectory intended to signify deliberate fiction; more particularly, I show that Susan is not a mere feature of plot, a returning daughter who organizes the "Story." Within the textual/contextual matrix I have been urging, Susan is the return-of-the-repressed. She is the resurfaced term that marketplace logic elides: the reader undeterred by generic confusion. Alien to business-as-usual, she broaches the potential breakdown of epistemological norms, the logical possibility that readers may refuse uncertainty as a condition of reading. Her rogue epistemology resegregates fiction and truth, challenging the family romance that consigns Roxana's children to a "romance" of infinitely deferred disclosure. Her insistent daughterhood threatens the family romance of Roxana/Lady Credit/Defoe, where each sustains the other's ambiguity as mutually evasive texts. Susan's insurgence, therefore, marks Defoe as thinking the unthinkable; eschewing complacent marketplace logic; exposing marketplace women to a woman who threatens their own, hence Defoe's, ability to remain players in the market.

None of Defoe's other narrative fictions presents a character that disrupts conditions of reading that govern (and perplex) the narratives' reception. Except for *A Journal* (which is scripted outside the market) Defoe's generically uncertain narratives assume a discourse in which reader discontent is cowed, managed through devices that proliferate uncertainty. Susan's singular relationship with Roxana/Lady Credit/ Defoe broaches in Defoean discourse the immanent complications of an uncertain market, a market whose unpredictability encompasses unpredictable, undisciplined readers.

Rather than approaching Susan through readings that decontextualize *Roxana*, I want to show how the "plottedness" she precipitates evinces *Roxana*'s engagement in context, its assimilation through ironic inversion of a cultural/commercial discourse that permeates Defoe's oeuvre. Within this discourse, *Roxana*'s relation (or nonrelation) to the "rise of the novel" can be tried comprehensively. *Roxana*'s position within Defoe's oeuvre indeed emerges as "new," not because it avows fictionality but because it confronts the fragility of a fictional enterprise that does not concede fictionality. *Roxana* bespeaks Defoe's queasy appraisal of marketplace strategies of infinite deferral, his discomfit with participation in them. *Moll Flanders*, which I also discuss, contemplates the fragility of a fictive persona, but not as the outcome of lapsed market discipline and the ascendancy of rogue readers. Consistent with market norms, *Moll* acknowledges chance, the ever-present potential of uninduced revelation. Viewed against its predecessors, *Roxana* is neither outside the market like *A Journal*, nor squarely within it like *Moll*. Rather, it addresses a market itself out of phase. It suggests that market uncertainty can pitch into reverse, tipping the laws of chance in favor of readers.

By focusing on *Roxana*'s preoccupation with a contest between author and reader, I interrogate theories of the novel's "rise" that eschew accommodation with nonaesthetic phenomena, and miss the text/context dialectic that constitutes (and obscures) authorial intent.[3] In effect, I seek to postpone the novel's "rise" insofar as that implies the localization of overt, intentional fictionality in a "literary" text. Accordingly, I question formalist approaches to *Roxana* insofar as they authorize readings of the Susan episode based on, indeed privileging, transparent authorial intent. I explore the anomaly of how irrecoverable "intent" – at the heart of Defoe's evasive strategy in *The Compleat English Tradesman* – is neutralized by formalism, becoming an open book. Such neutering of Defoe's fundamental, market-based discourse is the result of assumptions that if *Roxana* displays causal relationships; if the plotted coherence of Susan's pursuit and Roxana's response defies a lifelike randomness; then Defoe must *intentionally* have adopted means that *announce Roxana's* fictionality. It holds that the cause and effect arrangement perceptible in *Roxana*, moves the narrative beyond "the purely evenemental and giddy unpredictability we find in the picaresque" prenovelistic fictions,[4] into the penumbra of the generic Novel.

"Taking up an oft-reiterated theme," Michael Boardman has developed the formalist position as respects *Roxana*,[5] and his approach provides a useful contrast to my own. In *Defoe and the Uses of Narrative*, he states that "the [novel] reader recognizes that he is in a narrative world controlled by the guiding consciousness of an implied author, whose decisions are manifested on every page and dictate local responses to the likely direction of the story."[6] At the same time that Defoe creates fictions "with an illusion of truth so opaque as to be impenetrable," he "experiments with ways of subverting his own illusory structures, of including within an overall illusion of historicity the knowledge that the reader is participating in a basically fictional world" (6).

Equating perceptible causality with *avowed* fictionality casts *Roxana* as "a new kind of story . . . positively recognizable as a story made and not [as in *Moll*] remembered, as discourse." *Roxana* "extends the obvious and unashamed invitation that can be offered just as blatantly by a new kind of structure as by Fieldingesque commentary."[7] Such a view poses the issue of how we should read the Susan episode, and ultimately *Roxana*. Does *Roxana* dramatize a reader-in-the-text who would interrogate Roxana and enforce (dis)closure, or is the text concerned with the reader of *Roxana*, displaying a "delighted apprehension that he partakes of patterned, purposeful fantasy?"[8]

These approaches diverge over whether Defoe would risk inscribing an avowed fiction. More particularly, they differ over what type of readers inhabited the market, i.e. what "attitudes" towards potential fiction were plausible to Defoe. My interpretation (the former) posits a community of readers disciplined to accept uncertainty, and a rogue reader escaped from market discipline, determined to establish a text's generic affiliation. Such a reader threatens the very concept of sustainable uncertainty. Formalism, however, posits a discursive formation where Truth and Fiction are discrete; readers are receptive to fiction; authors and readers are allied. Such a view does not notice, much less attempt to assimilate, a Defoean oeuvre that both before and after *Roxana* is obsessed with generic evasion. Reading *Roxana* as continuous with a Defoean oeuvre that rearticulates contemporary commercial discourse, identifies Susan's murder as a blow that maintains indeterminacy.[9]

Roxana has been analyzed as an individuating consciousness, defining herself within an "environment [that] is ultimately a set of external problems to be analysed and solved rather than a set of involving and ineffable determinants."[10] I would suggest, however, that as a marketplace operative, Roxana *expects* to "analyze and solve" the Susan problem through marketplace strategies, i.e. by adopting an elusive persona, only to discover that Susan does not respond to marketplace norms. Such norms become "ineffable determinants," unable to constrain predictably. Roxana's "environment" turns on the author to baffle the author; it does not (as it should) surround the reader to baffle the *reader*. As Roxana ponders Susan, wondering "whether I was to be expos'd or not expos'd," the intractable reader emerges as an instrument of the market – an ambivalent Air-Money text – ceasing to behave as a frustrated *object* of discourse. The irony of *Roxana* is that the creditor/reader, no longer credulous, must herself be read, while manifesting the impenetrability of conventional marketplace texts. In a further, eerie dissemination of Lady Credit, *Susan* assimilates credit's instability *without* irony, shifting registers of knowability by seeming to know/not-know Roxana, goading Roxana toward infinite uncertainty.[11] It is as if in response to *Roxana*'s prefatorial warning "It is not always necessary that the Names of Persons shou'd be discover'd," Susan retorts "It is necessary for me!" If she resists the epistemology of the market, can she overcome it? In the ultimate ironic exchange of positions, the reader becomes uninterpretable, while the text she is reading, Roxana, opens towards clarity.

By envisioning the ironic reversal of a market characterized by irony, *Roxana* is crucially positioned between the logic of the credit-based market – confidently deployed from the *Review* through the preface of *Roxana* itself – and *The Compleat English Tradesman*, which massively seeks to rehabilitate that logic. In *Roxana*, Defoe explores the fragility of a regime that blurs the outlines of fiction and truth and insulates the author of fiction. He opposes to it an undaunted reader who daunts the author. In effect, *The Compleat English Tradesman* assaults Susan's potential acolytes, insisting for hundreds of pages that Susan's "success" is *sui generis*; that texts in the market are opaque; that author(ity) is dispersed, unaccountable, inculpable. Because I read *Roxana* as interrogating the viability of elusive potential fiction, and see Roxana as the ironic reincarnation of the most elusive of Defoe's fictions, I do not think *Roxana* "extends the obvious and unashamed invitation" to accept it as fictive. David Marshall apprehends Defoe's elusiveness when he identifies Susan as "*the* reader" (153), whose apparent murder abruptly terminates the (real) reader of a fictive text. By linking Susan to the market, I historicize Marshall's perception that *Roxana* concerns the detection of fiction. That is, I seek to ground the act of reading, and hence my response to formalist analysis, in an historically specific moment – the aftermath of the Bubble, the fall of Lady Credit, and the dependence (nonetheless) of marketplace texts on an impenetrable fictive potential. As Gary Waller observes with regard to the constitution of reading practices:

The history of reading is not merely a history of ideas about reading, constructing ideal models of reading as predictable from the "intentions" of texts; it is a history of real, material readers, men and women, and of the complex social formations that produced them as readers. Just as texts are written within particular social formations, so they are read within what [Tony] Bennett terms "reading formations," a selection or repertoire of assumptions, attitudes, material practices about how and to what ends to read, who should read, and for what purposes, as coded by institutional, class or gender, or other social factors. Reading is always culture specific, and what appear to be the natural practices by which reading occurs are in fact culturally produced, and so always a site of cultural struggle.[12]

Whether or not Defoe consciously constituted the Susan episode within a regime of causality, he need not have concluded (based on his own reading practices, i.e. without novels as models!) that causality necessarily betrays artistic intent. Indeed, the epistemology of the market founded "art" in the creation of narratives suspended between causal motivation and chance, where "cause" (in the form of an "author") could not be traced. Defoe's embeddedness in marketplace discourse would have deflected an impulse to produce anomalous texts whose outcome seemed controlled, "plotted," the work of an implied author. Authorial "intent" and historical process are coordinate in fashioning Defoe, as well as the rationalizations he offers to impede detection of fiction. The suggestion that Defoe would "blatantly" offer overt fiction isolates writerly intent, ignoring the dynamic between aspiration and the historical process to which it responds. Indeed, such an approach to *Roxana* is founded on a certain skepticism towards contemporaneity that (by ignoring the mutual engagement of text and context) overstates the case against historicism, at least New Historicism:

Historicism assumes that authors are invariably creatures of the social moment and that the most important thing about their fictions is how they reveal history behind the veil of fabulation . . . [T]here is no necessary relationship between the existence of a scene of historical conflict and the process, intensely personal and idiosyncratic, that results in a fictional text.[13]

The "scene of historical conflict" between author and reader is constituted by (and constitutes) commercial textuality. It exposes the generic elusiveness of such textuality; reader ennui; demands for certainty; the complication of elusive tropes. Defoe operates within this scene, whose instability is dramatized in *Roxana*.

Roxana lives in fear that revelation of her past will expose her negligence as a mother, as well as her previous whoredom. She cannot even approach the offspring that she wantonly abandoned:

I cou'd by no means think of ever letting the Children know what a kind of Creature they ow'd their being to, or giving them an Occasion to upbraid their Mother with her scandalous Life, much less to justifie the like Practice from my Example. (II, 9)

Roxana experiences conflict between desire for connection and fear of disclosure. While she needs to be read, she needs to evade being read, since apprehension – in terms of being understood – implies apprehension in terms of being caught, taken into custody by public evaluation. Roxana's past stalls her, it alienates aspiration. Her adopted persona, she hopes, will suppress her former identity, putting her "into some figure of Life in which I might not be scandalous to my own Family, and be afraid to make myself known to my own Children" (II, 10–11). Roxana wants *ultimately* to be read, but on terms that disown previous self-iterations. She would have the temporal maneuverability – the unaccountability – of a Defoe, who unwrites the narrative of another fallen Lady.

Amy becomes the agent of Roxana's flight from history, offering "a Scheme how you shall, if you have a-mind to it, begin and finish a perfect entire Change of your Figure and Circumstances in one day" (II, 13). The speech implicates Defoe, a controlling intelligence who in a day – literally from one edition of the *Review* to the next – transforms a whore into a Lady. This promise of instant change delivers Roxana to the discourse of credit: Lady Credit, Air-Money, the Funds. In the *modus operandi* of credit, such lack of fixity favors authors. Amy, and by devolution Roxana, affiliate to a matrix of expectations in which identity can be displaced, dispersed, disowned. They commit to a version of history constituted by the palimpsestual texts of credit, written over as if erased. Amy conscripts Roxana into this process. Roxana's recursive narrative, recording her venture into it:

I must go back here, after telling openly the wicked things I did, to mention something . . . (I, 220)

I must now go back to another Scene and join it to this End of my Story . . . (II, 82)

I must go back to [Amy's] Relation of the Voyage which they made to Greenwich together (II, 140)

becomes like palimpsest, laid down over what seemed a finished text. Thus *Roxana*, embedded in a type of history writing (as in *The Secret History of the Secret History*) that denies the ineffaceability of history, becomes the correlative of Defoe's effort to test – through Roxana – whether infinite elusiveness is consistent with unconstrained pursuit.

By adopting this "Scheme," changing costume and locale, Roxana positions herself as confident author, suppressing and rewriting narrative, planning to recur to the past in "some figure of Life" which "might not be scandalous." Taking up life as an apparent Quaker in another part of London (while giving out that she has left town), Roxana believes she has successfully displaced her person with a persona that bears no relation to it, that she is as invisible, for example, as The Right Honourable the Countess of —:

[T]here was not a QUAKER in town looked less like a Counterfeit than I did; But all this was my particular Plot to be the more completely conceal'd, and that I might depend upon being not known, and yet not being confin'd like a Prisoner, and be always in Fear . . . (II, 19)

Roxana thinks she can circulate (not be "confin'd") as if she were a shiny new-minted piece of counterfeit. In her own analysis, her lack of "intrinsick" value is compensated for by appearance. She fails to appreciate that appearance is not a barrier to history; it is a condition of history, unstable, inclined to elaborate itself in history. As John M. Warner observes, Roxana tries to mythicize history, that is to escape the diachronic, "but her past life in the figure of Susan, symbolizing all the inassimilable contingency of linear history, finally destroys her."[14]

In revising her appearance, Roxana's recourse to less elegant dress relies on the principle invoked in the preface to *Roxana*, whose Relator may be "dressing up the Story in worse Cloathes than the Lady, whose Words he speaks, prepar'd it for the World." Both Roxana, and the eponymous text circulating in the market, attempt to deflect attention from the "real" author of the text (in *Roxana* the "History" will "speak for itself" – for neither Roxana *nor* Defoe). Yet while the preface makes ambiguous claims (shabby "Cloathes" correspond to truth claims that may also be frayed), Roxana sallies forth as if she were indeed The Right Honourable the Countess of —. She adopts a totalizing strategy that reflects a belief that her fiction is completed, impervious to interrogation (i.e. history can be changed in an instant, and changed for good). The preface, "always in Fear," alternates between intimations of History and Story that impart the sense of radical nonclosure associated with marketplace texts. Roxana's posture is against the grain. Her sense of having finished disseminating fiction alerts the reader to an impending ironic reversal, a recursion to the condition of the preface, to the condition of texts in the market: congenital instability. In assuming that she can remove herself from necessities of texts in the market, Roxana assumes that no demands will be made that she account for herself; she assumes that she will not have to respond to such demands by continued invention. What *works* for marketplace texts works against Roxana. Her ironic relation to the market becomes apparent: Roxana doesn't know she will have to remain actively promulgating fiction. When Roxana begins to torture herself with guilt, we imagine an ironic reversal of her appearance; when Susan emerges, we are prepared for her as an agent of irony.

Yet while Roxana assumes that she can circulate, she fears intimacy. Initially, she resists the Dutch Merchant's renewed interest, fearing "if I shou'd come into a close Correspondence with him, he shou'd any-way come to hear what kind of Life I had led" (39). However, the Merchant is consistently indifferent to Roxana's past. Even after they marry, Roxana's fear that Susan's revelations "wou'd have been enough to have ruin'd me to all Intents and Purposes with my Husband" (89) are unfounded.[15] The Dutch Merchant greets the Captain's announcement that "your Lady has got a Daughter more than she expected" (119), as if the Captain "had brought a Tale by-halves, and, having heard it one way, had told it another" (120). Such complaisance before ambiguity evinces a reader disciplined by the market, insufficiently motivated to investigate a potential Daughter. As Lincoln Faller has pointed out, Susan is not a threat. To the people who know more about Roxana than she could bear, Roxana is "more an item of friendly gossip than of scandal" (235). I suggest, therefore, that Roxana's fear of impending ruin; her refusal to recognize Susan; her inability to abide in a new (seemingly airtight) persona, reflect an inability to escape the logic of narrative –

an inability to be a Lady Credit. Roxana is tortured by memory, even when she tries to erase public memory.

After an initial self-confidence, she feels intensely unsettled. Roxana is trapped in – one could say scripted by – the logic of her own past:

> There was a Dart struck into the Liver; there was a secret Hell within, even all the while, when our Joy was at the highest, but more especially *now*, after it was all over, and when according to all appearance, I was one of the happiest Women upon Earth; all this while, I say, I had such a constant Terror upon my Mind as gave me every now and then very terrible Shocks, and which made me expect something frightful upon every Accident of Life. (II, 75)

Roxana's "Hell within," which becomes the "Hell within" *Roxana*, is not so much *caused* by Susan's pursuit as *validated* by it. Susan is the objective correlative of narrative's resistance to closure (even "after it was all over," "it" wasn't), a resistance that confutes Roxana's attempt to retain a fixed, fictive persona. Roxana is the ironic version of Lady Credit because – in her own mind – the motility of history (the fluidity of narrative) is a source of pain, not triumph. The reader chasing Roxana is Roxana, unable to shed awareness of her own guilt: history keeps coming back. Susan is the projection of Roxana's self-perception. She becomes its agent, validating Roxana's guilt by seeming to know it, stimulating Roxana to imagine outsize consequences if "expos'd." For Roxana, Susan embodies the character of narrative in the market: open, unfixed, uncertain. The point is that if history convicts authors by the very quality of its unfixity, how can they pretend that the logic of the market works to their advantage, that history can be *suspended* in uncertainty? If the reader chasing Roxana is Roxana, the reader chasing both is Defoe, deploying Susan as a stalking horse. The "Terror" upon Roxana's "Mind," reflected in a fear that fiction collapses, is ultimately the sense that history does *not* collapse. History chases authors. In the vision of *Roxana*, the market is in a race with its own reality.

Susan is able to reconstitute History, to piece it together despite Story. Initially, she confronts Amy with "a broken Account of things" (II, 86), but she is dangerous because she has enough information to acquire more. Susan "said she did not question to find [Roxana], for she knew where she was gone to live privately, but tho' she might be remov'd again, for I know how it is, says she, with a kind of Smile, or a Grin, I know how it all is, well enough" (88). "She would go find

[Roxana] out; adding, that she made no doubt but she cou'd do it, for she knew where to enquire the Name of her new Husband" (90). For Susan, discourse does not disseminate Roxana; it renders her available, a congeries of data to be assembled. The market's mechanism has pitched into reverse. Discourse is a potential bearer of truth, not fiction; it permits consolidation of a person, rather than her dispersal. History can be retrieved, even where it is submerged or written over. The question is whether Amy's claims are just. Roxana must read her "mysterious" reader:

> Well, I set Amy to-work; and, give Amy her due, she set all her Wits to-work, to find out which way this Girl had her Knowledge; but more particularly, how much Knowledge she had, that is to say, what she really knew, and what she did not know . . . how she cou'd say she knew who Madam Roxana was, and what Notions she had of that Affair was very mysterious to me . . . (II, 89)

For Roxana, the issue is whether Susan can reconstitute coherent narrative from scattered discourse, whether the pieces of her "broken Account" can assume enough order to configure phenomena.

In a fascinating passage, Roxana's sense of the persistence of narrative, and hence of her own guilt, fuses with her fear of Susan's pursuit, and hence of being "discover'd":

> I must acknowledge, the Notion of being discover'd carried with it so many frightful Ideas, and hurry'd my Thoughts so much, that I was scarce myself, any more than Amy, so dreadful a thing is a Load of Guilt upon the Mind. (II, 91)

Internal and external pressures overwhelm Roxana to the point where she seems to inscribe, albeit not consciously, her own dissolution. The passage suggests that Roxana is not herself any more than *Amy* is Roxana; it also suggests that Roxana is not herself any more than she is Amy. If Roxana is not herself and not Amy, then who is she? Has she so lost control of her persona to history that she is totally discourse, and therefore totally available to Susan? I suggest that she has.[16]

The most excruciating episode in Susan's pursuit of Roxana occurs on the ship intended to take Roxana beyond Susan's reach. The irony of this reversal is so intense as to be emblematic, demonstrating that narrative openness works against the fixity of the fictive persona. As Susan and Roxana face each other, reading each other in public, Roxana was to expect that [Susan] wou'd discover that she knew me, and yet was, by all means possible, to prevent it; I was to conceal myself, if possible, and yet had not the least room to do any-thing towards it; in short, there was no retreat; no shifting any-thing off; no avoiding or preventing her having a full Sight of me; nor was there any counterfeiting my Voice, for then my Husband would have perceiv'd it; in short, there was not the least Circumstance that offer'd me any Assistance or any favourable thing to help me in this Exigence. (II, 97)

Roxana's difficulty is that she must submit to being read by Susan, since "retreat" could itself be read against her, by Susan and by others. Paradoxically, the only means of hiding is not-hiding. But by allowing Susan "a full Sight" of her, Roxana forgoes control, exposed to Susan's scrutiny. Such examination matters incrementally, since Susan is reading her in context with prior readings, putting data together with what has accrued. The crux is that Roxana does not advance reciprocally. For Roxana, Susan is inscrutable. Since Roxana does not know whether she is recognized, and since Susan does not disclose herself, Roxana experiences a lonely, desperate helplessness. As readers, we participate in her anxiety, since *we* do not know whether Susan recognizes Roxana, nor can we find out by reading Susan read Roxana. Restricted to the text before us (watching Susan's face, eavesdropping on her speech, i.e. reading *Roxana*) Susan is a hermeneutic blank. Her impassivity may or may not be feigned. Unlike us and our proxy Roxana, Susan has the advantage of constructing the object of *her* reading (Roxana) from textual/extratextual data; she is not limited by a text (Roxana's persona) that might otherwise be opaque.

In the foregoing scene, Defoe dramatizes the disequilibrium precipitated by a reader unrestricted by a text. By forcing us into the position of relatively disabled readers, we appreciate the threat posed by Susan, whose mobility beyond the text permits her to elaborate it back into a surrounding history. Susan, moreover, presses her case. When the Quaker visits the Captain's wife, she encounters Susan, "impertinently inquisitive" (I, 100). The report of this visit throws Roxana into consternation – reading at a distance, she is convinced that Susan "had artfully conceal'd her Knowledge" until she could expose it to Roxana's disadvantage (II, 101). The ironies or Roxana's evasion of Susan begin to tell as her evasionary tactics themselves create occasions for exposure. Claiming that she is indisposed, Roxana is visited by the Captain's wife, bringing Susan in tow. Her dress prompts an exclamation from Susan, who compares it with the Turkish dress Roxana wore when Susan was her servant. The Captain's wife asks Susan to describe its provenance, and once again Roxana is trapped: with "no Vent, nobody to open myself to, or to make a Complaint to for my Relief," she is "oblig'd to sit and hear her tell the story of Roxana, that is to say, of myself, and not know at the same time, whether she was in earnest or in jest" (II, 105). Susan's information confronts Roxana with an irrepressible narrativity that may well engulf her, forcing the narrative stasis she had planned to radically deconstruct. When the Quaker introduces "the kind Motion to me, *to let the Ladies see my Dress*" (II, 113), Roxana is carried by narrative to the point of becoming complicit against herself.

The irony of Roxana's position is underscored by her near-miss conscription into expounding a narrative she would suppress. Roxana is not only Susan's *reader*, indeed her ineffectual reader. Roxana's *authorship* of her own narrative is overdetermined by Susan's initiative; Roxana verges on assisting a reader she would evade. Accordingly, the power relations between author and reader implicit in the fluidity of narrative are reversed. It is Susan's intent, not Roxana's, that is problematic in Roxana's signature plaint, "whether I was to be expos'd or not expos'd."

Susan continues to remain opaque, and in a stunning analogy Roxana remarks "this impertinent Girl . . . *was now my Plague*" (126). The observation resonates with *A Journal*, where plague moves like "the Arrow that flies unseen, and cannot be discovered." For Defoe, plague baffles because it gains strength through "conversation"; it resists confinement; it can be located only after its damage has been done. In Roxana's tortured imagination, Susan is assimilated to an agent – plague – which defies efforts to understand it and blasts attempts at certainty. Roxana demands certainty of Susan, "whether I was to be expos'd or not expos'd," but receives only uncertainty. As a reader, Susan escapes confinement by marketplace epistemology; she does not accept uncertainty; she confines the author in uncertainty. The image of plague brilliantly concentrates *Roxana*'s ironic momentum, a momentum that (by her invoking plague) Roxana imputes to her own narration. Coming so late in the text the remark is definitive, evincing Roxana's profound comprehension of her lack of comprehension. Susan endorses the ironic momentum perceived by Roxana with an ironic observation of her own: "I believe she [Roxana] does not know me, but I know her; and I know that she is my Mother"

(II, 129). Of course Roxana does "know" Susan, but the knowledge that she *would* possess continually eludes her.

As Susan closes in on disclosure, she becomes a stalker, "haunting" the Quaker (II, 143), "hunt[ing]" Roxana "like a Hound" (II, 145). Roxana relates Susan's boast: "if I did not remove very quickly, she wou'd find me out" (II, 150). When Susan vanishes, and it seems that Amy has committed murder, Susan persists – "she haunted my Imagination, if she did not haunt my house" (II, 154). In Roxana's "imagination," Susan maintains her wonted venue; she was never "real" in the sense of being realized, quantifiable, understood. The gory shapes that she assumes – "her Throat cut . . . her Head cut . . . her Brains knock'd out . . . hang'd up upon a Beam . . . drown'd" (II, 154) – correspond in death to the indeterminacy by which she always "plagued" Roxana, who imagines that Susan knows/doesn't know her identity. In a final turn evincing the reversal of reader/author relations, Roxana pursues Susan:

I sent to the Captain's Wife in Redriff, and she answer'd me, She was gone to her Relations in Spittle-Fields, I sent thither, and they said, she was there about three Weeks ago; but that she went out in a Coach with the Gentlewoman that us'd to be so kind to her, but whither she was gone, they knew not . . . (II, 154)

Roxana in pursuit of her reader (indeed an apparently dead reader) demonstrates readerly author-ity over narrative, in particular the narrative that *we* are reading. Roxana, who would flee her reader, cannot psychologically let go her reader, and would almost bring her back to life. Indeed, without her reader Roxana's narrative ends abruptly, unable to sustain itself.

In reflecting on Amy's crime, Roxana submerges it in Susan's aggressiveness: "that unhappy Girl . . . broke in upon all our Measures . . . and by an Obstinacy never to be conquer'd or pacifi'd, either with Threats or Perswasions, pursu'd her Search after me (her Mother) as I have said, till she brought me even to the Brink of Destruction" (II, 157–158). Susan "broke in." Like a burglar, she would have made off with Roxana's persona and "expos'd" it. She *had* made off with Roxana's narrative, unsettling its static complacency. In Roxana's mind, Susan is the proximate cause of her own demise. Like the creditor/reader in *The Compleat English Tradesman* she demands certainty, and will not be "conquer'd or pacifi'd" with uncertainty. The discourse of the market – of the debtor/author – inhabits Roxana's logic. She absolves herself, invoking self-defense:

Susan "wou'd in all probability, have trac'd me out at last, if Amy had not by the Violence of her Passion, and by a way which I had no knowledge of, and indeed abhorr'd, put a Stop to her" (II, 158). In the market, the debtor/author must stay a step ahead of the creditor/ reader, but the latter puts him in that "abhorr'd" position. For Roxana, Amy's "Violence" is the ultimate offer of certainty to Susan, the end of narrative – of *the* narrative, which Susan herself precipitated; it fulfills a promise.

At another level implicating the market, Susan "broke in" to the logic of the market itself. Breaking into Roxana's narrative, hijacking her elusive fictivity, Susan disregards norms of reading that naturalized generic confusion, making indistinction between truth and fiction the acceptable, inevitable posture of a text. Such confusion protects the author of potential fiction from accountability. Thus Susan breaks into Roxana's persona because she breaks out of the credit/fiction bind, attempting to read by dispelling confusion. For this reason Susan threatens the real author, Defoe, whose own "intent" is veiled behind the epistemological impasse of marketplace textuality. Susan is no Polite Reader, but a rogue. Apparently she suffers the fate of one.

THE READER OF THE TEXT

Roxana's flashback to Susan comprises the most compelling narrative in Defoe's fiction. In formalist logic it transforms *Roxana* from a collation of events into a self-conscious artistic display that prefigures the Novel, that signals the reader that the text is fiction.[17] I argue, however, that approaching *Roxana* through a hypothetical reader outside the text, instead of reading the actual reader within it, discounts the contemporary scene of reading – which the reader-in-the-text, Susan, engages. Susan destabilizes power relations between author and reader by negotiating an epistemology founded on impenetrable texts. Her "impertinently inquisitive" momentum goes to the heart of Defoe's defense against accounting for fiction. To the suggestion of overt fictionality in *Roxana*, I would respond: *why would Defoe demonstrate that with effort texts can be penetrated, when that demonstration would weaken his own strategy?* Would it not be better, more historically "accountable," to read the text as aware that such strategy is itself already weak? We should not shrink from attributing Roxana's terror to a crisis in authority, to a realization (Defoe's) that unaccountable fiction may be running out of time.

Moreover, if there is pattern in *Roxana*; if the reader is drawn towards anticipating Roxana's tragic end (which, in fact, I did not when I first read the text); even if on reflection "justice" emerges in her "inevitable" punishment,[18] none of this adds up to an "intent" to signal fictionality. If "didacticism" means anything, and if, in fact, Defoe seeks to be didactic, then it must appear that a real woman could have experienced Roxana's torment, that a real daughter could have emerged from an inescapable, deplorable past.[19]

In *Roxana*, Defoe allows an ordinary reader to confront a fictive text of his creation – Roxana – with an impulse towards forcing disclosure. That reader apparently succeeds, and is apparently killed. If we transpose Susan back into the market that generated her, it seems impossible that Defoe might signal *through* her that Fiction and Truth are separate, that *Roxana* is Fiction *tout court*. The possibility of such a gesture goes to the heart of *Finance and Fictionality*, named so as to recognize a dynamic between market discourse and authorial volition. If Defoe manifests an intent to "innovate," if he is the volitional site of literary "technique," his technique is overdetermined by a discourse which writes him, and into which Defoe-as-author dissolves (even as he authorizes that discourse). Contrary to any potential expression of exuberant fictionality is the fact that Defoe cannot take "credit" for fiction. Rather, he must sustain an environment of uncertainty where fiction does not *discredit* him. I am not denying that Defoe may deliberately have set out to produce a patterned text (though one might mischievously argue that the flashback was an afterthought, an "After-cheat" as it were). I am suggesting, however, that Defoe would not have wanted any such initiative to be taken for avowed fiction; that no unavoidable pressures required him to assume that it would be; that in fact "art" in the market obscured causality. The generic uncertainty of *Roxana* does not ultimately depend on its preface, but on a whole discursive formation that makes the preface inevitable.

By failing to appreciate the dynamic between volition and the market – where products of volition are made manifest – formalism posits uncompromised authorial potency. However, Defoe was only potent by seeming not to be. He comes into being discursively by reinscribing a discourse that erases his authorial persona and muddles the fictionality of its product. Defoe knows this, and explores its ironic potential – the potential that he may be unerased – in *Roxana*. The text demonstrates that there *is* a "necessary relationship" between "a scene of historical conflict" and the "intensely personal" project of creating fiction. Indeed, there is a relationship between historical conflict and the project of reading, in which such conflict is characterized by author/reader opposition. An interpretation of *Roxana* (or any Defoean fiction) that posits the mutuality of interest between author and reader, insofar as both can participate in the certainty of avowed fiction, is ahistorical. In my view the reader in the text (Susan) is a better clue to the reader outside it – and to Defoe's attitude towards such a reader – than conjectures which project onto Defoe's texts our own preoccupation with the "rise of the novel."[20] Defoe's concern to resist accountability as a maker of fictions is perhaps the best indication that he knew his readers' resistance to fiction. It was a resistance he did not seek openly to transgress.

Indeed, *Roxana*'s centrality to a Defoean metanarrative concerned with the "inquisitive" reader is pointed up, one might say counter-pointed, by *Moll Flanders*. A great commonplace of Defoe scholarship is that Moll remains fluid, never allowing herself to be fixed by the gaze of history. As William Ray observes:

Even once she no longer needs to steal, she continues her one-woman show, making deceit and role-playing not only her profession, but her avocation... Her identity gradually establishes itself within this ongoing game of metamorphosis, fascinated not merely with deceiving people, but with deceiving them with *new* disguises and ploys. As Marie-Paul Laden aptly puts it, "in Moll's case, disguise and successive rejections of the past self (as it becomes fixed, alien, other) *constitute* the self."[21]

Yet if Moll has a genius for disengaging history, it is also true that she never encounters a reader such as Susan, with the will, perspicacity, and prior proximity to halt her metamorphoses – indeed to spin them in reverse towards an originary site. Moll even eludes the interrogation of an examining magistrate. When learning her name, he fails to connect it with a "Flanders"-woman whose "Name was so well known among the People at Hick's-Hall, the Old baily, and such Places" (II, 69). Compared to Roxana, Moll inhabits a normative market of appropriately baffled readers, willing in fact to deploy the rhetoric of uncertainty in her defense, as when a crowd shouts ironically "Which is the Rogue? Which is the Mercer?" (II, 67). Moll is not brought down by the Law, by determined institution-alized pursuit. She succumbs to chance, to the fifty-fiftyness of happenstance. Surprized red-handed with brocade, she is held by two furious (but otherwise disinterested) "Wenches" until a constable comes (II, 97).

Moll's implication in chance distinguishes her from Roxana. Roxana plays chess, calculating and responding.[22] She fears the random. Moll plays dice. Her repeated deceptive acts are discontinuous, "successive rejections of the past self." She cultivates a regime of randomness to avoid establishing *any* sustained persona, however elusive. The riskiness of randomness, however, is that past performance is no assurance of present success.[23] Her account confronts potential ruin when, after stealing some linen worth £22, she remarks:

> I could fill up this whole Discourse with the Variety of such Adventures, which daily Invention directed to, and which I manag'd with the utmost Dexterity, and always with Success.
> At length – as when does the Pitcher come safely Home that goes so often to the Well? – I fell into some Broils, which tho' they could not affect me fatally, yet made me known, which was the worst thing next to being found Guilty, that could befall me. (II, 60–61)

The transition from "Success" to acknowledging that pitchers too often dipped in the well encounter "Broils," marks Moll as pushing the envelope of chance. Moll falls into a time/present constituted only from a pile-up of random events; at any point during that pile-up, she could have escaped her personal past. Had she seized the opportunity to leave a life of crime (to put a period on "Success') antecedent events would not have pursued her – there would have been no Susan, who pursues Roxana as an indelible, inevitable fact of Roxana's narrative. Moll gambles with Success, with the throw of the dice, once too often; she faces the law of chance rather than a persistent, knowledgeable pursuer who stares at her face.[24]

In some circumstances, Moll is a great weigher of odds. Deciding against a career in coining, she observes: "my Business seem'd to lye another Way, and tho' it had hazard enough in it too, yet it was more suitable to me . . . and more Chances for a coming off, if a Surprize should happen" (II, 77). Moll prepares against Surprize, rather than against a known threat building up a data bank. In her last Adventure, surprised in the act of stealing plate, she pulls out a spoon that ostensibly she plans to match. Twenty pounds in her purse confirm her "intent," and since the law lacks points of reference tying her to past crimes (and therefore makes no effort to identify her in history) her intent escapes further scrutiny. Yet even so, Moll's triumph turns on the fact that within her universe (the market, normally constituted) the unknowability of intent is the mind's correlative to the randomness of things. It enacts in a subjective mode the world's resistance to perception, our inability to encompass how things will fall out. If it is possible that a dirty old spoon can deflect suspicion, it is possible that one's pocket may be picked of a spoon. Moll's downfall is that while she is prescient in preparing illusions, pocketing fictions that elide her intent, she fails to imagine that randomness may undo her when least she expects. She calculates "the chances for my coming off" should there be a surprise, but she might have inverted her formulation: the chances for *not* coming off, which on any given day may turn up. Unlike Roxana, Moll does not try to *control* the odds – she just plays it as it lays. After her caper with the plate, she reveals that she was "not at all made Cautious by my former Danger as I us'd to be" (II, 96). When on the very next page she is caught with brocade, she can only extenuate.

Since Moll inhabits purlieus of unregulated chance, she escapes the "plague" of astute readers who would reconstitute her history. Neither the law nor her scattered children have means or the will to invade her persona. She is a great chameleon in part because no persistent reader draws her back to the past. The "and then, and then" mode of her narrative corresponds to a market that baffles close readings, displacing origins and subsisting in deferral. The only hitch is that such a market is implicate in chance. Infinite deferral is possible, and we are meant to think that it is, but as Defoe himself avows, Air-Money can collapse. Disclosure is possible.

Thus *Moll* stands against *Roxana* as a baseline. It represents the inherent risk to any author foisting a persona on readers who have no special animus. Indeed, Moll's absence of terror (she "was not at all made Cautious") marks her text as peripheral to a Defoean concern (evinced in *Roxana*) with a market that has ceased to operate in its normal mode, turning against the authors of fiction. *Roxana* is a special case, not because it is a novel, but because it broaches the possibility of a market manipulable by *readers*.

Giving minimal space to a formalist argument, one might speculate that upon penning the last paragraph of *Roxana*, Defoe realized that he had stumbled upon Obvious Fiction and so murdered his own text. But then why publish it? One might suggest that he could not resist Roxana, as he could not resist Lady Credit, and had to display his new Mistress. But at that point *Roxana* becomes a "meer Allegory" of a career in love with fiction. I have argued, rather, that Defoe was indeed in love with fiction, but that it was a "closet" passion which he pursued without effusively "coming out." Of course if he did realize that *Roxana* disclosed his passion, this might explain why, rather than abandoning fiction and hoping to abscond from this element of his history, his next great work pursued fiction at the level of theory. *The Compleat English Tradesman*, laid down palimpsestually over fictions ranging from *The Secret History* to *Roxana*, pursues the fiction that there is no fiction; or at least you'll never know if there is. It seeks to decategorize preceding Defoean fiction, to destabilize a history of fictionality by invoking the fluidity of market discourse. It recapitulates Crusoe's thoughts in *Serious Reflections*, where he states that later works produce – give meaning to, amplify – their predecessors: "[T]he present Work is not merely the Product of the two first Volumes, but the two first Volumes may rather be called the Product of this: The Fable is always made for the Moral, not the Moral for the Fable." In Defoe's oeuvre, the Moral is *The Compleat English Tradesman*. The Fable[s] are all the fables that evade generic affiliation. They inhabit a market which inhabits them.

So does Defoe. As a consequence, *Roxana* broaches the question of whether obscure authors and generically obscure texts can dominate the market by dominating readers. Defoe seems to intuit that unavowed fiction could not sustain momentum indefinitely. John M. Warner observes that *Roxana*'s relentless ending "suggests how acutely Defoe sensed both the limitations of a purely human effort to resolve metaphysical problems in a post-mythic world and the narrative complications such efforts posed."[25] In the "post-mythic world" of a post-Bubble market, History without origin and without ending is exposed as potential myth. "Narrative complications" are not removed but revised, bound into a potential revelatory imperative. This does not make *Roxana* a novel, nor even predictive of novels. The text looks towards, frets over – perhaps concedes – potential (dis)closure by readers; it does not constitute a new paradigm of willing disclosure. In its essence, *Roxana* foresees radical destabilization of a mode of discourse that assumed its own impregnable uncertainty. If Defoe is prescient, then his concern is with accommodation, with counter-moves in the spirit of Roxana herself. He produces *The Compleat English Tradesman*. He looks over his shoulder, but not yet ahead to the Novel.

Notes

INTRODUCTION

1 Ian Watt's *The Rise of the Novel: Studies in Defoe, Richardson, and Fielding* (Berkeley: University of California Press, 1957, reprinted 1967) initiated a huge critical literature concerned with the genre's development. The most important study is Michael McKeon, *The Origins of the English Novel 1600–1740* (Baltimore: Johns Hopkins University Press, 1987). Other significant work includes Lennard J. Davis, *Factual Fictions: the Origins of the English Novel* (New York: Columbia University Press, 1983), and J. Paul Hunter, *Before Novels: the Contexts of Eighteenth-Century English Fiction* (New York: Norton & Company, 1990). Feminist readings such as Ros Ballaster's *Seductive Forms: Women's Amatory Fiction from 1684–1740* (Oxford: Clarendon Press, 1992) redirect scholarship on the novel, and numerous texts, such as Jane Spencer's *The Rise of the Woman Novelist: from Aphra Behn to Jane Austen* (Oxford: Basil Blackwell, 1986), broadly focus on women's place in the canon. Specialized studies of Defoe include John Bender, *Imagining the Penitentiary: Fiction and the Architecture of the Mind in Eighteenth-Century England* (Chicago: University of Chicago Press, 1987), Lincoln Faller, *Crime and Defoe: a New Kind of Writing* (Cambridge: Cambridge University Press, 1993), and Joseph Bartolomeo, *A New Species of Criticism: Eighteenth-Century Discourse on the Novel* (Newark: University of Delaware Press, 1994). In *Enlightenment and the Shadows of Chance: the Novel and the Culture of Gambling in Eighteenth-Century France* (Baltimore: Johns Hopkins University Press, 1993), Thomas Kavanagh argues that the eighteenth-century novel engages theories of probability implicit in the development of financial credit.

2 See, e.g., Davis, *Factual Fictions*, and Hunter, *Before Novels*.

3 On lingering religious opposition to fiction during the eighteenth century, see J. Paul Hunter, "The Loneliness of the Long-distance Reader," *Genre* 10 (1977), 455–484; George Starr, *Defoe and Casuistry* (Princeton: Princeton University Press, 1971) and David Marshall, *The Figure of Theater: Shaftesbury, Defoe, Adam Smith, and George Eliot* (New York: Columbia University Press, 1986), chapter 4. In *God's Plots and Man's Stories: Studies in the Fictional Imagination from Milton to Fielding*

(Chicago: University of Chicago Press, 1985), Leo Damrosch notes the arguments against fiction, and observes that Defoe's effort "[t]o write novels . . . was a subversive innovation" (204). Responding to *Robinson Crusoe*, Charles Gildon ridiculed its pretended authenticity, and argued that it lacked sufficient moral purport to be justified as fiction. See *The Life and Strange Surprizing Adventures of Mr. D . . . De F . . . of London, Hosier* (London, 1719). In *The Origins of the English Novel*, McKeon cites recent work demonstrating that "the cental phenomenon [of Puritan icono-clasm] is not a hostility to 'art' but a suspicion of traditional methods of mediating truth that also pervades much of early modern culture" (75).

4 *Robinson Crusoe* is frequently considered the first "novel" in spite of itself. See, e.g., Davis, *Factual Fictions*, 152.

5 "Naive empiricism" is attributed to Defoe by McKeon in *The Origins of the English Novel*, 206. He notes that "the naive empiricism of the claim to historicity purports to document the authentic truth" (48).

6 In *Defoe and the Idea of Fiction 1713–1719* (Newark: University of Delaware Press, 1983), Geoffrey Sill remarks that "A fully formed fiction is, in Henry James' phrase, one that 'cuts the string' that ties it to an external world . . . Defoe's writing in the second decade of the eighteenth century reveals a steady decline in the dependence of his work on realities that exist outside the text" (46–47).

7 On the meaning of "literary," see Peter Lamarque and Stein Olsen, *Truth, Fiction, and Literature* (Oxford: Clarendon Press, 1994), chapter 10. Lamarque and Olsen argue that the "literary" work is constituted in the author's intent to produce "literature" *and* in the reader's response to that intent:

> A text is identified as a literary work by recognizing the author's intention that the text is produced and meant to be read within the framework of conventions defining the practice (constituting the institution) of literature . . . [T]his intention is *the intention to invoke a literary response*. . . . The mode of apprehension which the practice defines is one of *appreciation*. The literary stance is defined by the expectation of (and consequently the attempt to identify) a certain type of value, i.e. literary aesthetic value, in the text in question. (255–256)

A "financial" text, while perhaps equally complex and coherent, does not elicit an aesthetic response; it is merely instrumental.

8 Defoe was held to account for a fiction, *The Shortest Way with the Dissenters* (1702), standing in the stocks and spending time in Newgate. When Gildon taunted him over *Crusoe*, Defoe deferred the issue of authorship in a haze of rhetoric.

9 See Eric Kerridge, *Trade and Banking in Early Modern England* (Manchester: Manchester University Press, 1988), on the broad reach of commercial credit during the period. John Scarlett's *The Stile of Exchanges: containing both their Law and Custom as Practiced in the most considerable places of Exchange in Europe* (London, 1682) evinces the thriving international market mediated by credit.

10 On the alienation of authors and readers during the period, see Susan Stewart, *Crimes of Writing: Problems in the Containment of Representation* (Oxford: Oxford University Press, 1991). Stewart argues that in the early eighteenth century "the classical public sphere of letters was beginning to disintegrate," creating a gap between the "context of production" and the "context of reception" (37). As a result, author and audience were becoming increasingly estranged. See also Hunter, *Before Novels*, noting that extended prefaces, dedicatory epistles, and modes of direct address sought to attenuate "the givens of mass print and the fact of an audience out of range" (238).

11 See Helen Grace, "Business, Pleasure, Narrative: the Folktale in our Times," in Rosalyn Diprose and Robyn Ferrel, eds., *Cartographies: Poststructuralism and the Mapping of Bodies and Spaces* (North Sydney: Allen & Unwin, 1991), 113–125, noting that "everyday economic life" has become "a fiction of terrifying realism," where so-called realities such as third world debt, corporate bonds, and futures trading seem quakingly unverifiable (118–119). Linguistic theorists routinely point out that "literary" language – rhyme, metaphor, fictivity – is found in non-literary language. See Steven Mailloux, *Interpretive Conventions: the Reader in the Study of American Fiction* (Ithaca: Cornell University Press, 1982), 134. In *Toward a Speech Act Theory of Literary Discourse* (Bloomington: Indiana University, 1977), 91, Mary Louise Pratt notes that "fictive" speech acts are present not only in literature, but in daily discourse, such as hyperbole, speculation, and verbal musings.

12 In *Customs in Common: Studies in Traditional Popular Culture* (New York: The New Press, 1993), E. P. Thompson describes the traditional eighteenth-century market as a "a social as well as economic nexus. It was a place where one-hundred-and-one social and personal transactions went on; where news was passed, rumour and gossip flew around" (256).

13 J. Paul Hunter, *The Reluctant Pilgrim: Defoe's Emblematic Method and Quest for Form in Robinson Crusoe* (Baltimore: Johns Hopkins University Press, 1966), 115.

14 David Marshall typifies critics who emphasize the nonmarket factors underlying Defoe's fictive practice: "It is generally agreed . . . that religious and social interdictions presented problems for Defoe – whether he believed in their validity or just pretended to or repeatedly contradicted in practice what he believed in theory." *The Figure of Theater*, 88.

15 See J. G. A. Pocock, *The Machiavellian Moment: Florentine Political Thought and the Atlantic Republican Tradition* (Princeton: Princeton University Press, 1975), and *Virtue, Commerce, and History* (Cambridge: Cambridge University Press, 1985). Swift attacked all forms of property except land as "imaginary." See *The Examiner, and Other Pieces Written in 1710–1711* (Oxford: Blackwell, 1987). Other outlets were equally opposed. See *Cato's Letters: or, Essays on Liberty, Civil and Religious, and Other Important*

Subjects (London, 1723), discussed in Pocock, *The Machiavellian Moment*, 267–277, and in Isaac Kramnick, *Bolingbroke and His Circle: The Politics of Nostalgia in the Age of Walpole* (Cambridge, MA: Harvard University Press, 1968). Augustan opposition to credit is also discussed in William Dowling, *The Epistolatory Moment: the Poetics of the Eighteenth-Century Verse Epistle* (Princeton: Princeton University Press, 1991).

16 The term "discursive formation," used together with "episteme," is from Michel Foucault, *The Archaeology of Knowledge* (New York: Pantheon, 1972):

> a world-view, a slice of history common to all branches of knowledge, which imposes on each one the same norms and postulates, a general stage of reason, a certain structure of thought that the men of a particular period cannot escape . . . By *episteme*, we mean, in fact, the total set of relations that unite, at a given period, the discursive practices that give rise to epistemological figures, sciences, and possibly formalized systems. (19)

> In *Writing and the Rise of Finance: Capital Satires of the Early Eighteenth Century* (Cambridge: Cambridge University Press, 1994), Colin Nicholson observes: "Poetry speaks politics in sometimes fiercely direct ways, while developing strategies of finance and commerce infiltrate rival assumptions and effects into literary structures of argument and response. In such transforming relations of power, writing and society constitute each other as an economics of the imagination" (xii).

17 Louis Montrose explains New Historicist rationale for broaching a continuum between the "literary" and "nonliterary" in "New Historicisms," in Stephen Greenblatt and Giles Gunn, eds., *Redrawing the Boundaries: the Transformation of English and American Literary Studies* (New York: Modern Language Association, 1992), 392–418. The classic statement of the necessity of this approach to an understanding of capitalist formations is Greenblatt's "Towards A Poetics of Culture," *Southern Review* (Australia) 20 (1987), 3–15, reprinted in H. Aram Veeser, ed., *The New Historicism* (New York: Routledge, 1989), 1–14. In "Fiction as Friction," in *Shakespearean Negotiations: the Circulation of Social Energy in Renaissance England* (Berkeley: University of California Press, 1988), 66–93, Greenblatt argues that Renaissance medical and theatrical practices establish "a shared code, a set of interlocking tropes and similitudes that function not only as objects but as the conditions of representation" (88). On the belated but necessary reception of New Historicism into eighteenth-century studies, see John Bender, "Eighteenth-Century Studies," in Greenblatt and Gunn, eds., *Redrawing the Boundaries*, 79–99.

18 Stephen Greenblatt observes that "New Historicists are sometimes said to be guilty of 'the principle of arbitrary connectedness'; that is, they conjoin what should by rights be kept apart, gluing together in a zany collage pieces that do not properly belong in the same place." See "The Eating of the Soul," *Representations* 48 (1994), 98–116, 99. In *Negotiating*

the Past: the Historical Understanding of Medieval Literature (Madison: University of Wisconsin Press, 1987), Lee Patterson phrases the charge with a neutrality bordering on irony: "No longer believing that cultural phenomena can be usefully explained as effects of anterior causes, New Historicism is released from the narrow criterion of relevance that constrained older literary historians" (67).

19 Compare Walter Benn Michaels, *The Gold Standard and the Logic of Naturalism: American Literature at the Turn of the Century* (Berkeley: University of California Press, 1987). In discussing Dreiser's *Sister Carrie*, Benn Michaels cites the rise of commodity futures trading, with its creation of fictitious excess value, and suggests that the novel is "structured by an economy in which excess is seen to generate the power of both capitalism and the novel" (58). Benn Michaels and I share the view that emergent capitalist phenomena and the structure of literary fictions are part of the same discursive formation.

20 In *Imagining the Penitentiary*, Bender confronts causal/homological relations, suggesting that neither excludes the other. See 4–6.

21 Arguments that the market conditioned reading practices, ostensibly invoke Stanley Fish's notion of "interpretive community," in which modes of interpretation exist antecedent to acts of reading. In *Is There a Text in This Class?* (Cambridge, MA: Harvard University Press, 1980), Fish states that "interpretive strategies . . . are finally not our own but have their source in a publicly available system of intelligibility" (332). See also "Change," in Stanley Fish, *Doing What Comes Naturally: Change, Rhetoric, and the Practice of Theory in Literary and Legal Studies* (Durham: Duke University Press, 1989), 141–162. However, my approach ironically reverses Fish: the market encourages an "interpretive strategy" that discourages interpretation, suppressing "intelligibility." Moreover, the "community" of the market (as I define it) comprises authors and readers at cross-purposes. Fish argues that since both share an objective of communication as well as common cues, texts are largely "interpretable."

22 *The Compleat English Tradesman*, I, 231–234.

23 In "Varieties of Literary Affection," in Leo Damrosch, ed., *The Profession of Eighteenth-century Literature: Reflections on an Institution* (Madison: University of Wisconsin Press, 1992), 26–41, Leo Braudy argues that Defoe deployed "edited" manuscripts to reinstate affective relationships with readers, thereby reifying himself as an author: "Defoe's fictional autobiographies parallel Pope's attempt to restore the presence of the author, who is *responsible* for what he writes and publishes" (32: original emphasis). I argue that the edited text defers such "responsibility."

24 See McKeon, *The Origins of the English Novel*, 108–109.

25 In *Writing and the Rise of Finance*, Colin Nicholson describes the implication of *Gulliver's Travels* in the discourse of credit, noting that Swift's "fictive form interrogates traditional categories that were

changing as investment expectations changed the ordering of social life
... The inventive freedoms his text consecrates, and the varieties of
different elements it permits and organizes correlate discursively with the
expanding processes of exchange, substitution, transference and equival-
ence of a market society and its credit-based paper-money machinery
and circulation" (119). In *The Economics of the Imagination* (Amherst:
University of Massachusetts Press, 1980), Kurt Heinzelman collates two
related phenomena: "(1) 'imaginative economics,' the way in which
economic systems are structured, by means of the imagination, upon
what are essentially fictive concepts – including, ultimately, 'the economy'
itself – and (2) 'poetic economics,' the way in which literary writers use
this fictive economic discourse, this body of systematized knowledge, as
an ordering principle in their own work" (11–12). See also Catherine
Gallagher, *Nobody's Story: the Vanishing Acts of Women Writers in the
Marketplace 1670–1820* (Berkeley: University of California Press, 1994),
especially chapter 3. Gallagher argues that anxiety about "the multiplication of nominal entities and the creation of imaginary worlds on paper
was closely bound to the anxiety ... about the new forms of paper
property – bills of exchange, stocks and shares" (130).

26 The classic formulation of Defoe as "homo economicus" is in Kramnick,
Bolingbroke and His Circle, 188–204. Kramnick suggests that "[i]n both his
career and his writing Defoe embodied the projecting spirit ...
Projecting man, free of any functional duty to any organic social
structure, stood alone, creating and shaping his own world and his own
destiny. His spirit was the spirit of Locke's man, of Robinson Crusoe, a
necessary ingredient of the capitalist creed" (193–194). See also Ian
Watt, "Robinson Crusoe as Myth," in the Norton Critical Edition of
Robinson Crusoe (New York: Norton, 1975), 311–331.

27 The capacity of credit to interfere with self-construction, subjecting
personal agency to forces beyond individual control, implies Defoe's
skepticism towards the "freedom" of modern, capitalist man. In *The
Subject of Modernity* (Cambridge: Cambridge University Press, 1992),
Anthony Cascardi observes that while Crusoe attempts to live auto-
nomously, insofar as he is "also bound to refashion society from the tools
that are salvaged from the ship, we are led to the view that culture is a
web from which we cannot break free, even if we recognize that it rests on
no absolute or original grounds" (88).

28 See Jürgen Habermas, *The Structural Transformation of the Public Sphere*
(Cambridge, MA: MIT Press, 1989).

29 The term "trope of selfhood" is applied by Deborah Wyrick to Jonathan
Swift in *Jonathan Swift and the Vested Word* (Chapel Hill: University of
North Carolina Press, 1988), xvi. I shall argue that Defoe's resistance to
acknowledging his status as author is "intended" but overdetermined
by the market for which he writes. See Roger Chartier, *The Order of
Books* (Stanford: Stanford University Press, 1994), noting that recent

criticism connects text and author, although in such representations the author

> is dependent in that he is not the unique master of the meanings of his text, and his intentions, which provided the impulse to produce the text, are not necessarily imposed either on those who turn his text into a book (bookseller-publishers or print workers) or on those who appropriate it by reading it. He is constrained in that he undergoes the multiple determinations that organize the social space of literary production and that, in a more general sense, determine the categories and the experiences that are the very matrices of writing. (28–29)

30 In "What is an Author?," in Josue Harari, ed., *Textual Strategies: Perspectives in Post–structuralist Criticism* (Ithaca: Cornell University Press, 1979), 141–60, Michel Foucault argues that "[t]exts, books, and discourses really began to have authors . . . to the extent authors became subject to punishment, that is, to the extent that discourses could be transgressive" (148). Defoe's antitransgressive strategies, coincident with those of credit texts, defer interrogation of him as an author of fiction.

31 Habermas, *The Structural Transformation of the Public Sphere*, 46.

32 While Richardson claimed merely to "edit" his epistolary novels, he pronounced Fielding to be less creative. Fielding, meanwhile, claimed to invent a new literary genre – hardly consistent with his own (tepid) truth claims. As Robert Newsom points out, Richardson "worried about" *Clarissa*'s verisimilitude, not about whether it was "verisimilar and untrue." *A Likely Story: Probability and Play in Fiction* (New Brunswick: Rutgers University Press, 1988), 172. He observes that such (attenuated) "worry" registers a new attitude towards the "truth" of fiction: "[t]he controversy surrounding Defoe's *Robinson Crusoe*, often thought to be the first modern novel in English, is significant in part because it is also the *last* such controversy of any moment. The beginning of the novel is largely marked, in other words, by the end of the worry" (172).

I CREDIT AND ITS DISCONTENTS: THE CREDIT/FICTION HOMOLOGY

1 War expenditures during the reigns of William and Anne amounted to £130 million. See Michael Jubb, "Economic Policy and Economic Development" in Jeremy Black, ed., *Britain in the Age of Walpole* (Saint Martin's Press, 1984), 121–144, 132. In *An Essay Upon Loans* (1710), Defoe stated that the war "has surmounted not all that ever went before it only, but all that it could be imagin'd, was possible for any Nation of our Dimensions in the World, to support" (6). Except where I refer to specialized studies, my account of the financial history of England during this period is based on P. G. M. Dickson, *The Financial Revolution in England: A Study in the Development of Public Credit 1688–1765* (London:

Macmillan, 1967). For broader insights, I have consulted John Brewer, *The Sinews of Power: War, Money and the English State, 1688–1783* (New York: Knopf, 1989).

2 Dickson, *The Financial Revolution*, 50, citing House of Commons Journal for January 12, 1692. Commenting on the end of this period, E. L. Hargreaves noted that "It cannot be assumed that the permanent existence of the debt was regarded as inevitable in 1714, but the change which had occurred both in its size and its composition indicated clearly that repayment and redemption could only be achieved by a gradual process extending over a considerable number of years." *The National Debt* (London: Frank Cass, 1930, reprinted New York: Augustus M. Kelley, 1966), 16.

3 Daniel Defoe, *An Essay Upon Loans*, 11.

4 *Review*, 7:137 (February 8, 1711), 546.

5 As an opponent of credit, Swift urged a stop to the war on grounds that "If the Peace be made this Winter, we are then to consider, what Circumstances we shall be in towards paying a Debt of about Fifty Millions, which is a fourth Part of the Purchase of the whole island, if it were to be sold." Sarcastically, he observed that "[i]t will, no doubt, be a mighty Comfort to our Grandchildren, when they see a few rags hang up in Westminster-Hall, which cost an hundred Millions, whereof they are paying the Arrears, and boasting, as Beggars do, that their Grandfathers were Rich and Great." *The Conduct of the Allies* (1711), reprinted in Herbert Davis, ed., *The Prose Works of Jonathan Swift* (Princeton: Princeton University Press, 1951), IV, 1–65, 54, 56.

6 *Fair Payment No Spunge: or, Some Considerations on the Unreasonableness of Refusing to Receive back Money lent on Publick Securities* (1717), introduction.

7 The Company cannot be compared to the old East Indies Company chartered by Queen Elizabeth, or to the other trading monopolies chartered by British monarchs. As Larry Neal observes, "From its beginning, the South Sea Company was primarily an organization for the conversion of government debt." See Neal, "How the South Sea Bubble was Blown Up and Burst: a New Look at Old Data," in Eugene White, ed., *Crashes and Panics: The Lessons from History* (Homewood, Illinois: Dow Jones-Irwin, 1990), 33–56, 38. In *Bolingbroke and His Circle* (Cambridge, MA: Harvard University Press, 1968), Isaac Kramnick notes that the Company was to be the Whig alternative to the Tory Bank of England, i.e. another source of funds to the government. Defoe, however, believed that it could be an agent for establishing British colonies in America. See *An Essay on The South Sea Trade; With An Enquiry into the Grounds and Reasons of the Present Dislike and Complaint Against the Settlement of a South Sea Company* (1712). In the same essay, however, he argued that failure to have consolidated the debt in exchange for South Sea stock would merely have postponed "the Evil Day . . . leaving the Debt a growing Disease" that would "at last infallibly prove mortal"

(20). Defoe made the same arguments in *A True Account of the Design and Advantages of the South-Sea Trade* (1711).

8 Archibald Hutcheson, *Some Calculations and Remarks Relating to the Present State of the Publick Debts and Funds. And a Proposal for the Intire Discharge of the National Debt and Incumbrance in Thirty Years Time,* "Fourth State" (12). Hutcheson was the most respected parliamentary commentator on the National Debt. Richard Steele, who disagreed with Hutcheson over major issues, described him as "the most celebrated modern Writer, concerning the publick Funds." *The Crisis of Property: An Argument Proving That the Annuitants for ninety-nine Years, as such, are not in the Condition of other Subjects of Great Britain* (London, 1720), 4. In *The Sinews of Power,* John Brewer notes that a portion of the government's debt was unfunded, though after 1714 this amount never exceeded 20 percent. See Brewer, 199.

9 Hutcheson, *Some Calculations,* "Sixth State," 15. In *The Discourse of the Sublime: Readings in History, Aesthetics, and the Subject* (Oxford: Basil Blackwell, 1989), Peter de Bolla argues that later in the century the National Debt raised questions of representation. See especially 131–139.

10 Government exactions had to increase relative to the revenue base, which was not expanding fast enough. Between 1700 and 1720, the ratio of public debt to gross national product climbed from 0.25 to 0.75. See Robert J. Barro, "Government Spending, Interest Rates, Prices, and Budget Deficits in the United Kingdom, 1701–1918," *Journal of Monetary Economics* 20 (1987), 221–247, 239. By 1720 taxes were 12 percent of national income, up from 8.9 percent in 1710, while national income had fallen from £59.8 to £47.5 million. See Paula Backscheider, *Daniel Defoe – His Life* (Baltimore: Johns Hopkins University Press, 1988), 451.

11 See, for example, John Holland, *The Directors of the Bank of England, Enemies to the Great Interests of the Kingdom* (London, 1715); Edward Leigh, *An Essay Upon Credit, Being A Proposal For the Immediate and Entire Payment of the Publick Debt* (London, 1715).

12 The Sinking Fund, established in 1715, was not a gimmick, but it was fragile. E. L. Hargreaves observes that "raiding of sinking funds has become so familiar that the impossibility of erecting a completely adequate legal safeguard is now generally recognized. Ultimately any legal agreement must break down in the face of the inability of a Parliament, however constituted, to bind its successors." *The National Debt* (London: Frank Cass & Co., 1930), 25. See Hargreaves' analysis of the Fund's specific vulnerabilities, chapter 2. Contentiousness surrounding the Fund is evident in *A State of the National Debt, as it stood December the 24th, 1716. With the Payments made towards the Discharge of it out of the Sinking Fund, &c. compared with The Debt at Michaelmas, 1725* (London, 1727), reprinted in John R. McCulloch, ed., *A Select Collection of Scarce and Valuable Tracts and Other Publications on the National Debt and*

the Sinking Fund (1857, reprinted New York: Augustus M. Kelley, 1966), 131–199, attributed to the Earl of Bath.

13 On the government's involvement with the South Sea Company, see Dickson, *The Financial Revolution*; Neal, "How the South Sea Bubble was Blown Up"; Neal, *The Rise of Financial Capitalism: International Capital Markets in the Age of Reason* (Cambridge: Cambridge University Press, 1990); Adam Anderson, *Origin of Commerce*, III, 1st edn (London, 1764); John Carswell, *The South Sea Bubble* (London: Cresset Press, 1960); William Scott, *The Constitution and Finance of English, Scottish and Irish Joint-Stock Companies to 1720* (Cambridge: Cambridge University Press, 1910); John Sperling, *The South Sea Company: an Historical Essay and Bibliographical Finding List* (Boston: Harvard Graduate School of Business Administration, 1962).

14 *The Crisis of Property*, 27.

15 Compare *A Letter To A Friend. In Which is shewn, The Inviolable Nature of Publick Securities* (London, 1717), "By A Lover of His Country," in John T. McCulloch, ed., *A Select Collection*, 19–46, 29: "Publick Credit, like Private, is entirely founded upon Integrity, and strict Performance of Contracts. If once Covenants are broke thro' by any Person, it necessarily alarms every body, and makes the parties concern'd Jealous, and upon their Guard, very suspicious of every Motion, and very apt to misinterpret, and to put the worst Sense upon every Action."

16 Among the warnings was a sober pamphlet, *Considerations Occasioned by the South-Sea Company's Bill* (London, 1720). Not only did it predict grave financial risk to individuals, it saw the concentration of financial power in the Company as a threat to British commerce. Also, James Milner saw no limit to what the Company might do: "[W]hatever is in their Interest, will be in their Power; and whatever their Power can accomplish, their Interest will push them on to do." Sounding like Defoe a decade earlier, he argued: "Must not every true Lover of Liberty of his Country be under the greatest Concern, to see it under such Hazards, to be stock-jobbed by a parcel of Men, who will have no regard to its Liberty, provided they can enrich themselves?" *Three Letters Relating to the South-Sea Company and the Bank* (London, 1720), 26. Defoe suggested in the *Commentator*, February 29, 1720, that only one in ten thousand would win the South Sea "gamble."

17 Hogarth's response to the scandal is examined in David Dabydeen, *Hogarth, Walpole, and Commercial Britain* (London: Hansib, 1987). Three generations after the debacle, Edward Gibbon's *Autobiography* still sighed over a lost family fortune.

18 *Applebee's Journal*, October 22, 1720; *The Weekly Journal and Saturday's Post*, October 19, 1720. Both are cited in Kramnick, *Bolingbroke and His Circle*, 68.

19 Charles Krindleberger, *Manias, Panics and Crashes: a History of Financial Crisis* (New York: Basic Books, 1978), 43. In *Enlightenment and the Shadows*

of Chance (Baltimore: Johns Hopkins University Press, 1993), Thomas Kavanagh argues that in early eighteenth-century France stock trading demanded "speculators' constant attention to what others exactly like them were doing. . . To sell was to bet that others were on the brink of selling and that stock prices would fall" (96).

20 *Considerations on the Present State of the Nation, as to publick credit, stocks, the landed and trading interests with a proposal for the speedy lessening of the publick debts* (London, 1720), 16–17.

21 The cited passage shows that "public" and "private" credit were inseparable. Defoe remarked that "all Publick Credit is deriv'd, tho' at some distance, from private Credit, and yet it reciprocally Contributes to the Support of its said remote Parent . . . If private Credit falls off, the Stock, the Trade, and by Consequence the Wealth of the Nation decays; and if the Trade of the Nation dies, the Fund of Publick Credit fails." *Review*, 7:118 (December 26, 1710), 470. Private credit relations displayed the same web-like characteristics as its public counterpart. For a discussion of the phenomenon, see Neil McKendrick, John Brewer, and J. H. Plumb, *The Birth of a Consumer Society: the Commercialization of Eighteenth-Century England* (Bloomington: Indiana University Press, 1982), especially 197–262. In *Britons: Forging the Nation, 1707–1737* (New Haven: Yale University Press, 1992), Linda Colley observes that "The men and women who benefited from [easy credit] found themselves caught fast in a complex web of dependency and obligation" (66).

22 Anthony Hammond, *A Modest Apology Occasion'd by the Late Unhappy Turn of Affairs, With Relation to Public Credit* (London, 1721), 15.

23 *Considerations on the Present State of the Nation*, 1–2. Backscheider remarks on the general fear of speaking out against the scheme for fear of seeming unpatriotic. See *Defoe*, 455. In addition, the "Frenzy" (and indifference to Jeremiahs) was part of a pervasive obsession with gambling. See e.g. Dickson, *The Financial Revolution*, 45. In *The Gamester: a Benefit-Ticket For all that Are Concern'd in the Lotteries* (London, 1719), Defoe satirized gambling, but still discussed how to play the odds.

24 On Law's scheme, see Kavanagh, *Enlightenment and the Shadows of Chance*, 67–104. Kavanagh does not compare French and English finances of the period, but argues that Law's scheme was theoretically respectable and without a trace of corruption.

25 Pressure for emulating the French succeeded because of economic competition. *The Present State of the French Revenues and Trade, and of the Controversy betwixt the Parliament of Paris, and Mr. Law* (London, 1720), argued that the French trading establishment

so united their Interest with that of the Government, as they seem to be inseparable, and by Consequence have assured themselves of so powerful a Protection, and have such a large Scene of Commerce in view, that it concerns all the Trading Nations in Europe, but us Britons more particularly, to be on our Guard, lest we should be out rivalled by them. (translator's preface)

26 Since Defoe wrote *The Chimera* shortly before the Bubble burst, he arguably participated in the split consciousness that permitted the English to criticize the French while accepting similar risks. Indeed, in *Fair Payment No Spunge*, Defoe called public credit in England a "chimera" (14), but the perception seems not to have influenced *The South-Sea Scheme Examin'd*. Early in 1720, Defoe expressed doubts about the scheme; his publicly articulated views softened towards the end of the year. Given his facility with numbers, and the fact that he sold his own shares in 1719, it is hard to imagine that his position was not calculated to support the government once the crisis became evident. In *Defoe*, Backscheider suggests that he was doing his patriotic best to uphold credit (457). Moreover, Defoe's suggestion in *Mr. Law* that nobody pressed a comparison with the French is untrue, and perhaps self-serving. Apart from his own *Chimera*, *Considerations Occasioned by the South-Sea Company's Bill* noted portentously that "The example of another Nation ought not to determine us to follow the same Measures, without examining whether that Nations was the better or the worse by such Measures" (36).

27 *Considerations on the Present State of the Nation*, 19.

28 *The Pangs of Credit: or, An Argument to Shew Where it is most reasonable to bestow the Two Millions . . . By An Orphan Annuitant* (1722), 2.

29 Hutcheson had raised the possibility of Company–government coziness on several occasions. His reissue of such animadversions hints that he knew of venality. See *A Collection of Calculations and Remarks Relating to the South Sea Scheme and Stock, which have been Already Published* (1720), e.g. at 66: "For, What may not a Corporation who are Masters of such Wealth, be able to effect? And having so many Opportunities of conferring beneficial Obligations, Peers of Parliament and Members of the House of Commons, may, in Time, become their humble Suppliants and Dependants."

30 *The Case of the Borrowers on the South-Sea Loans, Truly Stated* (London, 1721), 28–29.

31 *An Essay for Establishing a New Parliament Money: With Some Thoughts for the Service of the South-Sea Company* (London, 1721), 11.

32 My analysis draws on Pocock's *The Machiavellian Moment* (Princeton: Princeton University Press, 1975), and on *Virtue, Commerce, and History* (Cambridge: Cambridge University Press, 1985).

33 In *A Likely Story*, Newsom observes that in attempting to define a theory of probability, philosophers point to two antithetical concepts: a subjective, epistemological attitude, concerned with assessing belief, and an objective, statistical approach, concerned with the laws of chance. He argues that the two cannot be separated. In the discourse of credit they are intertwined: credit was often equated with gambling, even as it produced epistemological dilemma. See also the chapter "Duality" in Ian Hacking, *The Emergence of Probability: a Philosophical*

Study of Early Ideas About Probability, Induction, and Statistical Inference (Cambridge: Cambridge University Press, 1975), 11–17.

34 *A Collection of Calculations and Remarks*, 63.

35 Dream states were a commonplace of credit discourse. In *Some Calculations*, Hutcheson attributes "a pleasing Dream" to Parliament. Such identification of credit with dreaming invokes the nonlinear aspect of dreams already established in seventeenth-century psychology. Hobbes, for example, observed that he did not "remember so long a trayne of coherent thoughts, Dreaming, as at other times." *Leviathan* (Oxford: Clarendon Press, 1909, reprinted 1947), 15. Speaking of the origin of temporal ideas, Locke implicitly rules out the dream state: "The constant and regular succession of ideas in a waking man, is, as it were, the measure and standard of all other successions." *Essay Concerning Human Understanding*, II, chapter 14, section 12. The absence of linear sequence obliterates the assurance that an originary situs of meaning will yield a rational, predictable consequence.

36 In *The South-Sea Scheme detected; and the Management thereof Enquired Into* (London, 1720), the author argues: "Could the Advancing of Subscriptions . . . be any Thing else but the Building of a S – S-a Babel?" (7). The scheme garbles language, "Babel" itself is a garbling of "Bubble," enacting the concern expressed. It became a common pun. See e.g. "A South Sea Ballad," which states at stanza 9: "But should our South Sea Babel fall, / What numbers would be frowning? / The losers then must ease their gall, / By hanging or by drowning." The ballad is cited in Howard Erskine-Hill, *The Social Milieu of Alexander Pope* (New Haven: Yale University Press, 1975), 186–187. For background on "Babel" as a figure "used by those who were coming to see that language was no transparent medium," see Sharon Achenstein, "The Politics of Babel in the English Revolution," in *Pamphlet Wars: Prose in the English Revolution*, ed. James Holstun (London: Frank Cass, 1992), 14–44, 17.

37 Louis Althusser, *Lenin and Philosophy and Other Essays* (New York: Monthly Review Press, 1971), 172.

38 In "Defoe's Natural Philosophy and the Worlds of Credit," in John Christie and Sally Shuttleworth, eds., *Nature Transfigured: Science and Literature 1700–1900* (Manchester: Manchester University Press, 1989), 13–44, Simon Schaffer argues that Defoe sought to ground "credit," that is, credibility, in scientific notions of verifiability. However, the paradigm of financial credit was integral to Defoe's notions of credibility; imaginative enterprise was not displaced by procedures of contemporary empiricism.

39 *The Machiavellian Moment*, 459.

40 *Review*, 8:60 (August 11, 1711), 242. If "Reason" is subject to credit's deceptions, so too "All Credit built on the Foundation of Project, is a *Deceptio visus* upon the Imagination." *Review*, 3:126 (October 22, 1706).

41 *Review*, 6:30 (June 11, 1709), 120. In *A Collection of Calculations*, at 63,

Hutcheson had also cast schemes of public credit as a "Philosopher's Stone."

42 "Coining false news" is a brilliant conflation of counterfeiting (which was thriving) with linguistic enterprise, and reflects the metaphoric fertility of the money/language equation studied by Roland Barthes in *S/Z* (New York: Hill & Wang, 1974), and Sandra K. Fischer in *Econolingua – A Glossary of Coins and Economic Language in Renaissance Drama* (Newark: University of Delaware Press, 1985). False news, circulating through the economy like false coins, literally impoverishes all who receive it, since they act on its representation. For a discussion of the money/language exchange and its relation to credit, see J. S. Peters, "The Bank, the Press and the 'Return to Nature': On Currency, Credit, and Literary Property in the 1690s," in John Brewer and Susan Staves, eds., *Early Modern Conceptions of Property* (Routledge: London, 1995), 365–88.

43 *An Essay Upon Publick Credit,* 6, 9.

44 *Review,* 6:31 (June 14, 1709), 122.

45 In Alexander Pope's *The Rape of the Lock* (1712, 1714, 1717), "[t]he various Off'rings of the World appear" before Belinda, and on Belinda. They would have been imported subject to credit (e.g. bills of exchange), and Belinda probably purchased them on credit with income derived from credit (perhaps South Sea stock). On the development of international and metropolitan markets linked through credit, see Eric Kerridge, *Trade and Banking in Early Modern England.* Louis Landa discusses the involvement of *The Rape of the Lock* with international trade in "Pope's Belinda, the General Emporie of the World and the Wondrous Worm," *South Atlantic Quarterly* 70 (1971), 215–235, and in *Ends of Empire: Women and Ideology in Early Eighteenth-Century Literature* (Ithaca: Cornell University Press, 1993), Laura Brown argues that women's bodies became the site for a discursive exchange between aesthetic and economic theories.

46 *Review,* 1:88 (January 6, 1705), 365.

47 Alexander Pope, "Of the Characters of Women: an Epistle To a LADY," ll.41–42.

48 On seventeenth-century Dutch speculation in tulip bulbs, see Simon Schama, *The Embarrassment of Riches: an Interpretation of Dutch Culture in the Golden Age* (New York: Knopf, 1987), 350–366. Lady Credit may have an antecedent in the sixteenth- and seventeenth-century Dutch figure, Queen Money. See Schama's discussion at 323–343.

49 The *Oxford English Dictionary,* 2nd edn (1989), citing Shadwell and Richard Steele, states that in the early eighteenth century, "honest" still implied "chaste, virtuous, usually of a woman." It also meant that a phenomenon was "not seeming, other than it is; genuine."

50 Defoe introduced Lady Credit in the *Review,* 3:5 (January 10, 1706), where he notes ". . . nor did I design to have pursu'd the meer Allegory of CREDIT to the National Affairs; but I see such room for Publick Service in it, that I thought it my Duty" (20). She is denominated a Coy Mistress on

numerous occasions, as in "this *Coy Mistress of Treasure*, call'd CREDIT" (6:32, 127 [June 16, 1709].

51 On the capaciousness of allegory, and its ability to accommodate "realistic" narrative within an economy of symbols, see introductory discussion in Robert Kellogg and Oliver Steele, eds., *Edmund Spenser, Books I and II of the Faerie Queene, the Mutability Cantos, and Selections from the Minor Poetry*, (New York: Odyssey Press, 1965), 6–10.

52 See Paula Backscheider, "Defoe's Lady Credit," *Huntington Library Quarterly* 44 (1981), 89–100; Pocock, *Virtue, Commerce, and History*, chapter 5; Pocock, *The Machiavellian Moment*, chapter 13, and Janet Todd, *The Sign of Angelica: Women, Writing and Fiction 1660–1800* (New York: Columbia University Press, 1989), who remarks that "Defoe personified credit as feminine because of its link to unstable fortune" (20). In *Writing and the Rise of Finance*, Nicholson follows Pocock's account of Lady Credit. On the gendering of speculative activity, see Catherine Ingrassia, "The Pleasure of Business and the Business of Pleasure: Gender, Credit, and the South Sea Bubble," *Studies in Eighteenth-Century Culture* 24 (1995), 191–210.

53 Defoe habitually became involved with his own creations, which come to embody his personal predicament even as he has a personal stake in theirs. In *Serious Reflections During the Life and Surprising Adventures of Robinson Crusoe* (the third volume of the *Crusoe* trilogy, 1720), Crusoe argues, in what scholars see as a reference to Defoe himself, that "there is a Man alive, and well known too, the Actions of whose Life are the just Subject of these Volumes, and to whom all or most Part of the Story most directly alludes . . ." (preface). Even while denying authorship, Defoe apparently cannot resist an allegory of his suffering, much of which was caused as a result of his authorship. As to the probable reference by Crusoe to Defoe, see Lennard Davis, *Factual Fictions*, 159–160. David Marshall suggests that "*Roxana* becomes a psychological arena in which many of Defoe's preoccupations, anxieties, and fears are played out," and points to "Defoe's own investment in the situation and character of Roxana." He cites numerous critics' observations to the same effect. See *The Figure of Theater*, 254–255, n.6.

54 Feminist critics have shown that the female body traditionally represents textuality, the processes and predicaments of writing. In "'The Blank Page' and the Issues of Female Creativity," *Critical Inquiry* 8 (1981), 243–263, Susan Gubar observes that "[w]hen the metaphors of literary creativity are filtered through a sexual lens, female sexuality is often identified with textuality" (245). See also Charlotte Sussman, "The Other Problem with Women: Reproduction and Slave Culture in Aphra Behn's *Oroonoko*," in Heidi Hutner, ed., *Rereading Aphra Behn: History, Theory, and Criticism* (Charlottesville: University of Virginia Press, 1993), 212–233, and Ros Ballaster, *Seductive Forms: Women's Amatory Fiction from 1684 to 1740* (Oxford: Clarendon Press, 1992), chapter 5. This same approach has been applied to medieval texts. See Carolyn Dinshaw,

Chaucer's Sexual Poetics (Madison: University of Wisconsin Press, 1989). In *A Vindication of the Press* (1718), Defoe equates male writing with female deportment. Referring to necessitous hack writers, he suggests that they may be "entirely oblig'd to prostrate their Pens to the Town, as Ladies of Pleasure do their Bodies" (21); by contrast, he notes that "it is as necessary for a fine Writer to be endued with Modesty as for a beautiful Lady" (36). Recent studies link the hack writer to female figures responsive to the market. See Catherine Ingrassia, "Women Writing/Writing Women: Pope, Dulness, and 'Feminization' in the *Dunciad*," *Eighteenth Century Life* 14 (1990), 40–58, and Lance Bertelsen, "Journalism, Carnival, and *Jubilate Agno*," *ELH* 59 (1992), 357–384.

55 *Review*, 3:5 (January 10, 1706), 17–18.

56 *The Machiavellian Moment*, 453. In *Virtue, Commerce, and History*, Pocock is even more committed to connecting Credit with female stereotypes:

> Now it is an evident fact in the history and sociology of inter-sexual perception that masculine minds constantly symbolize the changeable, the unpredictable and the imaginative as feminine, though why they do so I would rather be excused from explaining. The random and the recurrent, the lunar and the cyclical, were summarized by Roman and Renaissance minds in the figure *Fortuna*. . . . It frequently occurs, in that Augustan journalism concerned with evaluating the impact of public credit upon society, that Credit is symbolized as a goddess having the attributes of the Renaissance goddess Fortune. (99)

While Lady Credit is not a goddess, Pocock correctly characterizes the symbology of "masculine minds." See Felicity Nussbaum, *The Brink of All We Hate: English Satires on Women 1660–1750* (Lexington: University of Kentucky Press, 1984). The irony in Defoe's appropriation of such satire is that he does not valorize it, but affiliates himself with its *objects*: uncertain, unpredictable women.

57 See for example Timothy Rogers, *The Character of a Good Woman, Both in a Single and Marry'd State* (London, 1697), 28–29: "a great Calmness and Quietness attends all [a Good Woman's] Actions. . . . She knows very well that those who are most passionate are most weak and simple." By hanging on "like a Beggar" who "never leaves" the indifferent male, Lady Credit becomes a histrionic caricature of the retiring, wilting femininity promoted by Richard Steele: "Modesty never rages, never murmurs, never pouts: When it is ill treated, it pines, it beseeches, it languishes." *The Tatler*, 217 (August 26–29, 1710).

58 *Review*, 3:5 (January 10, 1706), 18. In her relations with King Charles, Credit appears to drop her "coyness," her financial beneficence conflating with sexual complaisance. In the eighteenth century, "mistress" meant both "a woman who is loved and courted by a man," and also "a woman who illicitly occupies the place of a wife" (*OED*). Given Charles' reputation as a womanizer, Credit would have transcended her chariness merely by consorting with him; since she was "very kind" to the King, it seems that she transcended it all the way.

59 The term "jade" was "a term of reprobation applied to a woman," and

was also applied to Fortune in her personified form (*OED*). Defoe's usage distances Credit from a remote, disembodied ancestress, anchoring her in corporeality and diffusing her respectability. Three years later, the *Review* rearticulates Credit's history: "It was expected, that at the Restoration, she would come over from *Holland* with the young King *Charles* II, and indeed she was somewhere *incognita* in his Retinue" (6:31 [June 14, 1709], 124). She becomes disgusted with Charles' economic policy, however, and leaves. This contradicts the 1706 version of Credit's royal connection, and the shift in Credit's narrative (from mistress to mere lurking presence) leaves the reader perplexed. It epitomizes a market that cannot be encompassed (whose mysteries infiltrate Defoe's own discourse). By means of an elusive narrative, rather than by a stable signifying gender, Credit *engenders* epistemological confusion.

60 *Review*, 3:5 (January 10, 1706), 18. In popular usage, "elope" signified "a woman running away from home with a lover for the purpose of being married" (*OED*). While the term also meant "to run away," implications of sexual license and challenges to conduct book obedience hover about the word.

61 *Review*, 3:5 (January 10, 1706), 20.

62 The *Review*, 6:31 (June 14, 1709), 124, states that Lady Credit was raped by stockjobbers. In the following issue (June 16, 1709), she is in danger of being raped by present market manipulators, but Defoe nonetheless counsels financially sound measures "to get full possession of her" and gloats over her "Conquest" (126, 127).

63 Defoe admonishes that "if you will entertain this Virgin, you must act upon nice Principles of Honour, and Justice." *Review*, 7:116 (December 21, 1710), 463.

64 *Review*, 3:5 (January 10, 1706), 19.

65 Lady Credit's duality is not, for example, Duessa's in *The Faerie Queene*. Duessa appears virtuous, but hides moral and physical corruption. Lady Credit *is* virtuous and (at other times) *is not*. She is not deceptive because her "true" nature is hidden; she is deceptive because her nature is unstable, liable to slip from "chary" to "jade."

66 *Review*, 6:32 (June 16, 1709), 127.

67 *Review*, 6:31 (June 14, 1709), 124.

68 In *The Poetics of Sexual Myth: Gender and Ideology in the Verse of Swift and Pope* (Chicago: University of Chicago Press, 1985), Ellen Pollak observes:

As the text of Clarissa Harlowe made quite clear, and as social commentators throughout the century would affirm, the virginity of unmarried women was as fundamentally important as the chastity of wives; "a Slip in a Woman's Honour" (*Spectator*, 99) was considered damaging to her father before marriage as it was to her husband's afterwards. However innocent a woman might remain in the sight of God, the injury to her reputation in the world was, in either case, irreparable. Even such victimized fictional heroines as the young, innocent, and defenseless Teraminta, ruined by Decius and imprisoned in a life of debauch (*Tatler*, 45) or the pious orphan Caelia, deceived into a bigamous union with Palamede (*Tatler*,

198), must retire into poverty and shame, paying for their victimization by exchanging the material pleasures of this world for the spiritual consolations of the next. (54–55)

69 *Review*, 7:57 (August 5, 1710), 222.

70 *Review*, 3:6 (January 12, 1706), 23. To the same effect, Defoe states that "Credit, like the best Antidote ill applied, proves the worst Poison; and that which one way is the Foundation of our immense Trade in *England*, it being thus boldly invaded, misapplied and presum'd upon, is one of the worst Mischiefs that we can be exposed to." *Review*, 3:7 (January 15, 1706), 26. On Defoe's bi-valent attitude towards credit, see Robert Markley, "'So Inexhaustible a Treasure of Gold': Defoe, Capitalism, and the Romance of the South Seas," *Eighteenth-Century Life* 18, 3 (1995), 148–67.

71 Thus even as Credit is "the Mother of great Designs," it is also true that "Credit, like all other Species, begets its kind; the Canker runs through all sorts of Trade." *Review*, 3:6 (January 12, 1706) 22.

72 In *The Compleat English Tradesman* (1725–7), Defoe recommends that husbands introduce their wives to the family business (vol. 1, Letter 21), but he never suggests that women display themselves like signs over doorways.

73 In the *Review*, Lady Credit's narrative has generic affinities to romance. In *The Romance* (London: Methuen, 1970), Gillian Beer observes that "The characteristic device [of medieval romance] is that of 'entrelacement,' interlacing stories so that nothing is ever finally abandoned or circumscribed. [Eugene] Vinaver compares the effect to that of medieval ornament: 'The expansion is not, as in classical ornament, a movement towards or away from a real or imaginary centre – since there is no centre – but towards *potential infinity*'" (21). The text cited is *Form and Meaning in Medieval Romance* (Cambridge: Humanities Research Association, 1966). See also Carolyn Dinshaw, *Chaucer's Sexual Poetics*, noting that "romance narrative, considered generically, itself proceeds by dilation, delay, incessant deferral" (52). The classic discussion linking women's bodies and narrative dilation is Patricia Parker, "Literary Fat Ladies and the Generation of the Text," in *Literary Fat Ladies: Rhetoric, Gender, Property* (London: Methuen, 1987), 8–35. Epistemological uncertainty, as produced by credit and romance, is expressed in the incommensurability of narrative, the absence of a characterological, situational stability. Consistent with such antiepistemology, Mary Carleton created a late seventeenth-century personal romance, an autobiographical persona suspended between gentility and whoredom. See Hero Chalmers, "'The Person I Am, Or What They Made Me Be': the Construction of the Feminine Subject in the Autobiographies of Mary Carleton," in *Women, Texts and Histories 1575–1760*, ed. Clare Brant and Diane Purkiss (New York: Routledge, 1992). For a discussion of late seventeenth to early eighteenth-century romance emphasizing the female body as the site of

open-ended narrative, resistant to closure, see Ros Ballaster, *Seductive Forms*, chapters 2 and 5. Viewed against romance paradigms, the female Credit figures that appeared in early eighteenth-century periodicals, notably the *Spectator* and *Examiner*, bear only nominal relation to Lady Credit. These figures, discussed by Backscheider in "Defoe's Lady Credit," do not generate uncertainty through personal narrative. They are hypostatizations akin to emblemata, mere static vignettes.

74 *Review*, 6:31 (June 14, 1709), 122. Compare Defoe's *An Essay Upon Publick Credit*: "Credit is a Consequence, not a Cause; the Effect of a Substance, not a Substance; 'tis the Sun-shine, not the Sun" (9).

75 *Review*, 6:31 (June 14, 1709), 122.

76 In *Factual Fictions*, 167–173, Lennard Davis examines Defoe's orchestration of multiple identities, and manipulation of multiple competing print outlets. For a thorough discussion of Defoe's propagandistic subterfuges, see James Sutherland, *Defoe* (Philadelphia: J. B. Lippincott, 1938), 126–226. Defoe's letters chronicle his shape changing as, in disguise, he spreads Harley's line in Scotland. A famous letter dated November 26, 1706, states that for maximum effect, Defoe's ostensible business on the scene alters to suit his interlocutor: "I am all to Every one that I may gain some." George Healey, ed., *The Letters of Daniel Defoe* (Oxford: Clarendon Press, 1955), no. 68.

77 David Marshall notes that "undone" had both sexual and textual implications. If it meant to be "ruined" as a woman, it also meant to be "understood," interpreted as a text: the *OED* cites a 1654 usage that speaks of undoing a text. The sexual/textual connection, embedded in language, reified ironically in Lady Credit's narrative (wherein her periodic sexual undoing precludes a conclusive undoing of the text), is the basis of her capacity to allegorize Defoean narrative. On the sexual/textual ramifications of the term "undone" in *Moll Flanders* and *Roxana*, see David Marshall, *The Figure of Theater*, 152.

78 On narrative transvestism, that is, male authors' speaking in the voices of females, see Madeleine Kahn, *Narrative Transvestism: Rhetoric and Gender in the Eighteenth-Century Novel* (Ithaca: Cornell, 1991). For a broad theoretical exploration of the phenomenon, see *Men Writing the Feminine: Literature, Theory, and the Question of Genders*, ed. Thais Morgan (Albany: SUNY Press, 1994). Defoe does not abdicate his persona to Credit as he does to Moll and Roxana, but he uses this female self-reflexively. Lady Credit is identified with narrative contingency, deploying arts that Defoe's situation demands that he master.

79 *Review*, 6:32 (June 16, 1709), 127–128.

80 *Review*, 3:6 (January 12, 1706), 22.

81 Jeremy Taylor, whom Defoe cites in *Conjugal Lewdness*, argued in *Holy Living* (1650) that "chastity" consisted in the "suppression of all irregular desires," which included not only fornication and adultery but also "concerning meats and drinks: there being no certain degree of frequency

or intention prescribed to all persons, but it is to be ruled by the other actions of man, by proportion to the end, by the dignity of the person in the honour and severity of being a Christian." See *The Whole Works of Jeremy Taylor*, 10 vols. (London, 1861), III, 55–56. For lack of being "chary," Lady Credit compromises her "chastity" in one sense, endangering it in the other. The bivalent connotations of the term renders her gobbling of candies a punning intimation of potential sexual indulgence. Moreover, as early as the seventeenth century, excessive consumption of sugar was thought to damage health. James Hart argued that "the immoderate uses thereof, as also sweetconfections, and Sugar-plummes, heateth the blood, ingendreth the *landise obstructions, cachexias, consumptions*, rotteth the teeth, making them looke blacke, and withall, causeth many a loathsome stinking-breath." *Klinike or the Diet of Diseases* (1633), 97. Sugar's effect on the body was hotly debated into the eighteenth century, so that Lady Credit's "immoderate uses thereof" could hardly reflect a disposition "chary" towards her physical wellbeing. On the history of sugar consumption, see Sidney Mintz, *Sweetness and Power: the Place of Sugar in Modern History* (New York: Viking, 1985), especially chapter 3.

82 "Defoe's Lady Credit," 96–97.

83 *Review*, 7:58 (August 8, 1710), 226. Pocock suggests that if earlier depictions of Lady Credit signified "volcanic and irrational social innovations," then in 1710 Defoe had to find new means to suggest "Credit as a stabilizing, virtuous, and intelligent agency." *The Machiavellian Moment*, 454. Defoe perceived a threat to the nation's credit, and hence to its capacity to trade and conduct war; he therefore had to refurbish Lady Credit's image. I shall argue, however, that this "image" hardly remains stable. The instability already established in her persona overcomes the imperatives of a makeover.

84 *Review*, 7:59 (August 10, 1710), 230.

85 Dr. Johnson's *Dictionary* (1755) defines the falling sickness as "the epilepsy; a disease in which the patient is without any warning deprived at once of his senses, and falls down." See also Owsei Temkin, *The Falling Sickness: a History of Epilepsy from the Greeks to the Beginnings of Modern Neurology* (Baltimore: Johns Hopkins University Press, 1945), especially 193–242.

86 *Review*, 7:102 (November 18, 1710), 405.

87 *Ibid.* and 7:120 (December 30, 1710), 478.

88 *Review*, 7:134 (February 1, 1711), 534. The term "epiphany" is not too strong to apply to Defoe's encounter with Lady Credit. He calls himself "her humble Votary," noting that "I . . . threw my self at her Feet, and beg'd I might have the Liberty to speak to her" (534). Lady Credit does not materialize as a goddess, however.

89 *Review*, 7:135 (February 3, 1711), 539.

90 Following Gerard Genette, *Palimpsestes: la littérature au second degré* (Paris: Seuil, 1982), R. Barton Palmer defines hypertextuality as "a relation . . . dominated by a gesture of transformation (the hypertext alters, in some fashion, the hypotext [original text])." See Palmer, "Transtextuality and the Producing-I in Guillaume de Machaut's Judgment Series," *Exemplaria* 5.2 (1993), 283–304, 289.

91 Defoe collapses the metaphor, "text as woman," freeing it from discourse so that the text is woman. In this Pygmalion-like gesture, Defoe succumbs to the fascination of his own creation. In "Reading Like a Man," a brilliantly suggestive chapter in *Chaucer's Sexual Poetics*, Carolyn Dinshaw argues that for the critic E. Talbot Donaldson, Chaucer's Criseyde, "never fully understood, [is the] focus of desire in narrative" (35). Donaldson, who characterizes one manuscript reading over another in terms of sexual allurement, "is fascinated by Criseyde precisely because he sees her as the essential indeterminacy of the text" (36). In this sense, Defoe is "reading like a man."

92 The reception of Defoe's texts was fraught, and the *Review* is filled with self-defensive rhetoric. Defoe's tactic is instructive. In the Preface to volume 9, for example, Defoe complains that he is unjustly "Condemn'd by common Clamour, as Writing for Money, Writing for particular Persons, Writing by great Men's Direction, being Dictated to, *and the like*; every tittle of which, I have the testimony of my own Conscience, is absolutely false, and the Accusers must have the Accusation of their own Consciences, that they do know it to be true" (A2). Defoe offers as testimony his subjective knowledge, which is unverifiable.

93 *Eleven Opinions of Mr. Harley* (May 14, 1711), 41.

94 The association of whorishness with obtaining money by shape-changing was well established in seventeenth-century pornography and satire against women (often the same thing). For example, in Ferrante Pallavicino's immensely popular *The Whores Rhetorick Calculated to the Meridian of London and Conformed to the Rules of Art in Two Dialogues* (London, 1683), an old whore instructs her pupil that "you must put on a seeming modesty, even when you exercise the most essential parts of your Profession. . . . Your avarice must be insatiable, you must therefore never shy any occasion of increasing your stock: and your whole life must be one continued act of dissimulation" (40). The instruction is remarkably similar to Lady Credit's *modus operandi*: "This part of the Rhetorick is necessary to fit you on all occasions, to use ambiguous expressions . . . to equivocate, vary and double" (42–43). It is necessary that "when fortune deserts the man, let the Whore do so too, without retaining the least sense of her old acquaintance, their mutual joys, or his past generosity" (90).

95 *Review*, 8:60 (August 11, 1711), 243.

2 DEFOE AND FICTIONALITY

1 In *Defoe and the Idea of Fiction 1713–1719* (Newark: University of Delaware Press, 1983), Geoffrey Sill notes that after the *Review* ceased publication in 1713, Defoe "began using fictions . . . not merely to illustrate political ideas – as he had done for years in the *Review* – but rather as the very *form* of those ideas" (24). He argues that "propaganda" is inseparable from the rest of Defoe's fiction, and that in "Defoe's hands, ideology and fiction were related and independent forms of knowledge . . . a way of . . . changing the world" (25).

2 See generally, John Robert Moore, *A Checklist of the Writings of Daniel Defoe* (Bloomington: University of Indiana Press, 1971).

3 *The Converting Imagination: Linguistic Theory and Swift's Satiric Prose* (Carbondale: Southern Illinois University Press, 1994), 50. Francus argues that through complex translations, Swift demonstrates "the verbal distance to be spanned between [himself] and his creations" (51). See also Deborah Wyrick, *Jonathan Swift and the Vested Word* (Chapel Hill: University of North Carolina Press, 1988), 96–102. Wyrick argues that Swift wanted his texts to be identified with him, so long as they were not definitively identified for purposes of prosecution.

4 In *Addison and Steele are Dead: the English Department, its Canon, and the Professionalization of Literary Criticism* (Newark: University of Delaware Press, 1990), Brian McCrea argues that where the author's values and opinions are known, one can "triangulate them with the values and opinions of the created character, and chart the degree of irony . . . But if the author, the fixed point, is elusive, then the irony becomes infinitely complicated and impossible to chart with any certainty" (61). McCrea addresses the case where readers know that the persona did not create the text, but cannot measure irony since they do not know who did create it. In Defoe's case, a reader is supposed to assume that whoever wrote the text (if it is anonymous) is still not wearing a mask, and that there is therefore no irony.

5 While Sill correctly denominates Defoe's political narratives as "fictions," he insufficiently pursues Defoe's *sub rosa* interventions into the public sphere.

6 Francus, *The Converting Imagination*, 52.

7 The *Drapier's Letters*, which do not satirize the purported author, M. B. Drapier, were never attributed to a person by that name.

8 For a list of sources on "reader entrapment" in Swift, see Francus, 206, n.4. See also Fredrick Smith, "The Danger of Reading Swift: the Double Bind of Reading *Gulliver's Travels*," in Karl Kropf, ed., *Reader Entrapment in Eighteenth-Century Literature* (New York: AMS Press, 1992), 109–130.

9 See also Jurgen Habermas, *The Structural Transformation of the Public Sphere* (Cambridge, MA: MIT Press, 1989), noting that "the state-

governed public sphere was appropriated by the public of private people making use of their reason" (51), and that "the public process of critical debate lay claim to being in accord with reason" (54).

10 Terry Eagleton, *The Function of Criticism: From "The Spectator" to Post-Structuralism* (London: Verso, 1984), 15.

11 "Introduction: Habermas and the Public Sphere," in Craig Calhoun, ed., *Habermas and the Public Sphere* (Cambridge, MA: MIT Press, 1992), 13. On the importance of reason to Habermas' conception of the public sphere, see also Neil Saccamano, "The Consolations of Ambivalence: Habermas and the Public Sphere," *MLN* 106 (1991), 685–698, noting that Habermas attributes political agency to "the public of private persons, capable of judging art and debating rationally about politics" (686), and Donald Guss, "Enlightenment as Process: Milton and Habermas," *PMLA* 106 (1991), 1156–1169.

12 For interpretations, see Sill, *Defoe and the Idea of Fiction*, 87–93, Paula Backscheider, *Daniel Defoe – His Life* (Baltimore: Johns Hopkins University Press, 1988), 353–56, G. V. Bennett, *The Tory Crisis in Church and State 1688–1730* (Oxford: Clarendon Press, 1975), J. A. Downie, *Robert Harley and the Press* (Cambridge: Cambridge University Press, 1979).

13 Ros Ballaster observes that "the scandal chronicle had a directly political and often incendiary purpose, and its authors display an attendant wariness with regard to their claims to veracity in order to avoid legal reprisals or ostracism at court. . . . [It] took the epistemological play between fact and fiction to new heights of ambiguity." *Seductive Forms: Women's Amatory Fiction from 1684–1740* (Oxford: Clarendon Press, 1992), 56–57, 60–61.

14 Discussing the *chronique scandaleuse* popularized by the Female Wits, Ballaster notes that Mary Manley created "political allegory with the purpose of making and breaking political careers," and "trod a delicate path seeking to protect herself from legal retribution while ensuring that her allegorical structure was not so obscure that her readers could not recognize her fiction as the party political propaganda it was" (*Seductive Forms*, 128–129). Maximillian Novak notes that Defoe "never wrote a romance in the manner of Aphra Behn, Mrs. Haywood or Mrs. Manley, and while he may have admired these writers for their ingenuity, he probably regarded them as trivial." See "Defoe's Theory of Fiction," *Studies in Philology* 61 (1964), 650–668, 651. See also Michael McKeon, *The Origins of the English Novel 1660–1740* (Baltimore: Johns Hopkins University Press, 1987), 59–63, crediting the *chronique scandaleuse* with a powerful political potential.

15 John Oldmixon, *A Detection of the Sophistry and Falsities of the Pamphlet, Entitul'd, the Secret History of the White Staff*, 1st edn (1714), 8. In *Robert Harley and the Press*, J. A. Downie states that Oldmixon "wrote the Whig rejoinders" (187).

16 See Backscheider, *Defoe*, 355; Bennett, *The Tory Crisis*, 190.

17 *The Secret History of the Mitre and Purse, In Which The First and Second parts of the Secret History of the White Staff are fully considered, and the Hypocrisy and Villanies of the staff are laid open and Detected* (1714), n.p. (preceding p. 4).

18 Backscheider, *Defoe*, 356.

19 In part 2, Defoe shuffles the author's identity. One of the few passages in which the anonymous writer refers to himself suggests that he is a prominent propagandist, but deflects suspicion from Defoe by attributing his work to someone else: "I have many Tracts written about the Years 1708–9–10, to prove this [the "old Whigs"' coalition with the Jacobites]; and a long Recapitulation thereof is found in an anonymous Pamphlet of that Time, which, on that very account, made much noise, entituled *The October Club*, written, as was said, by the late Sir G. H." (8).

20 *The Secret History of the Secret History of the White Staff, Purse & Mitre* (1715), 6.

21 In *Grub Street: Studies in a Subculture* (London: Methuen, 1972), Pat Rogers states that "in the millions of words Defoe set down on paper, the incidence of the term ["Grub Street"] is negligible. And he assuredly never made any effort to body forth the full Grub Street conceit in the manner of the *Dunciad*. He was too near the game to be able to afford that" (398). Perhaps Rogers missed *The Secret History of the Secret History*.

22 Regarding Defoe's claims that *The Shortest Way* was intended to be read ironically, see J. A. Downie, "Defoe's *Shortest Way With the Dissenters*: Irony, Intention and Reader Response," *Prose Studies* 9 (1986), 120–139. Downie notes that Defoe gave conflicting versions of his intent, first claiming that no one could read the text literally, while later suggesting that he had hoped some people would. See also Maximillian Novak, "Defoe's *Shortest Way With the Dissenters* – Hoax, Parody, Paradox, Irony and Satire," *Modern Language Quarterly* 27 (1966), 402–417, and "Defoe's Use of Irony" in *The Uses of Irony*, ed. Maximillian Novak and Herbert Davis (Los Angeles: University of California Press, 1966), 7–38. In *An Appeal to Honour and Justice*, Defoe argues that several of his incendiary tracts were ironic.

23 Of course there must be a nominal author, one who mechanically puts pen to paper. Defoe identifies William Pittis, whom he claims was working for Edmund Curll, the notorious Grub Street publisher. Defoe goes so far as to avow that Pittis showed him the manuscript of *The Secret History*, and "proves" that Pittis is the author because he has written on both sides of the issue of war with France. The accusation is ironically, audaciously self-reflexive, since Defoe was himself accused of writing on both sides of issues. Indeed, in *A Vindication of the Press* (1718) Defoe would write (without a whiff of irony) that booksellers and authors "should be permitted the Liberty of Writing and Printing of either Side for bread, free of Ignominy; and as getting Money is the chief Business of the World, so these measures cannot by any means be esteem'd Unjust

or Disreputable" (21). Defoe can be on either side of writing on either side.

24 The crux in *The Secret History of the Secret History* is the manner in which it risks embarrassment to Harley, first by suggesting that *The Secret History* is untrue, then by leaving open the possibility that Harley commissioned the response even after he was criticized for involvement in *The Secret History*. Harley sought to disavow any connection with *The Secret History*, and did so in private letters and a public advertisement *after* publication of *The Secret History of the Secret History*. In *The Tory Crisis*, Bennett notes that "When [Harley] wrote to Dr. Stratford to disclaim any connection with the *Secret History*, the good canon was politely incredulous" (191). See also J. A. Downie, *Robert Harley*, 187–188, citing portions of the letter to Stratford and the advertisement. Downie suggests that Defoe misjudged the potential response to the pamphlets; assuming Harley's involvement, he may have done the same. While it is possible that Defoe consulted Harley on *The Secret History of the Secret History*, it is such a bizarre, rogue text that Harley's acquiescence seems unlikely.

25 See "The Precession of Simulacra" in Jean Baudrillard, *Simulations*, trans. Paul Foss, Paul Patton, Philip Beitchman (New York: Semiotext(e), 1983), 1–79. "Simulation" (attributed to late capitalism) is opposed to representation. It is "a question of substituting signs of the real for the real itself" (4), cancelling referentiality, hence originality, in any text or material phenomenon.

26 *A Detection of the Sophistry and Falsities*, part III (1715), 3.

27 Defoe's suspicion of the public sphere, evident in *An Appeal to Honour and Justice*, pervaded his texts. In *The Structural Transformation*, Habermas calls coffeehouses "centers of criticism – literary at first, then also political – in which began to emerge, between aristocratic society and bourgeois intellectuals, a certain parity of the educated" (32). But Defoe deprecates coffeehouses. In *The Compleat English Tradesman*, he argues that they are "devoted to scandal," "where the characters of all kinds of persons and professions are handled in the most merciless manner . . . nor is it less hard, that the Credit of a Tradesman, which is the same thing in its nature as the virtue of a Lady, should be tossed about, shuttlecock like, from one table to another in the coffee house" (I, 188). In *A Vindication of the Press* (1718), he states: "you'll find very few Coffee-Houses in this opulent City, without an illiterate Mechanick, Commenting upon most material Occurrences, and Judging the Actions of the greatest Councils in Europe" (17). Such attacks bolster a strategy dependent on the perceived unreliability of public sphere discourse.

28 See Davis, *Factual Fictions*, reviewing Defoe's dizzying cross-pollination of Whig and Tory newspapers. See also Sill's account of Defoe's interpolating a preface into a Jacobite pamphlet, suggesting an interpretation opposite to that intended. *Defoe and the Idea of Fiction*, 115–117.

29 *The Fortunes and Misfortunes of the Famous Moll Flanders . . . Written from her own Memorandums* (Oxford: Basil Blackwell, 1927), vol. I, vii.

30 *The Fortunate Mistress or a History of the Life and Vast Variety of Fortunes of Mademoiselle de Beleau, Afterwards Call'd The Countess De Wintelsheim, In Germany, Being the Person known by the Name of the LADY ROXANA, in the Time of King Charles II* (Oxford: Basil Blackwell, 1927), vii.

31 Joseph Bartolomeo, *A New Species of Criticism: Eighteenth-Century Discourse on the Novel* (Newark: University of Delaware Press, 1994), 35, citing Laura Curtis, *The Elusive Daniel Defoe* (London: Vision Press, 1984), 103. Curtis argues that irrespective of Defoe's commercial objectives, the "actual product, which he could not completely analyze, seemed somewhat uncanny to him." She avoids discussing Defoe's "general theory of fiction," therefore, since "Defoe himself was not sure of what he was doing and why."

32 The "objectivity" attributed to print must be refracted through the collaborative culture that produced heavily marketed texts. In this sense I demur from unqualified statements such as McKeon's:

> Print contributes to and reinforces an "objective" standard of truth which is also, especially in narrative, a "historical" standard of truth, of historicity: did it happen, and how did it happen? And the verifying potential of print is so powerful that the historicity of the act of publication itself could seem to supplant, and to affirm, the historicity of that information which print putatively exists only to mediate. (*The Origins of the English Novel*, 46)

33 Even today, manuscript "submission" correlates to the author's relinquishing full control. In *Printing Technology, Letters & Samuel Johnson* (Princeton: Princeton University Press, 1987), Alvin Kernan observes that "What [the printed text] corresponds to in its accuracy is not . . . obvious; it is usually said to be the author's intention, but in fact it turns out to be some form of itself generated and fixed in the process of writing, editing, and printing" (165). By bringing to the surface mediating personae elided by the author's (printed) "intent," Defoe demystifies the print text: "accuracy" is a surface phenomenon, contingent on processes of negotiation and deference. In "Lessons from the 'Literatory,': How to Historicise Authorship," *Critical Inquiry* 17 (1991), 479–507, David Saunders and Ian Hunter cite "the fluid distribution of bibliotechnical capacities, the closeness of intellectual and entrepreneurial activities [which] had arisen with print technology" (496). In *The Printing Press as an Agent of Change: Communications and Cultural Transformations in Early Modern Europe*, 2 vols. (Cambridge, MA: Harvard University Press, 1979), Elizabeth Eisenstein observes that the "early capitalist entrepreneur . . . hired scholars, translators, editors and compilers when not serving in these capacities himself," and that "the divisions of literary labor remained blurred" (I, 153–154). Johnson's *Dictionary* defined "Editor" as "Publisher" as well as "he that revises or prepares any work for publication."

34 On the commerciality of eighteenth-century publishing, which produced fierce contests between pirates and proprietors of canonical texts, see Mark Rose, *Authors and Owners: the Invention of Copyright* (Cambridge, MA: Harvard University Press, 1993).

35 David Burgin, *The End of Art Theory: Criticism and Postmodernity* (London: Macmillan, 1986), 174.

36 In *The Imprint of Gender: Authorship and Publication in the English Renaissance* (Ithaca: Cornell University Press, 1993), Wendy Wall observes that Renaissance authors frequently wrote elaborate prefaces, disavowing complicity in publication of the text. Authors thereby preserved a posture aloof from the market, even as the claim was a "marketing strategy" (187), enticing readers with the prospect of illicit disclosure. See Wall's brilliant chapter, "Prefatorial Disclosures: 'Violent Enlargement' and the Voyeuristic Text" (169–226). Even in the sixteenth century, therefore, authors hid behind commerciality, obscuring their own intent. Defoean self-reflexivity differs in that the author does not claim to have withheld the text; rather, print production overdetermined by capitalism is shown to be inimical to authorial, indeed generic integrity.

37 *A New Species of Criticism*, 40.

38 A generation after *Crusoe*, Richardson wrote in a letter that in *Pamela*, he deployed "the umbrage of the editor's character to hide myself behind." See William Warner, *Reading Clarissa: the Struggles of Interpretation* (New Haven: Yale University Press, 1979), 129. Editorial "umbrage" was common, as in Bentley's infamous edition of Milton. Shakespeare was emended by Pope and Theobold. On editorial practice in the early eighteenth century, which clearly tolerated substantive (or suggested substantive) emendation, see Peter Seary, *Lewis Theobold and the Editing of Shakespeare* (Oxford: Clarendon Press, 1990), and Margreta DeGrazia, *Shakespeare Verbatim: the Reproduction of Authenticity and the 1790 Apparatus* (Oxford: Clarendon Press, 1991). Each successive edition of Shakespeare vied with predecessors; editing was tied to the *sale* of editions. Thus the relationship between textual intervention and commerciality was a commonplace. Both Johnson's *Dictionary* and the *Oxford English Dictionary* cite Pope in his own edition of Shakespeare's *Henry V*: "This nonsense got into all the editions by a mistake of the editors."

39 Delight and instruction were commonplace Horatian grounds on which to recommend texts. In *Crusoe*, however, such grounds are offered not for their own sake, but to deflect from the text's generic uncertainty. Horace is conscripted into a commercial project, creating a curious counterpoint to the text's undeniable moral purport. *Crusoe* uses its "morality" amorally to mollify readers concerned with the truth of texts.

40 David Marshall observes that "[t]he fiction of history shifts the question of truth from the specific events of the narrative to the author who supposedly speaks the text." From this he concludes "Defoe's anxieties

about fiction and deception focus less on the act of writing fiction than on the act of impersonation." *The Figure of Theater*, 93–94.

41 The preface to *The Farther Adventures* appears immediately after the preface to *The Life & Strange Surprising Adventures* in the Blackwell edition. The cited portion is at vii.

42 On the abridgments of *Crusoe*, see Pat Rogers, "Classics and Chapbooks," in Isabel Rivers, ed., *Books and Their Readers in Eighteenth-Century England* (New York: St. Martin's, 1982), 27–45. On piracies of the text, see Pat Rogers, *Robinson Crusoe* (London: Allen & Unwin, 1979), 7–8.

43 On the view that moral teaching justified the practice of fiction, see Starr, *Defoe and Casuistry*, 190–211. In *The Reluctant Pilgrim: Defoe's Emblematic Method and Quest for Form in Robinson Crusoe* (Baltimore: Johns Hopkins University Press, 1966), J. Paul Hunter states: "[Timothy] Cruso's 'middle way' [mixing parable and history] was by no means universally approved, but by the end of the seventeenth century the use of such a form had at least become a legitimate subject of debate. Those who favored fiction at all based their stand on the didactic usefulness of such material, which is the argument advanced by Defoe in his hedging Preface to *Robinson Crusoe*" (118). Starr and Hunter are supported by David Marshall in *The Figure of Theater*.

44 On relations between authors and publishers during the early eighteenth century, see Rose, *Authors and Owners*. Paula Backscheider examines Defoe's arrangements with *Crusoe*'s publisher in *Daniel Defoe*, 605, n.77.

45 *A Full and True Account of a Horrid and Barbarous Revenge by Poison, On the Body of Mr. Edmund Curll, Bookseller*, in Norman Ault, ed., *The Prose Works of Alexander Pope* (Oxford: Blackwell, 1936, vol. 1), 262. On Curll's notorious manipulation of book sales, including his changing the names on title pages and denial of association with vilified authors, see Ralph Straus, *The Unspeakable Curll* (London: Chapman & Hall, 1927). In "An Author to Let" (attributed to Richard Savage), the writer claims that in Curll's service "I wrote Obscenity and Profaneness, under the names of Pope and Swift . . . translated from the French what they never wrote." *The Works of Richard Savage Esq.* (1777), vol. 1, 266.

46 Jonathan Swift, *A Tale of a Tub*, ed. A. C. Guthkelch and D. Nichol Smith (Oxford: Clarendon Press, 1958), 207. Using a persona, Lady Mary Wortley Montagu attacked high-handed proprietors, noting that an "Ingenious printer had thrown in a little Bawdy at the end of a Paragraph." Citing his subservience to the market, the printer argued that "Hawkers refuse to sell [your Paper], the coffee houses won't take it in . . . if you will rail at no body, nor put in no feign'd names." *The Nonesense of Common-Sense* (1738), in *Lady Mary Wortley Montagu: Essays and Poems and Simplicity, a Comedy*, ed. Robert Halsband and Isobel Grundy (Oxford: Clarendon Press, 1993), 127.

47 Gildon's pamphlet appears in Paul Dottin, *Robinson Crusoe Examin'd and Criticis'd* (London: J. M. Dent, 1923), 81–128. Portions cited are at

112–113. In "Classics and Chapbooks," Rogers notes that Gildon may have authored the first abridgment of *Crusoe*, which appeared a few weeks after its publication.

48 On the impossible metaphysics of Crusoe's argument, see Davis, *Factual Fictions*, 156–161 and McKeon, *The Origins of the English Novel*.

49 Crusoe's appearance is the mirror image of Harley's. In *The Secret History of the Secret History*, the real Harley became a fiction claiming he was not real in *The Secret History*. In *Serious Reflections*, a fictional Crusoe claims to be real, and claims he was real in the previous texts.

50 For an illuminating discussion of novelistic prefaces, *Moll Flanders*, and the culture of print, see Maurice Couturier, *Textual Communication: a Print-based Theory of the Novel* (London: Routledge, 1991), chapter 2.

51 *Jonathan Swift and the Vested Word* (Chapel Hill: University of North Carolina Press, 1988), 134. On the history of the clothes metaphor, see 140.

52 According to Johnson's *Dictionary*, "garble" meant "to sift, to part, to separate the good from the bad." Yet the term could also imply an effort to misrepresent. The *OED* states that to "garble" was "to make selections from with a (usually unfair or malicious) purpose."

53 The slippage is by design, and in fact seems heavy-handed. It does not reflect an indifference to "fact" and "fable." On Defoe's sense of historicity, see Ulrich Suerbaum, "Storm into Story: the Development of Defoe's Theory and Technique of Narrative," in *Modes of Narrative: Approaches to American, Canadian, and British Fiction* (Wurzburg: Koningshausen & Neumann, 1990), 265–277.

54 My position is an ironic turn on Chartier's in *The Order of Books*: "The new economics of writing supposed the full visibility of the author, the original creator of a work from which he could legitimately expect to profit" (39).

3   CREDIT AND HONESTY IN *THE COMPLEAT ENGLISH TRADESMAN*

1 See for example Robert Weisberg, "Commercial Morality, the Merchant Character, and the History of the Voidable Preference," *Stanford Law Journal* 39 (1986), 3–138, and Peter Earle, *The Making of the English Middle Class: Business, Society and Family Life in London, 1660–1730* (Berkeley: University of California Press, 1989). In *Defoe and the Defense of Commerce* (Victoria: University of Victoria Press, 1987), Thomas Meier dismisses the text's lessons on accounting as "pedantic detail" (56), though "intensive" reading demonstrates that they engage questions of textual veracity.

2 *Defoe and Economics: the Fortunes of Roxana in the History of Interpretation* (New York: St. Martin's Press, 1987), x. In *Before Novels: the Contexts of Eighteenth Century English Fiction* (New York: Norton & Company, 1990),

J. Paul, Hunter suggests that "one reason that popular reading materials antecedent to the novel have not been studied more fully is that most of them seem to a modern sensibility inherently wrongheaded, narrow, ineffectively focused, and boring" (226). I shall argue that Hunter's own "reading" of *The Compleat English Tradesman* does not materially change that view.

3 In *Daniel Defoe – His Life* (Baltimore: Johns Hopkins University Press, 1988), Paula Backscheider sees the text as part of a "detailed, carefully ordered construct toward which Great Britain might aspire," in which "Defoe characterizes the English people, identifies their strengths and advantages, and charts their course to greatness" (510–511). She groups the text with such others as *A Plan of the English Commerce*. William Dowling observes that the "emergent bourgeoisie [is] celebrated," and that the text "represents a benign vision of commerce" associated with "Whig panegyric." *The Epistolary Moment: the Poetics of the Eighteenth-century Verse Epistle* (Princeton: Princeton University Press, 1991), 17, 107. In *Defoe and Middle Class Gentility* (Cambridge, MA: Harvard University Press, 1968), Michael Shinagel sees it as "a practical manual on how to succeed in business but also a conduct book designed to dignify the profession and polish the men who practice it" (134). Most reductively, Laura Curtis argues that "the main content" of the text "is its information for beginners about practical matters," setting a standard that is "impossibly idealistic." *The Versatile Defoe* (Totowa: Rowman and Littlefield, 1979), 378. In *Defoe and Casuistry* (Princeton: Princeton University Press, 1971), George Starr recognizes that the text implicates Defoe's theory of fiction, but he fails to examine the complex negotiations in the text itself. James Sutherland sees the text's numerous extended dialogues in relation to Defoe's novels, but he does not examine the text's engagement with the problem of fictionality itself. See "The Relation of Defoe's Fiction to His Nonfictional Writings," in *Daniel Defoe*, ed. Harold Bloom (New York: Chelsea House, 1987), 49. The best reading of the text is in Lincoln Faller, *Crime and Defoe* (Cambridge: Cambridge University Press, 1993), but Faller still uses the text to illuminate the "meaning" (not the technique) of Defoe's novels.

4 "The Good Clerk," in *The Complete Works of Charles Lamb*, ed. R. H. Shepherd (London, 1875), 354–358, 356. Lamb also suggested that the text could be read in "an *ironical sense*, and as a piece of *covered satire*." Letter to Walter Wilson, December 16, 1822, excerpted in Pat Rogers, *Defoe: the Critical Heritage* (London: Routledge & Kegan Paul, 1972), 86.

5 In *The Economics of the Imagination* (Amherst: University of Massachusetts Press, 1980), Kurt Heinzelman states: "'economics' does not issue forth in a psychologically consistent way or in a single discursive form. Or, to state the thesis positively, the economic complicity of literature is integrally connected to the discursive complexity of economics" (9).

6 Rick Altman, *The American Film Musical* (Bloomington: Indiana

University Press, 1987), 4, 5. Ian Reid suggests an approach to genre more conducive to my analysis: "genre is uncategorical: it is a shifting semiotic space where a certain range of textual possibilities may be framed in order to interact meaningfully." See "When is an Epitaph Not an Epitaph: a Monumental Generic Problem and a Jonsonian Instance," *Southern Review* 22/3 (1989), 198–210, 209. See also Nigel Smith, *Literature and Revolution in England, 1640–1660* (New Haven: Yale University Press, 1994), who views genres "not [as] fixed categories, but [as] interacting *foci* of intelligibility" (8). In *The Ideology of Genre: a Comparative Study of Generic Instability* (University Park: Pennsylvania State University Press, 1994), Thomas Beebee argues: "a text's generic status is rarely what it seems to be. . . . [S]ince a 'single' genre is only recognizable as difference, as a foregrounding against the background of its neighboring genres, every work involves more than one genre, even if only implicitly" (27, 28).

7 Steele was a Protestant minister, not the essayist/MP cited in chapter 1.

8 The Institute of Chartered Accountants in England and Wales classifies *The Compleat English Tradesman* as an early accounting text. See "Bibliography: Books on Accounting in English, 1543–1800," in B. S. Yamey, H. C. Edey, and H. W. Thomson, *Accounting in England and Scotland: 1543–1800 – Double-Entry in Exposition and Practice* (London: Sweet and Maxwell, 1963), 202–224.

9 In *Economics and the Fiction of Daniel Defoe* (Berkeley: University of California Press, 1962), Maximillian Novak identifies Defoe's economics with contemporary mercantilism, but does not discuss his massive interest in credit. Basically, mercantilism held that it was necessary to maintain a favorable balance of trade (exports exceeding imports), and that full employment was the object of trade. It was split over whether high wages (hence high purchasing power) or low wages (hence competitive overseas pricing) would serve that end. In general, Defoe favored high wages, though he thought servants were paid too much. On mercantilist theory, see Eli Hecksher, *Mercantilism* (London: Allen & Unwin, 1955); Edgar Furniss, *The Position of the Laborer in a System of Economic Nationalism: a Study of the Labor Theories of the Later English Mercantilists* (New York: A. M. Kelley, 1965); Joyce Appleby, *Economic Thought and Ideology in Seventeenth Century England* (Princeton: Princeton University Press, 1978); J. A. W. Gunn, *Politics and the Public Interest in the Seventeenth Century* (London: Routledge and Kegan Paul, 1969).

10 Such principles are ironic in light of Defoe's last ignominious flight from creditors. The gentleman-tradesman finally becomes one persona that Defoe cannot inhabit undetected.

11 Defoe is seen as a derivative economic thinker. However, insofar as he connects economic structures and psychological, epistemological phenomena, his conventionality is overstated. In *Tradeful Merchants: the Portrayal of the Capitalist in Literature* (London: Routledge & Kegan Paul,

1981), John McVeagh argues that "Defoe never achieves significance as an economic thinker" because his technical analyses always trail off into a concern for "human issues" (53). Yet the two are not opposed! Defoe's analysis of the impact of economic formations on psychology is a breakthrough.

12 Hunter, *Before Novels*, 242.

13 Hunter elaborates the Puritan provenance of the Guide in *The Reluctant Pilgrim*, 28–50.

14 Richard Steele indicated what such diligence might mean, noting that trade was "an Affair that takes up six parts of seven of their [tradesmen's] Time." *The Trades-man's Calling*, Epistle to the Reader (London, 1684). Since Steele opposed excessive sleep, he appears to assume a workday of twelve to fourteen hours.

15 *Before Novels*, 252. In *The Reluctant Pilgrim*, 45, Hunter also assimilates *The Compleat English Tradesman* to a religious, moralizing tradition.

16 The opening chapters of *The Trades-man's Calling* are devoted to the choice of a "particular" calling, which differs from one's "general" calling to serve God only in that it is a "setled Imployment in some special Business of God's appointment, for our own and others good." He notes that "The former and this latter are both elegantly mention'd in one Verse, 1 Cor. 7.20. Let every Man abide in the same [earthly] Calling, wherein he was called [by his heavenly calling]" (2). On the notion of "particular calling," see Hunter, *The Reluctant Pilgrim*, 34ff., R. H. Tawney, *Religion and the Rise of Capitalism* (New York: Harcourt Brace & Company, 1926), 249–246; Charles and Catherine George, *The Protestant Mind and the English Reformation 1570–1640* (Princeton: Princeton University Press, 1961), chapters 3 and 4.

17 According to Defoe, a promisor's denial of his promise's silent conditionality implies a *lack* of Christianity, suggesting that he intends his commitments to override God's disposition in the world (1, 232–234). Defoe turns Steele on his head, claiming the high road for himself while it diminishes the sanctity of promises.

18 See Lawrence Klein, "The Third Earl of Shaftesbury and the Progress of Politeness," *Eighteenth Century Studies* 18 (1984–5), 186–214, and *Shaftesbury and the Culture of Politeness: Moral Discourse and Cultural Politics in Early Eighteenth-century England* (Cambridge: Cambridge University Press, 1994); "From Texts to Manners – A Concept and its Books: *Civilité* between Aristocratic Distinction and Popular Appropriation," in Roger Chartier, *The Cultural Uses of Print in Early Modern France* (Princeton: Princeton University Press, 1987), 71–109; Jacques Revel, "The Uses of Civility," in Roger Chartier, ed., *A History of Private Life*, 4 vols. (Cambridge, MA: Harvard University Press, 1987–90), III, 164–185; Peter France, "The Commerce of the Self," in *Comparative Criticism* 12 (Cambridge: Cambridge University Press, 1990), 39–56, reprinted in France, *Politeness and Its Discontents: Problems in French*

Classical Culture (Cambridge: Cambridge University Press, 1992), 97–112; Harold Mah, "The Epistemology of the Sentence: Language, Civility, and Identity in France and Germany, Diderot to Nietzsche," *Representations* 47 (1994), 64–84.

19 France states that "The politeness manuals published in France, Britain and elsewhere, all contribute to inculcating the ideal of *doux commerce*. They stress the need for negotiation between selves, and do not eschew talk of buying and selling." One French definition of politeness finds that it functions

> not simply out of altruism, however, but because this is the best rational calculation of self-interest. . . . The pay-off for successful negotiation is sympathy, the penalty for failure is isolation. . . . However, the commerce of the self that I have been outlining – the negotiation, bartering, giving and taking of feelings, attitudes, gestures and words – and the relation of all this to "true" feeling is one of the constant subjects of all kinds of literary works. . . . A great deal of the literature of the seventeenth and eighteenth centuries is concerned with offering positive or negative models of sociability for a privileged society in which "commerce" in the sense of conversation and social intercourse is probably what matters most. (44–45)

20 In *Shaftesbury and the Culture of Politeness*, Klein states: "On the surface, politeness oriented individuals towards each other's needs and wishes: it seemed to arise in a generous concern for the comfort of others. In reality, the polite concern for others might be a secondary effect of a far more basic self-concern. Thus, the altruistic or charitable appearance of politeness might conceal opportunistic egoism" (4). In "The Epistemology of the Sentence," Mah observes that "it was immediately apparent that in practice, civility's sensuous forms were easily detached from their supposed moral purpose and placed in the service of other intentions or made into ends in themselves" (70).

21 In "From Texts to Manners," Chartier emphasizes the element of disguise in a type of "polite" conversation that in the eighteenth century would make its way to England:

> *Civilité*, then does not necessarily signify the agreement of the "good within" with the "graceful comeliness without" . . . The concept of *civilite* stands at the very heart of the tension between appearance and existence that epitomizes baroque sensitivity and etiquette. The *civilite* of the seventeenth century . . . is best understood as above all a social seeming. . . . Then *civilite* becomes pretense; it changes from a legitimate representation to a hypocritical mask. (85, 87)

See also Klein, "The Third Earl of Shaftesbury," noting the theatrical aspects of polite self-presentation. He cites statements by Mandeville and Abel Boyer to the effect that politeness implied a disagreement between appearance and intrinsic reality: "It appeared to break the continuity between moral and social personality, exploring the disponibility of the social self and pioneering its transformation into a role-player" (191). See also Klein, *Shaftesbury*, 72–80.

22 A few pages later the text suggests that the Tradesman can seek "a happy
    medium," neither "rude" nor "sullen and silent" (256). Yet that
    medium must always be co-opted by a forebearing politeness, which
    permits an accurate description of the goods but excludes any statement
    by the Tradesman reflecting on the dynamics between himself and the
    customer.

23 Steele is much less sanguine than Defoe about abating an announced
    price. For him, the issue turns on calculations of a "just price." See *The
    Trades-man's Calling*, 151–152. On pre-capitalist notions of the "just
    price," enabling each man to have the necessaries of his station, see R. H.
    Tawney, *Religion and the Rise of Capitalism*, 40–41.

24 The process of debt collection heavily favored the creditor during the
    eighteenth century. See J. Innes, "The King's Bench Prison in the Later
    Eighteenth Century: Law, Authority, and Order in a London Debtor's
    Prison," in John Brewer and John Styles, eds., *An Ungovernable People: the
    English and their Law in the Seventeenth and Eighteenth Centuries* (New
    Brunswick: Rutgers University Press, 1985), 250–298. So long as the
    creditor could prove the debt, he had a high probability of recovery, with
    the debtor required to pay costs as well. See also Earle, *The Making of the
    English Middle Class*, 123–130.

25 Regarding the legal aspects of Bills, see James Milnes Holden, *The History
    of Negotiable Instruments in English Law* (London: Athlone Press at the
    University of London, 1955). On their development and usage, see Eric
    Kerridge, *Trade and Banking in Early Modern England* (Manchester:
    Manchester University Press, 1988), especially chapter 3. In "Money
    and the Structure of Credit in the Eighteenth Century," *Business History*
    12 (1970), 85–101, B. L. Anderson discusses the need for bills in light of
    an inadequate money supply. Anderson notes that

    > the regulation of bills was always difficult and open to abuse, so that opportunities
    > existed for stretching their credibility to someone's advantage. It seems likely,
    > for example, that many were endorsed and circulated even while the issuers
    > were unable to honour them. Indeed it appears from the evidence that the
    > practice of "protesting" an inland bill was much less closely adhered to than in
    > the case of its foreign counterpart, perhaps because its more local transmission
    > allayed doubts about its reliability, but also because it was to the advantage of
    > many bill users to prolong the circulation of even a dubious bill in order to delay
    > settlement. (93)

    The Bills' unregulated manipulability underlies Defoe's discussion.

26 Later, Defoe suggests that "there is no fraud against his own reflections, a
    man is very rarely an hypocrite to himself" (1, 103). But the text suggests
    that temporizing is the vice of debtors, and that it is frequently
    accompanied by self-delusion.

27 Steele cites the Golden Rule as the basic measure of trading ethics. For
    example, in discussing honesty he states "This Veracity and Justice are so

conjunct, that he cannot be just in his Dealings, that is false in his Words: For the same Law that commands us to do by others, as we would be done unto, equally obliges us to speak in our Commerce to them, as we would be spoken to" (*The Trades-man's Calling*, 141).

28 See *Defoe and Casuistry*, esp. 122–124. Starr cites Defoe's arguments supporting such propositions, and their manipulation by Moll and Roxana.

4 FICTIONS OF STABILITY

1 According to the Royal Society, "facts" could be constituted through witnessing their production in a public space. Texts could recapitulate the production of facts, creating endless "virtual witnesses" (readers) who confirm these facts. See Steven Shapin and Simon Schaffer, *Leviathan and the Ai-Pump: Hobbes, Boyle, and the Experimental Life* (Princeton: Princeton University Press, 1985).

2 Pacioli's work on accounting appears as part of a mathematical treatise, the *Summa de Arithmetica Geometria Proportioni and Proportionalita*. There are several translations of all or part of this text, including John Geijsbeek-Molenaar, *Ancient Double Entry Book Keeping* (Denver: Geijsbeek, 1914). On the history of double entry, see James Winjum, *The Role of Accounting in the Economic Development of England: 1500–1750* (Urbana: University of Illinois, 1972); A. C. Littleton, *Accounting Evolution to 1900* (New York: American Institute Publishing Co., 1933); Basil Yamey, *Essays on the History of Accounting* (New York: Arno Press, 1978); A. C. Littleton and E S. Yamey, *Studies in the History of Accounting* (New York: Arno Press, 1978); B. S. Yamey et al., *Accounting in England and Scotland: 1543–1800* (London: Sweet & Maxwell, 1963).

3 Hugh Oldcastle, *A Profitable Treatyce called the Instrument of Boke to learne to knowe the good order of the kepyng of the famouse reconynge called in Latyn, Dare and Habere, and in Englyshe, Debitor and Creditor* (London, 1543).

4 See the bibliography in Yamey, *Accounting in England and Scotland*.

5 Defoe would have used accounting in his early career as a hosier and pantile manufacturer, and in 1695 he was appointed accountant to a commissioner of the glass duty. He thought enough of his proficiency to mention it to Harley on two occasions when seeking patronage. In a letter of May–June, 1704, Defoe states that "Matters of Accounts are my perticular Element, what I have Allways been Master of." In a letter of June 10, 1707, he suggests work such as "Accompta or Compttr of the Accounts, things I pretend to Master of." *The Letters of Daniel Defoe*, ed. George Healey (Oxford: Clarendon Press, 1955).

6 On the uniformity of accounting technique as demonstrated in these early manuals, see Winjum, 47–49. On the evolution of accounting pedagogy, see J. G. C. Jackson, "The History of Methods of Exposition

of Double-Entry Book-Keeping," *Studies in the History of Accounting*, 288–312.

7 Classical accounting assumes that the world can be represented in a text. For example, it assumes that items reflected in one's books under a system of perpetual inventory will appear on one's shelves – not be pilfered by staff, eaten by mice, spoiled, or fallen in value. Accounting is paradoxical in that even while one's accounts may be maintained with up-to-the-minute accuracy, time itself can erode their accuracy.

8 Accounting protocol punishes anyone who produces a lying text. North notes that if a tradesman interpolates a fraud into his books,

> if he insists on the Advantage, as a common Thief, and being never after trusted, or dealt with by [other merchants], is from thenceforth (in his Reputation) crack'd, and soon after (probably) bankrupt, and broke; so sacred a Thing is to keep Books of Accompts in Time, and with the utmost Rigor of truth and Justice, in the Matter and Form of them. (32)

9 See *Principles of Book-keeping, explain'd* (Edinburgh, 1718), 9–10.

10 Seventeenth- and eighteenth-century accounting manuals emphasize that if applied properly, double-entry makes an account universally accessible and acceptable. The same is true today by following Generally Accepted Accounting Principles promulgated by the Financial Accounting Standards Board.

11 *Idea Rationaria* (London, 1683), preface.

12 Under double entry, the ledger is theoretically out of phase whenever a new entry in anterior texts is not yet carried over. However, the system can always be brought into phase, and one's exact position established (in theory), by making the proper entries. The *system* of texts, therefore, always generates Truth.

13 North acknowledges that some businesses not dependent on credit do not employ double entry. However, he does not teach any other method, and "absolutely require[s], that whatever is wrote, be a Part of, and approach in some degree towards the ultimate Perfection of Form, that Accompts can possibly receive" (56). Other accounting texts disparage methods not compliant with double entry. In *Debtor and Creditor Made Easy* (1708), Stephen Monteage asks of tradesmen using such methods: "[W]hat ballance can they bring these Books to? None at all" (preface). Defoe's method is not without *some* similarity to double entry, in that it permits integration of texts, but it omits the crucial matter of trial balance, required to detect error.

14 *A Journal of the Plague Year* (New York: Norton, 1992), 47.

15 In the episode of the cloud that looks like an avenging angel, the populace responds to shapes that are "but Air and Vapour" (22), prompted by imagination. "Appearance pass'd for as real" (24). Potential victims are bilked by quacks and mountebanks (29, 186), just as mountebank/stockjobbers had set upon Lady Credit. In "Defoe's Natural Philosophy," Simon Schaffer states "It has been persuasively

argued that Defoe used Plague reports as a means of treating the 'possession' of London by South Sea fever in 1720–21. His personation as a reporter with no credit among those possessed nicely reveals the crisis of credit and authority which he applied to the diagnosis of these moral ills" ("Defoe's Natural Philosophy," in John Christie and Sally Shuttleworth, eds., *Nature Transfigured: Science and Literature 1700–1900* [Manchester: Manchester University Press, 1984] 22–23). Schaffer cites, *inter alia*, Pat Rogers, "This Calamitous Year: *A Journal of the Plague Year* and the South Sea Bubble," in *Eighteenth Century Encounters* (Brighton: Harvester Press, 1985), 151–167. The best discussion of this connection is in Maximillian Novak, "Defoe and the Disordered City," *PMLA* 92 (1977), 241–252. I have already noted comparisons between the plague and the Bubble in contemporary tracts. *The Battle of the Bubbles* (anon: London, 1720) states: "Closed were Robin's well-frequented Doors, as in the Time of Plague," referring to the "multifarious monsters" about to ravage the town (5). *Considerations on the Present State of the Nation* (London, 1720), speaking of the brewing financial calamity, notes that "the Infection spread like the Pestilence" (16). Alluding to the plague's French provenance, Stanhope's *Epistle to His Royal Highness the Prince of Wales* (London, 1720) states: "And South-Sea shuts more houses than Marseilles" (8). See also *The History of the Rise and Fall of the South Sea Stock* (London, 1721), 14, and James Milner's *Three Letters Relating to the South-Sea Company and the Bank* (London, 1720), 18. Defoe's own *Anatomy of Exchange Alley* (1719) notes that ambition will in time ruin the jobbers, but "'twill be only like a general Visitation, where all Distempers are swallow'd up in the Plague, like a common Calamity" (40). In *The Social Milieu of Alexander Pope* (New Haven: Yale University Press, 1975), Howard Erskine-Hill notes that Francis Atterbury, speaking before the Lords in 1721, "'justly compared' the ill-effects of the [South Sea] scheme 'to a pestilence'" (200).

16 *Considerations on the Present State of the Nation*, 18.

17 *The Compleat English Tradesman*, 234–235. The universality of credit reinforces the relational quality of the market: "He that gives no trust, either by wholesale or by retail, and keeps his cash all himself... is not yet born, or if there ever was any such, they are all dead." *The Compleat English Tradesman*, I, 268.

18 On words as carriers of plague, see Richard Rambuss, "'A Complicated Distress': Narrativizing the Plague in Defoe's *A Journal of the Plague Year*," *Prose Studies* 12 (1989), 115–131.

19 On semiotic obscurity in *A Journal*, see Rambuss, "'A Complicated Distress,'" and Carol Houlihan Flynn, *The Body in Swift and Defoe* (Cambridge: Cambridge University Press, 1990), 8–13.

20 In "H. F.'s Meditations: *A Journal of the Plague Year*," *PMLA* 87 (1972), 417–422, Everett Zimmerman suggests that H. F. "seems almost temperamentally incapable of reaching a conclusion" (419). H. F.'s

inconclusiveness is not so much a personal quirk, however, as a consequence of plague's resistance to (en)closure.

21 H. F. observes that he spent his time "writing down my Memorandums of what occurred to me every Day." He refers to no revision other than "What I wrote of my private Meditations I reserve for private Use" (65–66). "Design" is associated with publication in *Crusoe, Moll*, and *Roxana*.

22 Paul Alkon, *Defoe and Fictional Time* (Athens: University of Georgia Press, 1979), 211.

23 In "'A Complicated Distress,'" Rambuss cites "the contest staged in the text between H. F.'s strain towards the limits of natural representation and the internal pressure exerted by an epidemic *not* to be represented in naturalistic terms" (129). But in fact H. F. does not "strain." The lacunae in his text are *part* of the "representation," rendering plague honestly.

24 See Austin Flanders, "Defoe's *Journal of the Plague Year* and the Modern Urban Experience," *The Centennial Review* 16 (1972), 328–348, arguing that *A Journal* "give[s] expression to a sense of the tenuousness of life and the moral order, to anxiety at witnessing the spectacle of civilization" (331). Flanders links the text to "apocalyptic forebodings" in *The Hind and the Panther*, the *Dunciad*, and Gibbon's *History*. In "The Unmentionable and the Ineffable in Defoe's Fiction," *Studies in the Literary Imagination* 15 (1982), 85–102, Maximillian Novak suggests that in *A Journal* language falls into noncommunication. While he relates this to a Defoean preoccupation with the insufficiency of language, I suggest that Defoe's ultimate concern is with the constitution of a nonfictive rhetoric when faced with the "ineffable." For a summary of contemporary theories concerning the insufficiency of words, and the relationship of such theories to *Roxana*, see Lincoln Faller, *Crime and Defoe* (Cambridge: Cambridge University Press, 1993), 218–220.

25 Compare Benjamin Moore, "Governing Discourses: Problems of Narrative Authority in *A Journal of the Plague Year*," *The Eighteenth Century: Theory and Interpretation* 33 (1992), 133–147, arguing that H. F. is the site of competing discourses that promote and subvert his narrative authority.

26 See Louis Landa's introduction to *A Journal of the Plague Year* (Oxford: Oxford University Press, 1969), x.

5   LADY CREDIT'S REPRISE: *ROXANA*

1 In *The English Business Company After the Bubble Act – 1720–1800* (New York: The Commonwealth Fund, 1938), Armand B. DuBois observes that "The situation in England after 1720 is in many regards reminiscent of America in 1930; a lethargic government, in some quarters a sense of public outrage, in others a profound feeling of depression" (11). Susan's

indecorum reflects such "public outrage," callously scorned by Parliament's adoption of the "Bubble Act" in May 1720. The legislation, 6 Geo.i, c. 18, prohibited false or irregular charters and the taking of subscriptions for enterprises backed thereby. However it originated when the South Sea Company, colluding with friendly MPs, sought to suppress rivals lacking royal charters. A leading lawyer of the time, Thomas Pengelly, opined that "the Words of the Act are general and ambiguous." Cited in DuBois, *The English Business Company*, 4. The Act reinscribed the market's uncertainty, and DuBois notes the framers must have known that it raised "problems of proof that could be molded to suit" any government policy (5).

2 In *An Essay Upon Projects* (1697), four years prior to *The Villainy of Stock-Jobbers Detected* (1701), Defoe refers to "shares in joint-stocks, patents, engines and undertakings blown up by the air of great words, and the name of some man of credit concerned," and to "stock-jobbed" as "the fine new word for nothing-worth." See *The Earlier Life and Chief Earlier Works of Daniel Defoe*, ed. Henry Morley (New York: Burt Franklin, 1889, reprinted 1970), 24–164, 35.

3 New Historicism opposes the formalistic view of literature as "an autonomous aesthetic order that transcends the shifting pressure and particularity of material needs and interests." See Louis Montrose, "Renaissance Literary Studies and the Subject of History," *ELH* 16 (1986), 5–12, 8.

4 Thomas Kavanagh, *Enlightenment and the Shadows of Chance* (Baltimore: Johns Hopkins University Press, 1993), 118.

5 Lincoln Faller, *Crime and Defoe* (Cambridge: Cambridge University Press, 1993), 245.

6 Michael Boardman, *Defoe and the Uses of Narrative* (New Brunswick: Rutgers University Press, 1983), 158. Boardman continually defines the novel in terms that broach the reader's awareness of fictional intent: "[T]raditional novels exhibit, along with much classical drama, a kind of teleological 'tightness' that narrative fiction before Richardson ordinarily does not; they are all closed, internally referring, probabilistic, causally patterned narratives we accept as avowed fictions" (17–18). Such texts "allow us to experience them as positively and not just accidentally fictional" (18). Boardman notes "the inapplicability of the paradigm to most of Defoe, except *Roxana*" (17–18). In *Narrative Innovation and Incoherence: Ideology in Defoe, Goldsmith, Austen, Eliot, and Hemingway* (Durham: Duke University Press, 1992), he asserts that the novel's apparent "realism is designed to be 'read through.'. . . The psychological demands upon the reader of the action's formal structures proclaim them as things wrought unapologetically as purposeful fictions" (27–28). See also Ralph Rader, "Defoe, Richardson, Joyce, and the Concept of Form in the Novel," in William Matthews and Ralph Rader, *Autobiography, Biography, and the Novel* (Los Angeles: University of

California Press, 1973) and "Defoe's 'Almost Invisible Hand': Narrative Logic as a Structuring Principle in *Moll Flanders*," *Eighteenth-Century Fiction* 6 (1993), 1–28.

7 Boardman, *Narrative Innovation and Incoherence*, 27, 141.

8 Boardman, *Defoe and the Uses of Narrative*, 16.

9 In *The Novel and the Police* (Berkeley: University of California Press, 1988), D. A. Miller pursues a tack analogous to mine. He posits "a radical *entanglement* between the nature of the novel and the practice of the police," i.e. between discursive and disciplinary practices. He asks "How do the police systematically function as a topic in the 'world' of the novel? And how does the novel – as a set of representational techniques – systematically participate in a general economy of policing power?" (2). If one substitutes "Susan" for "police" on grounds that she pursues, interrogates, disciplines Roxana and her allies, then *Roxana* may be said to respond to Miller's inquiry without needing to posit a "novel," i.e. when fiction is still "a set of representational techniques" not yet consolidated in a genre. Miller's approach integrates text and context, around circumstances broadly analogous to *Roxana*, in just the mode I pursue as a counterweight to formalism.

10 John Richetti, *Defoe's Narratives: Situations and Structures* (Oxford: Clarendon Press, 1975), 195. In *Story and History: Narrative Authority and Social Identity in the Eighteenth-Century French and English Novel* (Oxford: Basil Blackwell, 1990), William Ray states that Roxana embodies "selfhood as an ongoing activity of bargaining, planning, and representation," and that "all [her] attention is absorbed by the intricate management of [her] material situation and appearance" (79).

11 In the space of a few pages, Roxana remarks "I was to expect [Susan] wou'd discover that she knew me . . . " (11, 97); "I thought I perceiv'd that the Girl did not know me" (97); "I began to be thorowly convinc'd by this time, that the Girl did not know me" (98); "I was quite discourag'd, not-at-all doubting but that the jade had a right Scent of things, and that she knew and remember'd my Face" (101); "This [Susan's belief that Roxana was dead], I say, a little reliev'd my Thoughts, but I was soon down again" (103).

12 Gary Waller, *The Sidney Family Romance: Mary Wroth, William Herbert, and the Early Modern Construction of Gender* (Detroit: Wayne State University Press, 1993), 153–154. Waller cites Tony Bennett, "Texts in History," *Journal of the Midwest Modern Language Association* 18 (1985), 1–18. See also Robert Darnton, "First Steps Toward a History of Reading," in *The Kiss of Lamourette* (New York: W. W. Norton, 1990), 154–187. Darnton argues that "Reading has a history. It was not always and everywhere the same . . . Interpretive schemes belong to cultural configurations, which have varied enormously over time" (187). For a discussion of a shift in eighteenth-century reading practices, demonstrating the need to attend to their specificity, see Elizabeth

Harries, *The Unfinished Manner: Essays on the Fragment in the Later Eighteenth Century* (Charlottesville: University of Virginia Press, 1994), chapter 4.

13 Boardman, *Narrative Innovation and Incoherence*, 11–12.

14 John M. Warner, *Joyce's Grandfathers: Myth and History in Defoe, Smollett, Sterne and Joyce* (Athens: University of Georgia Press, 1993), 53.

15 On Roxana's exaggerated fears regarding the affect of Susan's revelations on her marriage, as well as on her relations generally, see Madeleine Kahn, *Narrative Transvestism: Rhetoric and Gender in the Eighteenth-century Novel* (Ithaca: Cornell, 1991), 99, and Faller, *Crime and Defoe*, 325. A contrary view is advanced by Boardman in *Defoe and the Uses of Narrative*, 146–147.

16 For another reading of this passage, see Kahn, *Narrative Transvestism*, 96.

17 In *Defoe and the Uses of Narrative*, Boardman argues: "[A]s a function of the causal nature of [*Roxana's*] plot, one can have an *anticipatory* experience; one perceives in advance the nature of a promised fate for a character, which may justly be called tragic." (140).

18 In *Narrative Innovation and Incoherence*, 44–47, Boardman argues that *Roxana's* plot suggests inevitability, instituting poetic justice.

19 In *Narrative Innovation and Incoherence*, Boardman argues that the pseudofactual mode precludes didacticism (26). Yet the *Crusoe* texts argue that much Improvement can be gained irrespective of genre – fact or fiction is equally servicable.

20 Referring to *Defoe and the Uses of Narrative*, Faller argues against "premature foreclosures that come with thinking about the past as if its future had already happened. Defoe was not reaching toward the writing of novels. . . . He was improvising, making complex gestures in a complex moment with little aim beyond the moment." *Crime and Defoe*, 245–246.

21 William Ray, *Story and History*, citing Marie-Paul Laden, *Self-Imitation in the Eighteenth-Century Novel* (Princeton: Princeton University Press, 1987), 67.

22 Roxana's elaborate "moves," calculated to elude Susan, comport with strategies that constitute the hide-and-seek concerns of Game Theory. For a compelling application of such theory to literature, see Steven J. Brams, *Theory of Moves* (Cambridge: Cambridge University Press, 1994), especially 60–66.

23 In *Enlightenment and the Shadows of Chance*, Kavanagh notes that Buffon described the chance event as "characterized by its lack of any causal relation to past or future, by the absence of any relation to what has gone before as cause or to what will come after as effect" (113). For a discussion of *Moll's* relation to contemporary views of gambling, see Gary Hentzi, "'An Itch of Gaming': the South Sea Bubble and the Novels of Daniel Defoe," *Eighteenth-Century Life* 17 (1993), 32–45. In *Crime and Defoe*, Faller observes that "it is as though Moll were shooting

dice and Roxana playing cards" (232–233); I suggest chess as more nearly Roxana's mode. For a discussion of *Moll* and *Roxana* as texts engaged with early capitalism, see Ann L. Kibbie, "Monstrous Generation: The Birth of Capital in Defoe's *Moll Flanders* and *Roxana*," *PMLA* 110 (1995), 1023–34.

24 Defoe was fascinated by Chance, and while he ridiculed gambling, he wrote treatises on betting. In *The Gamester* (1719), he juxtaposed the "laws of Chance" to the Law, suggesting that each had a place in genteel education. In *The Gamester II* (1719), he characterized "Chance" as the absence of skilled, attentive play, using dice as his model. Had Moll read his text, she would have learned that "where there is anything of Hazard, [it] will be reduc'd to this at last, viz. in dubious Cases, to calculate on which Sides are the most Chances" (sig. A).

25 *Joyce's Grandfathers*, 55.

Index